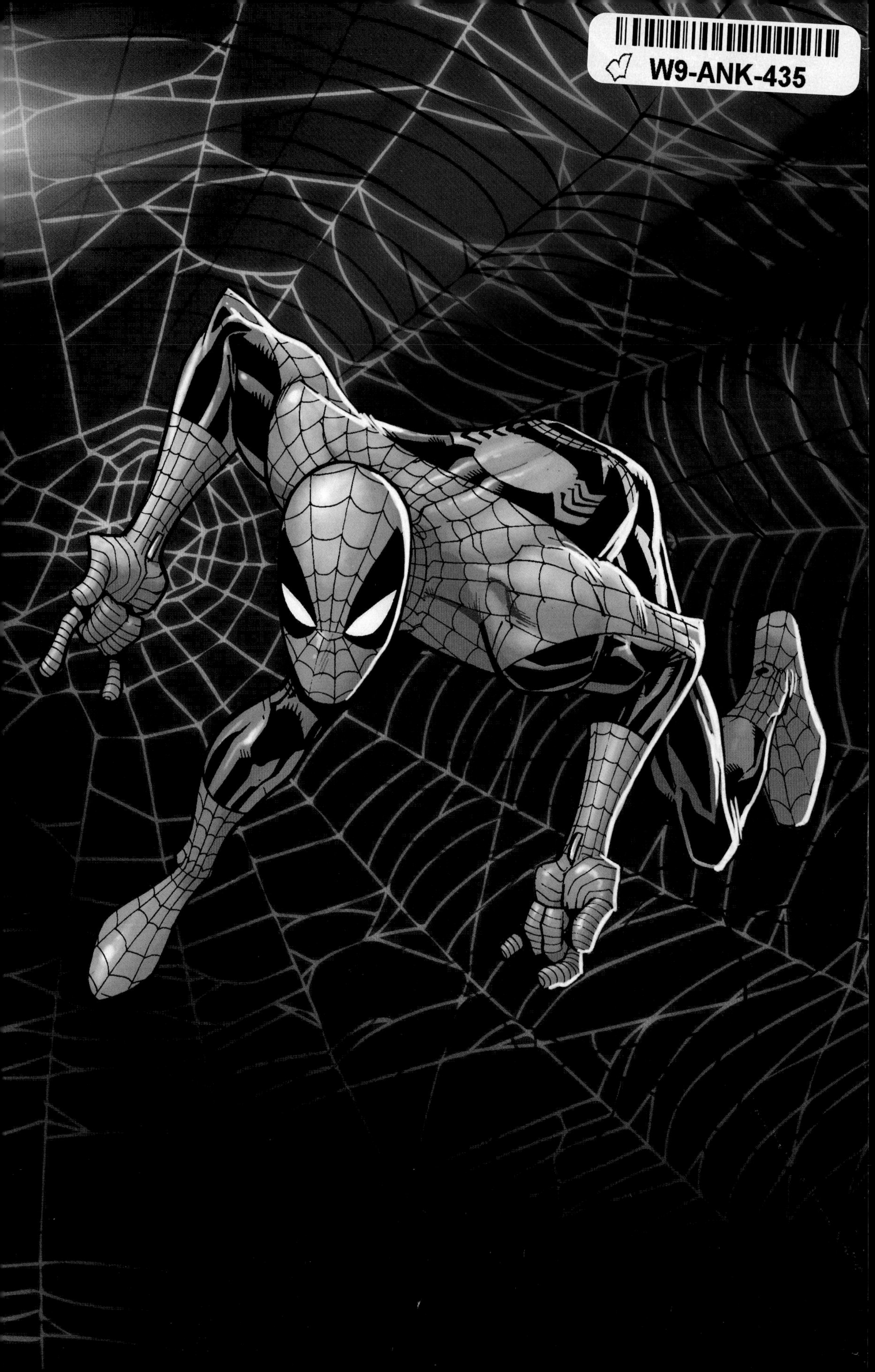

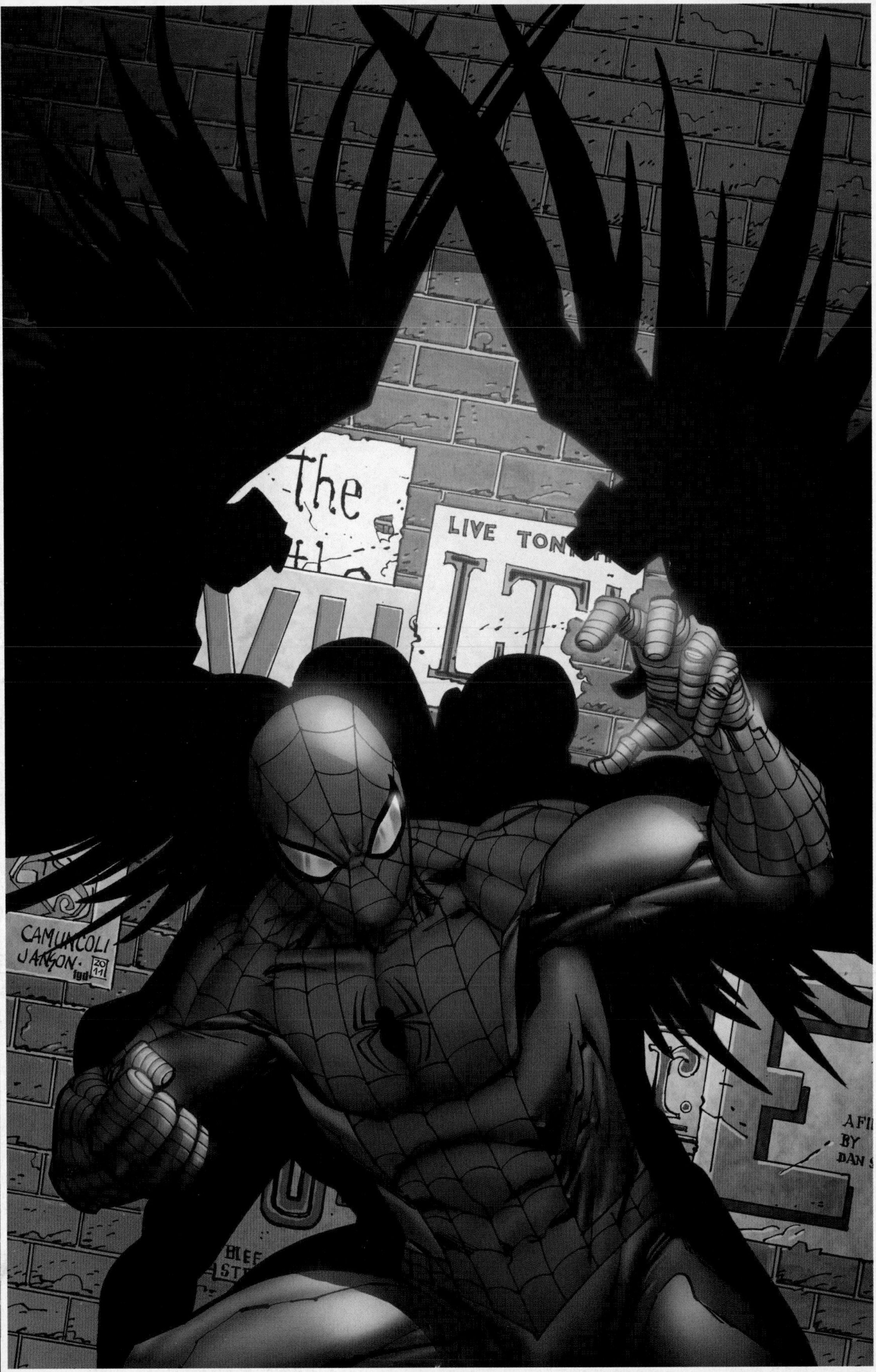
The
LIVE TON
CAMUNCOLI
JANSON
2011

AMAZING SPIDER-MAN #674

COVER BY GIUSEPPE CAMUNCOLI, KLAUS JANSON & FRANK D'ARM

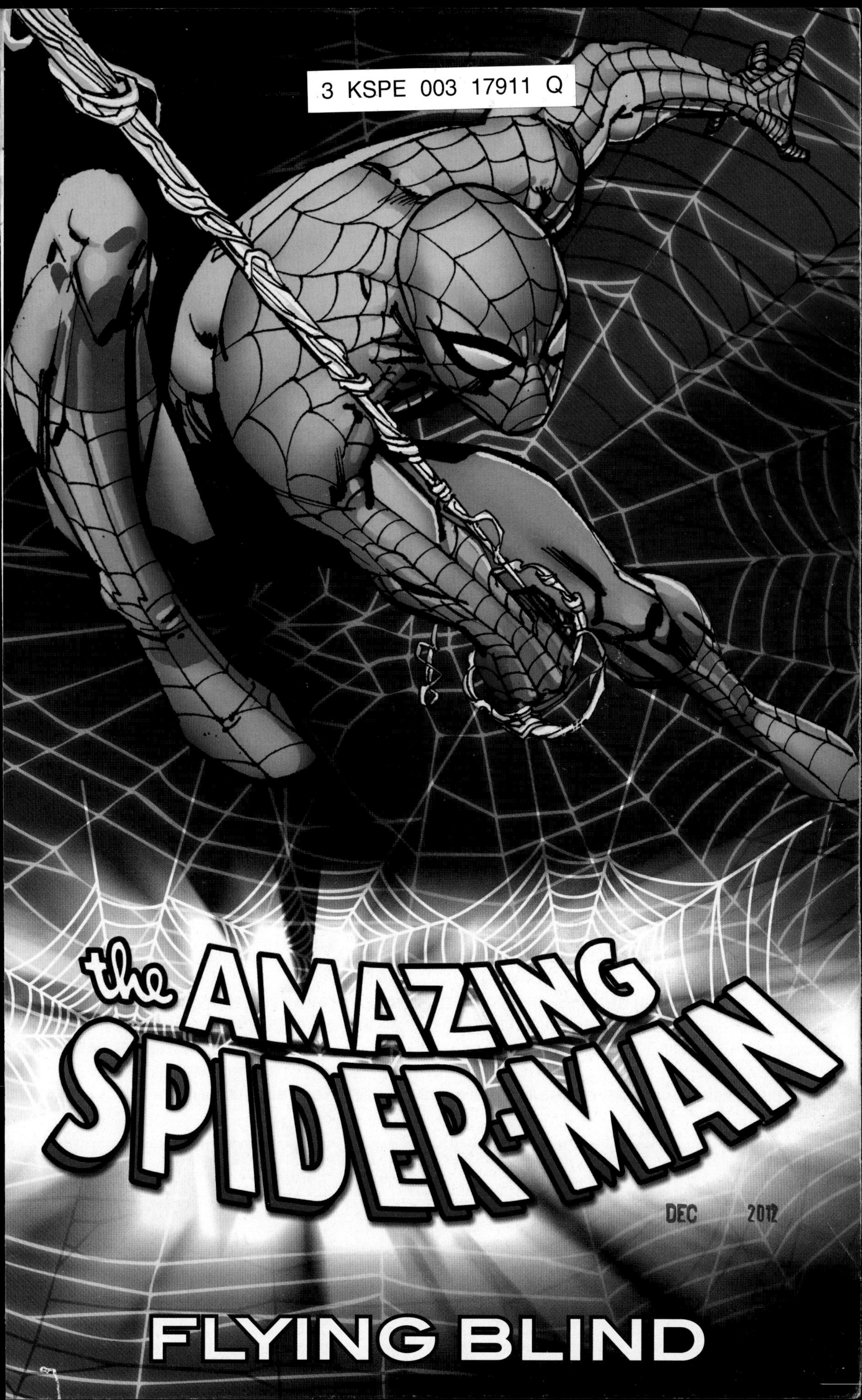
the AMAZING
SPIDER-MAN
DEC 2012
FLYING BLIND

the AMAZING SPIDER-MAN

FLYING BLIND

AMAZING SPIDER-MAN #674-675
Writer: **DAN SLOTT** • Penciler: **GIUSEPPE CAMUNCOLI**
Inker: **KLAUS JANSON**
Colorist: **FRANK D'ARMATA**
Cover Art: **GIUSEPPE CAMUNCOLI, KLAUS JANSON** & **FRANK D'ARMATA**

AMAZING SPIDER-MAN #676
Writer: **DAN SLOTT** • Penciler: **HUMBERTO RAMOS**
Inker: **VICTOR OLAZABA**
Colorist: **EDGAR DELGADO** • Cover Art: **HUMBERTO RAMOS** & **EDGAR DELGADO**

AMAZING SPIDER-MAN #677
Writer: **MARK WAID** • Artist: **EMMA RIOS**
Colorist: **JAVIER RODRIGUEZ** • Cover Art: **HUMBERTO RAMOS** & **EDGAR DELGADO**

DAREDEVIL #8
Writer: **MARK WAID** • Artist: **KANO**
Colorist: **JAVIER RODRIGUEZ** • Cover Art: **PAOLO RIVERA**

Letterer: **VC'S JOE CARAMAGNA** • Assistant Editor: **ELLIE PYLE** • Senior Editor: **STEPHEN WACKER**

Collection Editor: **JENNIFER GRÜNWALD** • Assistant Editors: **ALEX STARBUCK** & **NELSON RIBEIRO**
Editor, Special Projects: **MARK D. BEAZLEY** • Senior Editor, Special Projects: **JEFF YOUNGQUIST**
Senior Vice President of Sales: **DAVID GABRIEL** • SVP of Brand Planning & Communications: **MICHAEL PASCIULLO**

Editor in Chief: **AXEL ALONSO** • Chief Creative Officer: **JOE QUESADA** • Publisher: **DAN BUCKLEY** • Executive Producer: **ALAN FINE**

SPIDER-MAN: FLYING BLIND. Contains material originally published in magazine form as AMAZING SPIDER-MAN #674-677 and DAREDEVIL #8. First printing 2012. Hardcover ISBN# 978-0-7851-6001-4. Softcover ISBN# 978-0-7851-6002-1. Published by MARVEL WORLDWIDE, INC., a subsidiary of MARVEL ENTERTAINMENT, LLC. OFFICE OF PUBLICATION: 135 West 50th Street, New York, NY 10020. Copyright © 2011 and 2012 Marvel Characters, Inc. All rights reserved. Hardcover: $19.99 per copy in the U.S. and $21.99 in Canada (GST #R127032852). Softcover: $16.99 per copy in the U.S. and $18.99 in Canada (GST #R127032852). Canadian Agreement #40668537. All characters featured in this issue and the distinctive names and likenesses thereof, and all related indicia are trademarks of Marvel Characters, Inc. No similarity between any of the names, characters, persons, and/or institutions in this magazine with those of any living or dead person or institution is intended, and any such similarity which may exist is purely coincidental. **Printed in the U.S.A.** ALAN FINE, EVP - Office of the President, Marvel Worldwide, Inc. and EVP & CMO Marvel Characters B.V.; DAN BUCKLEY, Publisher & President - Print, Animation & Digital Divisions; JOE QUESADA, Chief Creative Officer; DAVID BOGART, SVP of Business Affairs & Talent Management; TOM BREVOORT, SVP of Publishing; C.B. CEBULSKI, SVP of Creator & Content Development; DAVID GABRIEL, SVP of Publishing Sales & Circulation; MICHAEL PASCIULLO, SVP of Brand Planning & Communications; JIM O'KEEFE, VP of Operations & Logistics; DAN CARR, Executive Director of Publishing Technology; SUSAN CRESPI, Editorial Operations Manager; ALEX MORALES, Publishing Operations Manager; STAN LEE, Chairman Emeritus. For information regarding advertising in Marvel Comics or on Marvel.com, please contact John Dokes, SVP Integrated Sales and Marketing, at jdokes@marvel.com. For Marvel subscription inquiries, please call 800-217-9158. **Manufactured between** 3/12/2012 and 4/9/2012 (hardcover), and 3/12/2012 and 10/8/2012 (softcover), by R.R. DONNELLEY, INC., SALEM, VA, USA.

10 9 8 7 6 5 4 3 2 1

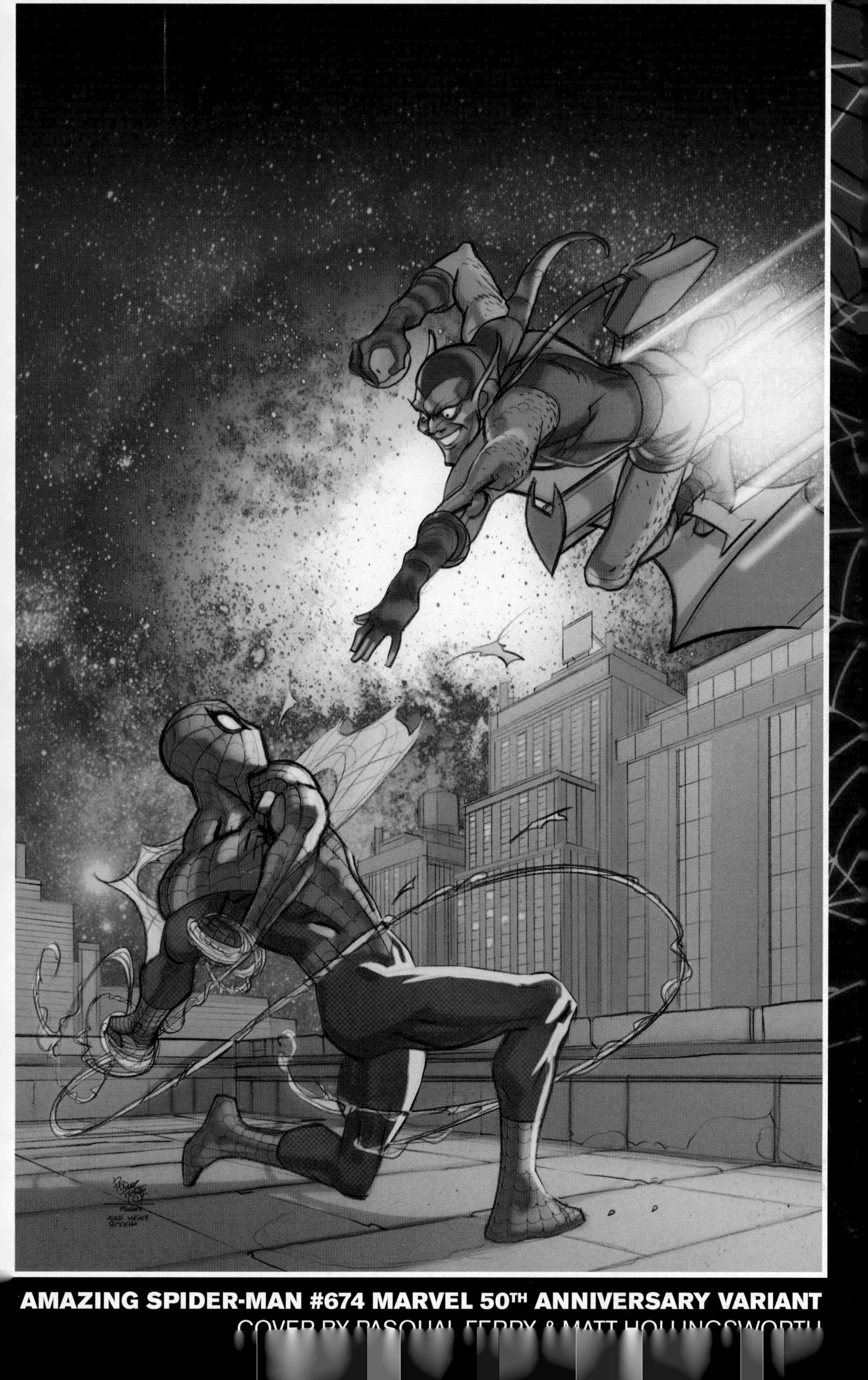

AMAZING SPIDER-MAN #674 MARVEL 50TH ANNIVERSARY VARIANT
COVER BY PASQUAL FERRY & MATT HOLLINGSWORTH

FINAL ☆☆☆☆

DAILY BUGLE®

NEW YORK'S FINEST DAILY NEWSPAPER

SINCE 1897 ☆☆☆☆
$1.00 (in NYC)
$1.50 (outside city)

INSIDE: THE NEW ORGANIZED CRIME – PART 4: THE EXCHANGE BY NORAH WINTERS; MARATHON OVERRUN BY MOLOIDS!; A.D.A. KIRSTEN MCDUFFIE SPOTTED AT THE WAKE, THE HOTTEST NEW NIGHTCLUB IN TOWN.

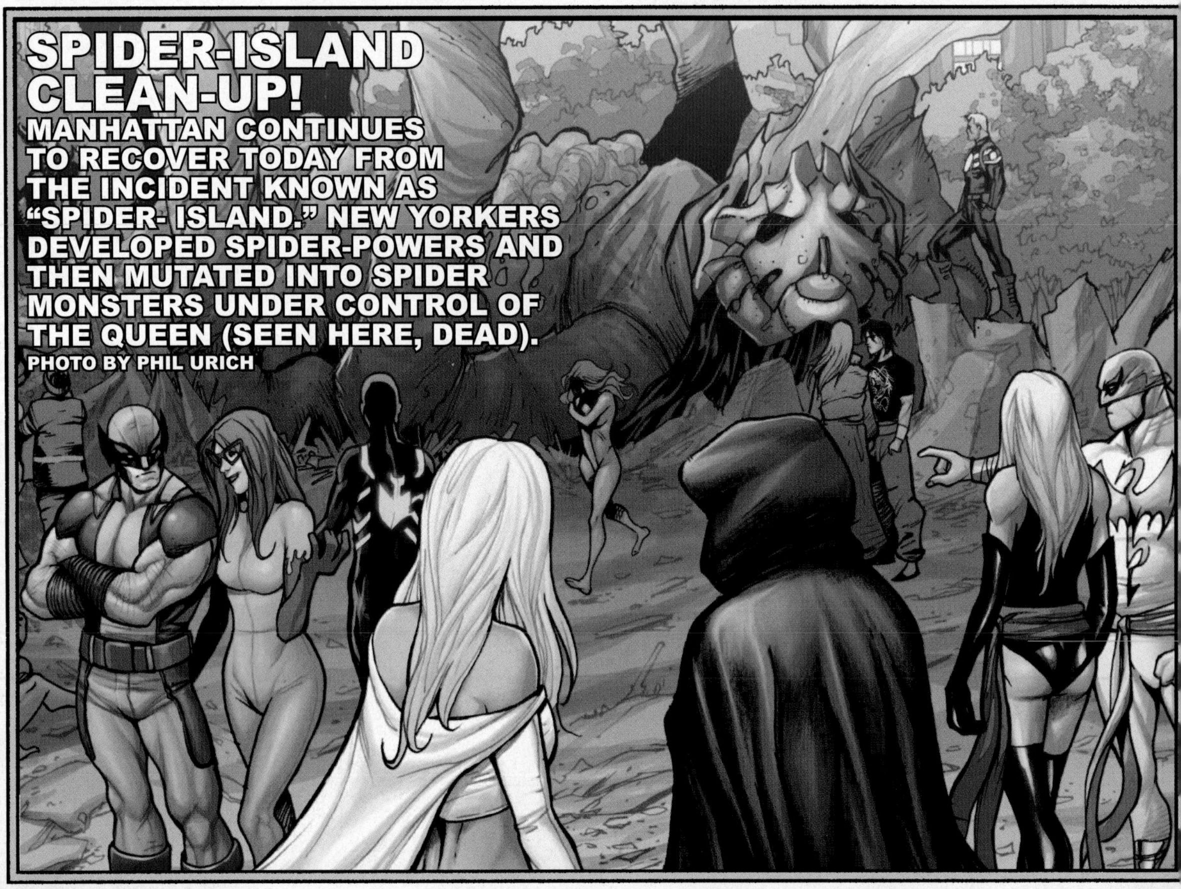
SPIDER-ISLAND CLEAN-UP!
MANHATTAN CONTINUES TO RECOVER TODAY FROM THE INCIDENT KNOWN AS "SPIDER- ISLAND." NEW YORKERS DEVELOPED SPIDER-POWERS AND THEN MUTATED INTO SPIDER MONSTERS UNDER CONTROL OF THE QUEEN (SEEN HERE, DEAD).
PHOTO BY PHIL URICH

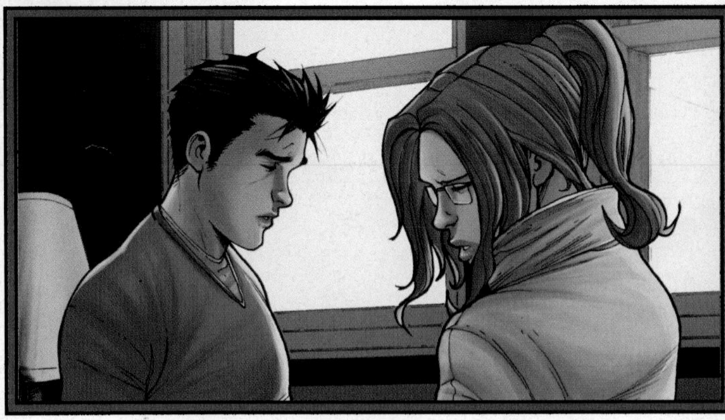

SPIDER-ISLAND BREAK-UP!

MOLLY MANTON, OUR RELATIONSHIP EXPERT, WEIGHS IN ON LIVES AND RELATIONSHIPS DESTROYED BY FINDING OUT ABOUT YOUR LOVER'S ARACHNID SIDE.

DAN SLOTT
WRITER

GIUSEPPE CAMUNCOLI
PENCILS

KLAUS JANSON
INKS

FRANK D'ARMATA
COLOR ART

VC'S JOE CARAMAGNA
LETTERING

ELLIE PYLE
ASSISTANT EDITOR

STEPHEN WACKER
EDITOR

AXEL ALONSO
EDITOR IN CHIEF

JOE QUESADA
CHIEF CREATIVE OFFICER

DAN BUCKLEY
PUBLISHER

ALAN FINE
EXEC. PRODUCER

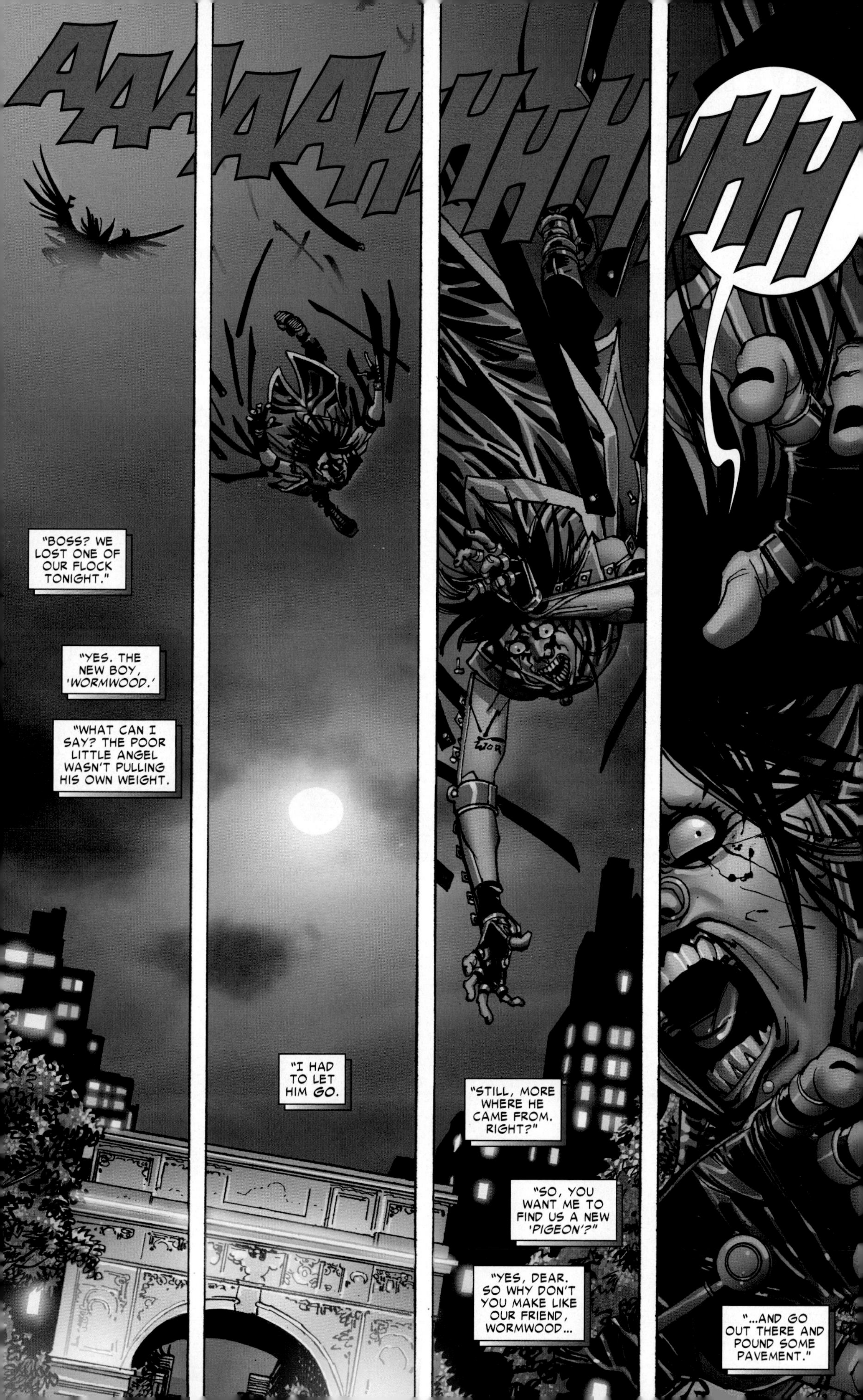
AAAAAAHHHHHH
"BOSS? WE LOST ONE OF OUR FLOCK TONIGHT."
"YES. THE NEW BOY, 'WORMWOOD.'
"WHAT CAN I SAY? THE POOR LITTLE ANGEL WASN'T PULLING HIS OWN WEIGHT.
"I HAD TO LET HIM GO.
"STILL, MORE WHERE HE CAME FROM. RIGHT?"
"SO, YOU WANT ME TO FIND US A NEW 'PIGEON'?"
"YES, DEAR. SO WHY DON'T YOU MAKE LIKE OUR FRIEND, WORMWOOD...
"...AND GO OUT THERE AND POUND SOME PAVEMENT."

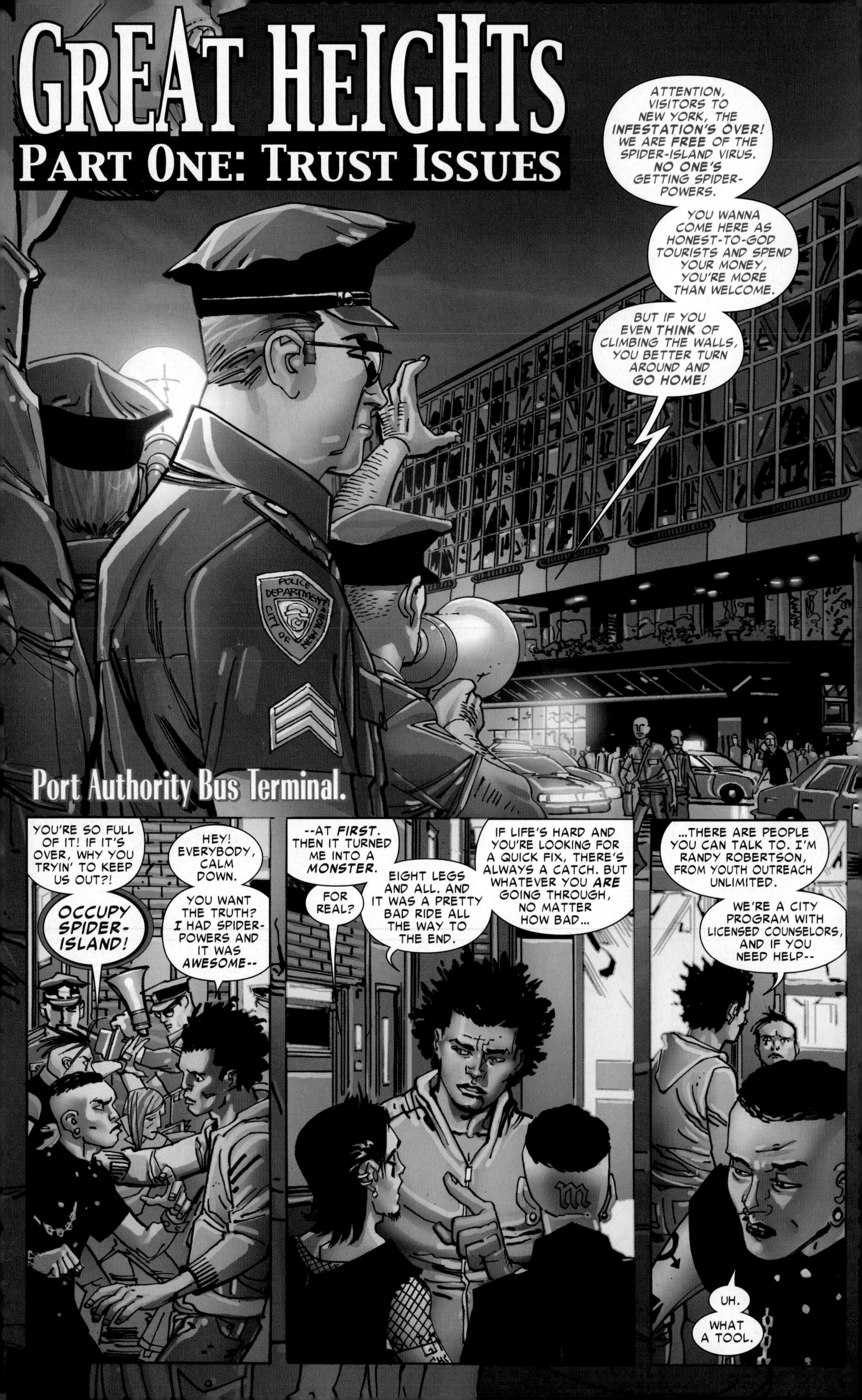
GREAT HEIGHTS
PART ONE: TRUST ISSUES
ATTENTION, VISITORS TO NEW YORK, THE INFESTATION'S OVER! WE ARE FREE OF THE SPIDER-ISLAND VIRUS. NO ONE'S GETTING SPIDER-POWERS.
YOU WANNA COME HERE AS HONEST-TO-GOD TOURISTS AND SPEND YOUR MONEY, YOU'RE MORE THAN WELCOME.
BUT IF YOU EVEN THINK OF CLIMBING THE WALLS, YOU BETTER TURN AROUND AND GO HOME!
Port Authority Bus Terminal.
YOU'RE SO FULL OF IT! IF IT'S OVER, WHY YOU TRYIN' TO KEEP US OUT?!
OCCUPY SPIDER-ISLAND!
HEY! EVERYBODY, CALM DOWN.
YOU WANT THE TRUTH? I HAD SPIDER-POWERS AND IT WAS AWESOME--
--AT FIRST. THEN IT TURNED ME INTO A MONSTER.
FOR REAL?
EIGHT LEGS AND ALL. AND IT WAS A PRETTY BAD RIDE ALL THE WAY TO THE END.
IF LIFE'S HARD AND YOU'RE LOOKING FOR A QUICK FIX, THERE'S ALWAYS A CATCH. BUT WHATEVER YOU ARE GOING THROUGH, NO MATTER HOW BAD...
...THERE ARE PEOPLE YOU CAN TALK TO. I'M RANDY ROBERTSON, FROM YOUTH OUTREACH UNLIMITED.
WE'RE A CITY PROGRAM WITH LICENSED COUNSELORS, AND IF YOU NEED HELP--
UH.
WHAT A TOOL.

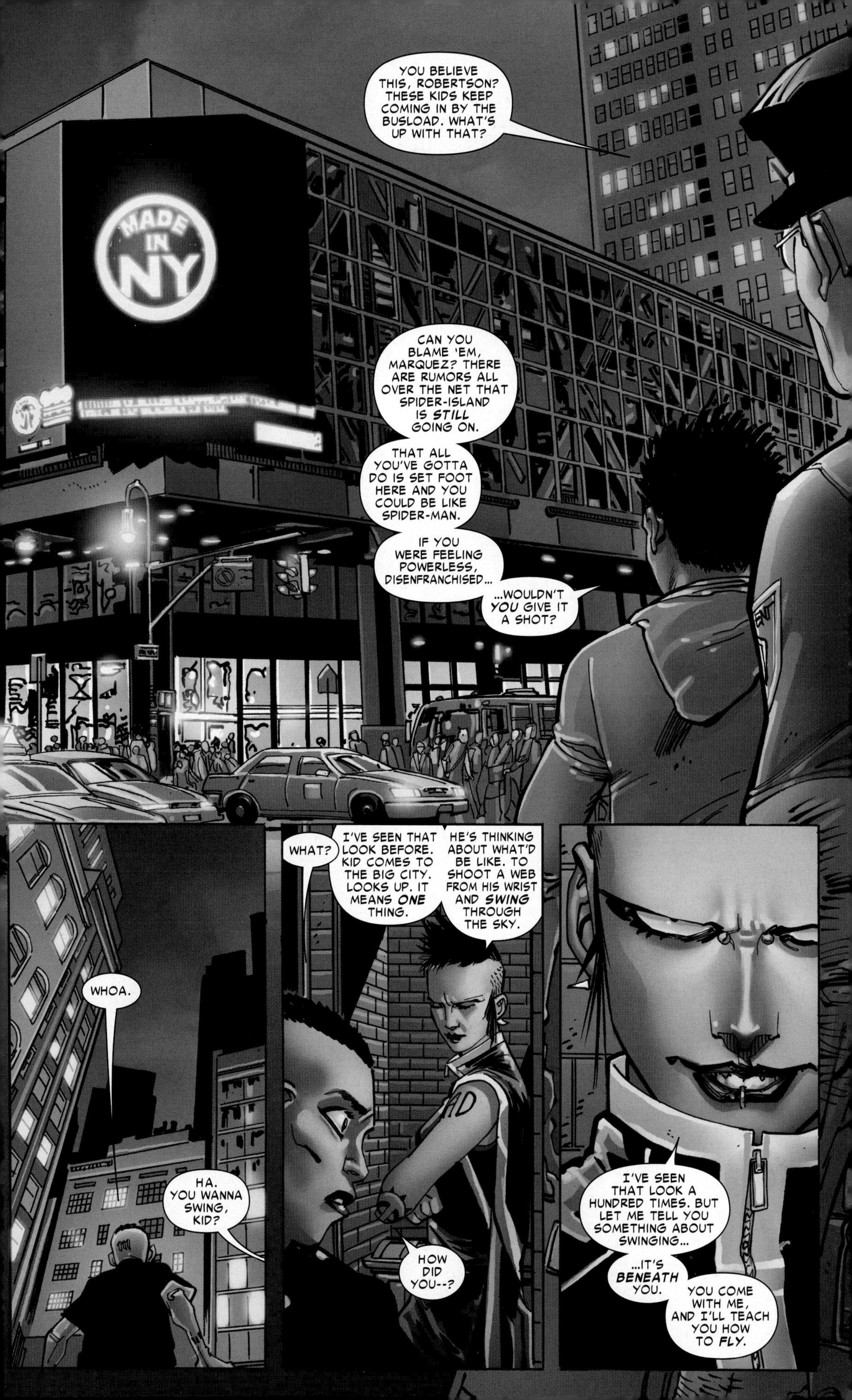
MADE IN NY
YOU BELIEVE THIS, ROBERTSON? THESE KIDS KEEP COMING IN BY THE BUSLOAD. WHAT'S UP WITH THAT?
CAN YOU BLAME 'EM, MARQUEZ? THERE ARE RUMORS ALL OVER THE NET THAT SPIDER-ISLAND IS STILL GOING ON.
THAT ALL YOU'VE GOTTA DO IS SET FOOT HERE AND YOU COULD BE LIKE SPIDER-MAN.
IF YOU WERE FEELING POWERLESS, DISENFRANCHISED...
...WOULDN'T YOU GIVE IT A SHOT?
WHOA.
HA. YOU WANNA SWING, KID?
WHAT?
I'VE SEEN THAT LOOK BEFORE. KID COMES TO THE BIG CITY. LOOKS UP. IT MEANS ONE THING.
HE'S THINKING ABOUT WHAT'D BE LIKE. TO SHOOT A WEB FROM HIS WRIST AND SWING THROUGH THE SKY.
HOW DID YOU--?
I'VE SEEN THAT LOOK A HUNDRED TIMES. BUT LET ME TELL YOU SOMETHING ABOUT SWINGING...
...IT'S BENEATH YOU.
YOU COME WITH ME, AND I'LL TEACH YOU HOW TO FLY.

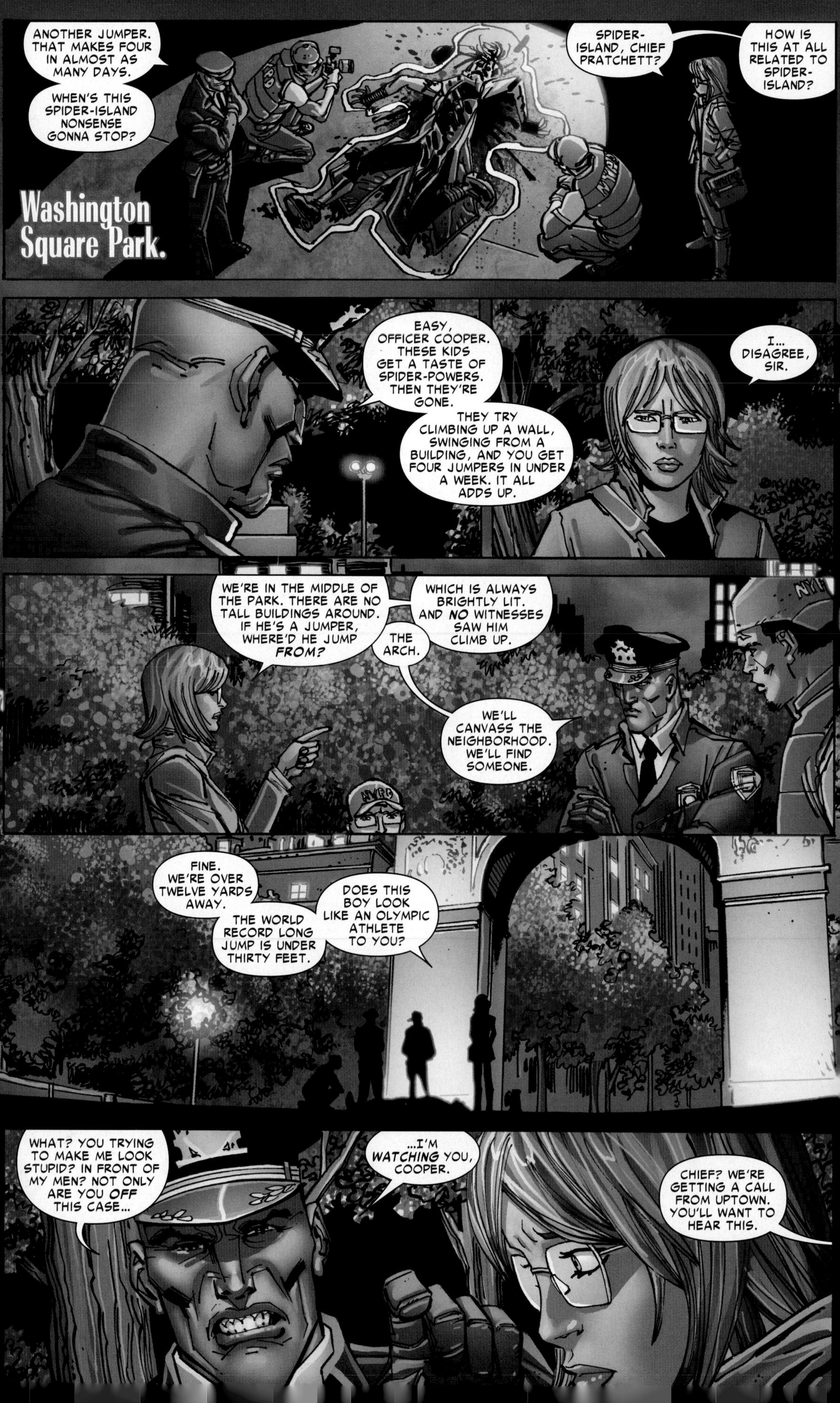
ANOTHER JUMPER. THAT MAKES FOUR IN ALMOST AS MANY DAYS.
WHEN'S THIS SPIDER-ISLAND NONSENSE GONNA STOP?
HOW IS THIS AT ALL RELATED TO SPIDER-ISLAND?
SPIDER-ISLAND, CHIEF PRATCHETT?
Washington Square Park.
EASY, OFFICER COOPER. THESE KIDS GET A TASTE OF SPIDER-POWERS. THEN THEY'RE GONE.
THEY TRY CLIMBING UP A WALL, SWINGING FROM A BUILDING, AND YOU GET FOUR JUMPERS IN UNDER A WEEK. IT ALL ADDS UP.
I... DISAGREE, SIR.
WE'RE IN THE MIDDLE OF THE PARK. THERE ARE NO TALL BUILDINGS AROUND. IF HE'S A JUMPER, WHERE'D HE JUMP *FROM?*
WHICH IS ALWAYS BRIGHTLY LIT. AND *NO* WITNESSES SAW HIM CLIMB UP.
THE ARCH.
WE'LL CANVASS THE NEIGHBORHOOD. WE'LL FIND SOMEONE.
FINE. WE'RE OVER TWELVE YARDS AWAY.
THE WORLD RECORD LONG JUMP IS UNDER THIRTY FEET.
DOES THIS BOY LOOK LIKE AN OLYMPIC ATHLETE TO YOU?
WHAT? YOU TRYING TO MAKE ME LOOK STUPID? IN FRONT OF MY MEN? NOT ONLY ARE YOU *OFF* THIS CASE...
...I'M *WATCHING* YOU, COOPER.
CHIEF? WE'RE GETTING A CALL FROM UPTOWN. YOU'LL WANT TO HEAR THIS.

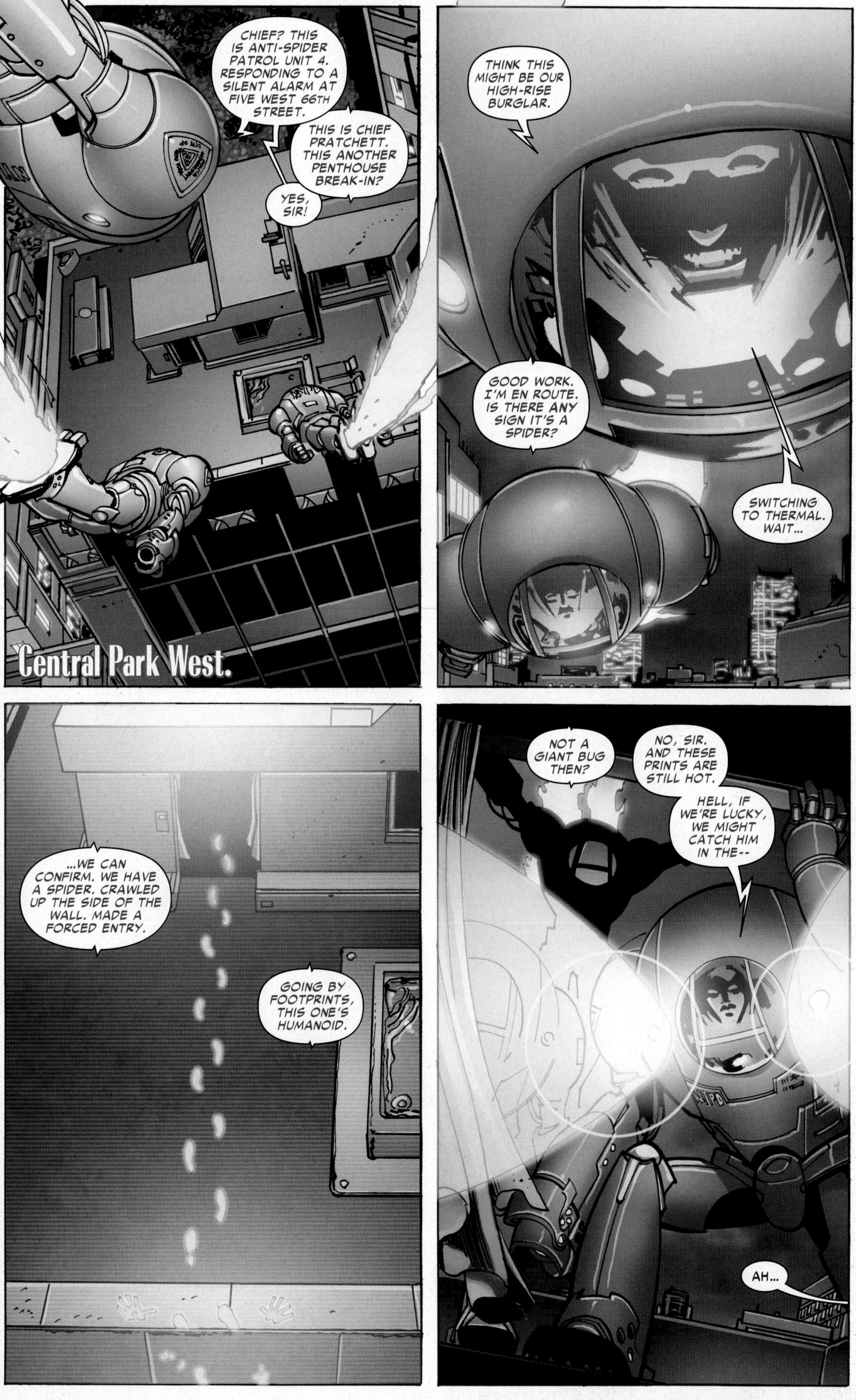
Central Park West.
CHIEF? THIS IS ANTI-SPIDER PATROL UNIT 4. RESPONDING TO A SILENT ALARM AT FIVE WEST 66TH STREET.
THIS IS CHIEF PRATCHETT. THIS ANOTHER PENTHOUSE BREAK-IN?
YES, SIR!
THINK THIS MIGHT BE OUR HIGH-RISE BURGLAR.
GOOD WORK. I'M EN ROUTE. IS THERE ANY SIGN IT'S A SPIDER?
SWITCHING TO THERMAL. WAIT...
...WE CAN CONFIRM. WE HAVE A SPIDER. CRAWLED UP THE SIDE OF THE WALL. MADE A FORCED ENTRY.
GOING BY FOOTPRINTS, THIS ONE'S HUMANOID.
NOT A GIANT BUG THEN?
NO, SIR. AND THESE PRINTS ARE STILL HOT.
HELL, IF WE'RE LUCKY, WE MIGHT CATCH HIM IN THE--
AH...

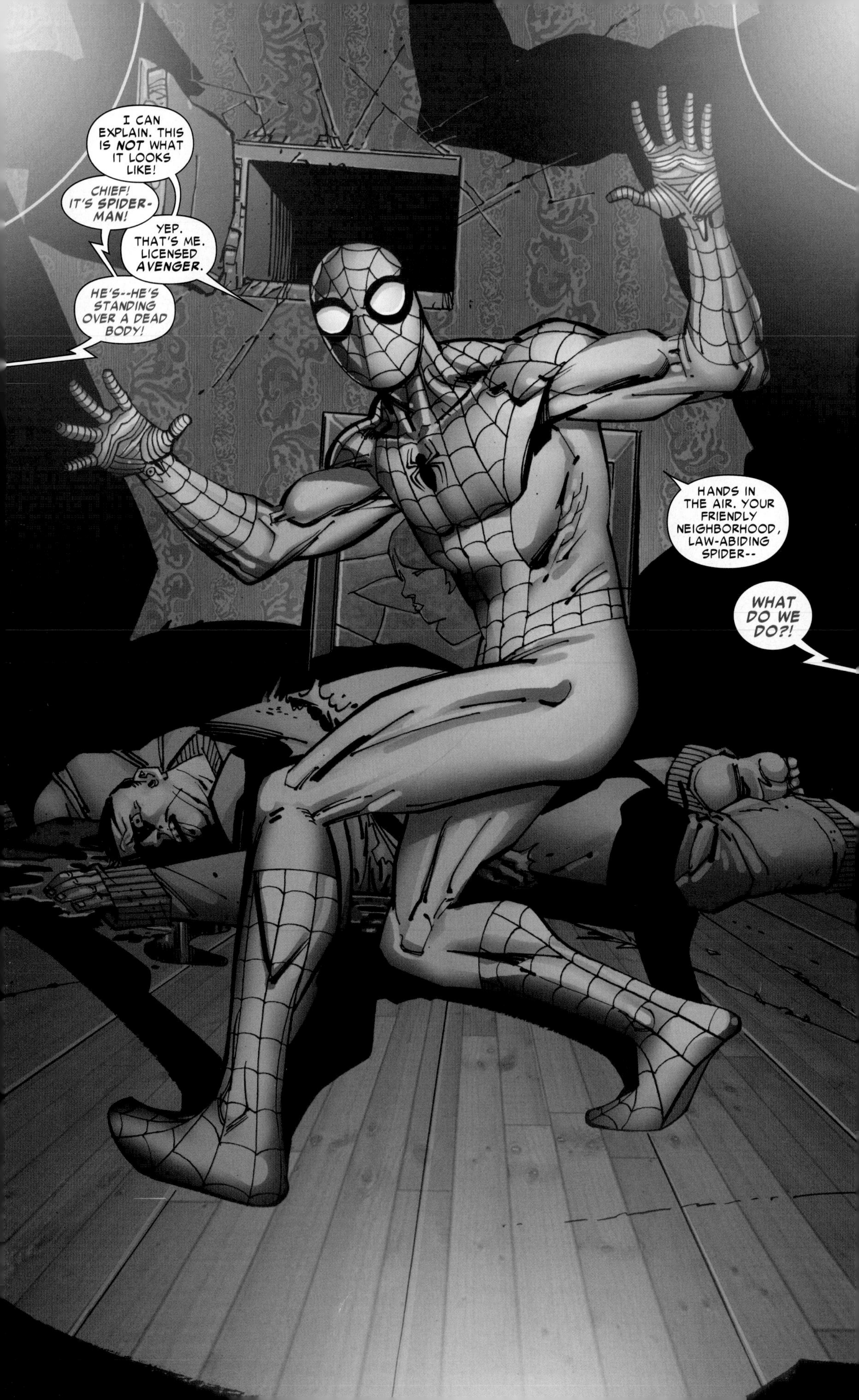
I CAN EXPLAIN. THIS IS *NOT* WHAT IT LOOKS LIKE!
CHIEF! IT'S SPIDER-MAN!
YEP. THAT'S ME. LICENSED **AVENGER**.
HE'S--HE'S STANDING OVER A DEAD BODY!
HANDS IN THE AIR. YOUR FRIENDLY NEIGHBORHOOD, LAW-ABIDING SPIDER--
WHAT DO WE DO?!

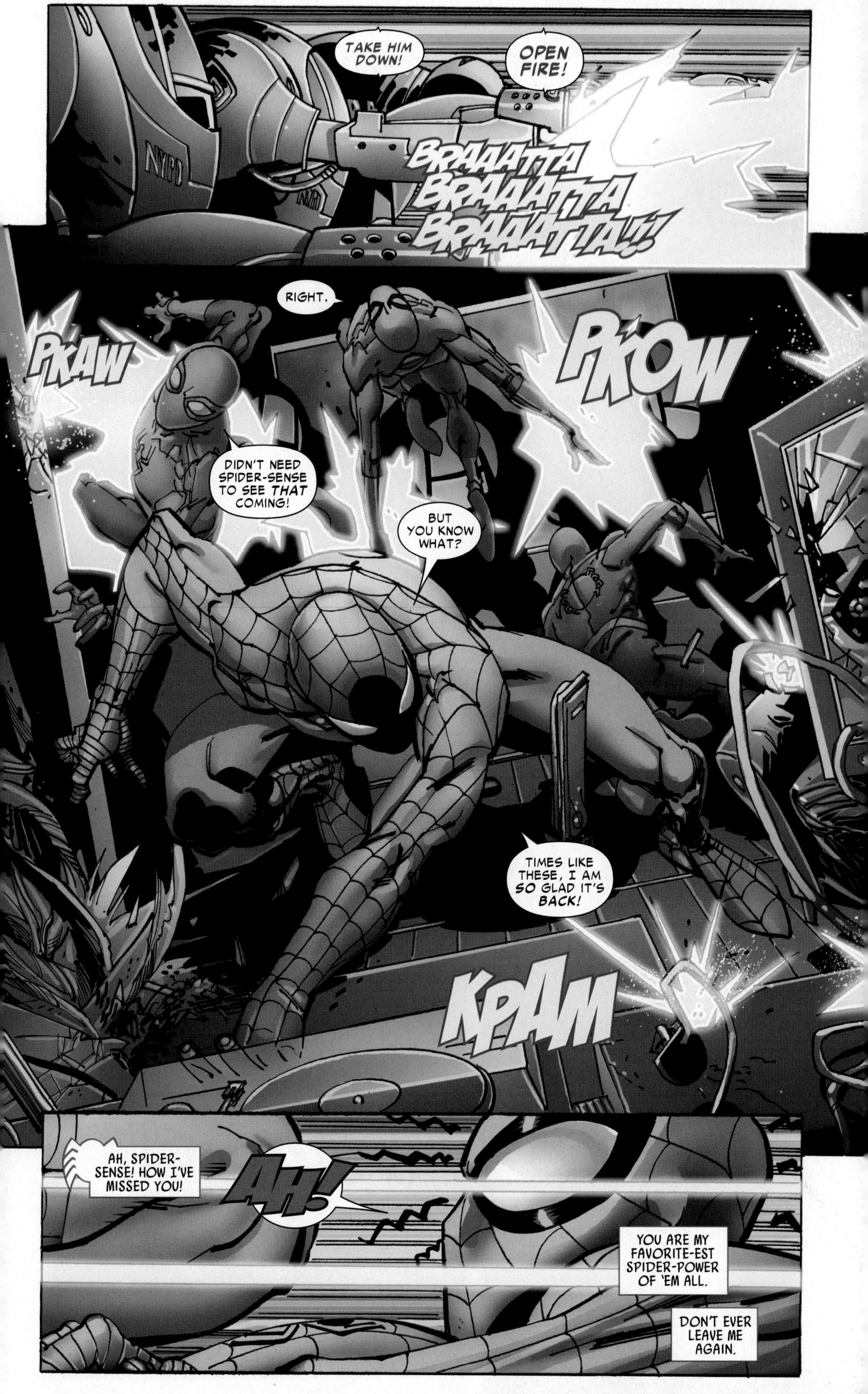
TAKE HIM DOWN!
OPEN FIRE!
BRAAATTA BRAAATTA BRAAATTA!!!
RIGHT.
PKAW
PKOW
DIDN'T NEED SPIDER-SENSE TO SEE THAT COMING!
BUT YOU KNOW WHAT?
TIMES LIKE THESE, I AM SO GLAD IT'S BACK!
KPAM
AH, SPIDER-SENSE! HOW I'VE MISSED YOU!
AH!
YOU ARE MY FAVORITE-EST SPIDER-POWER OF 'EM ALL.
DON'T EVER LEAVE ME AGAIN.

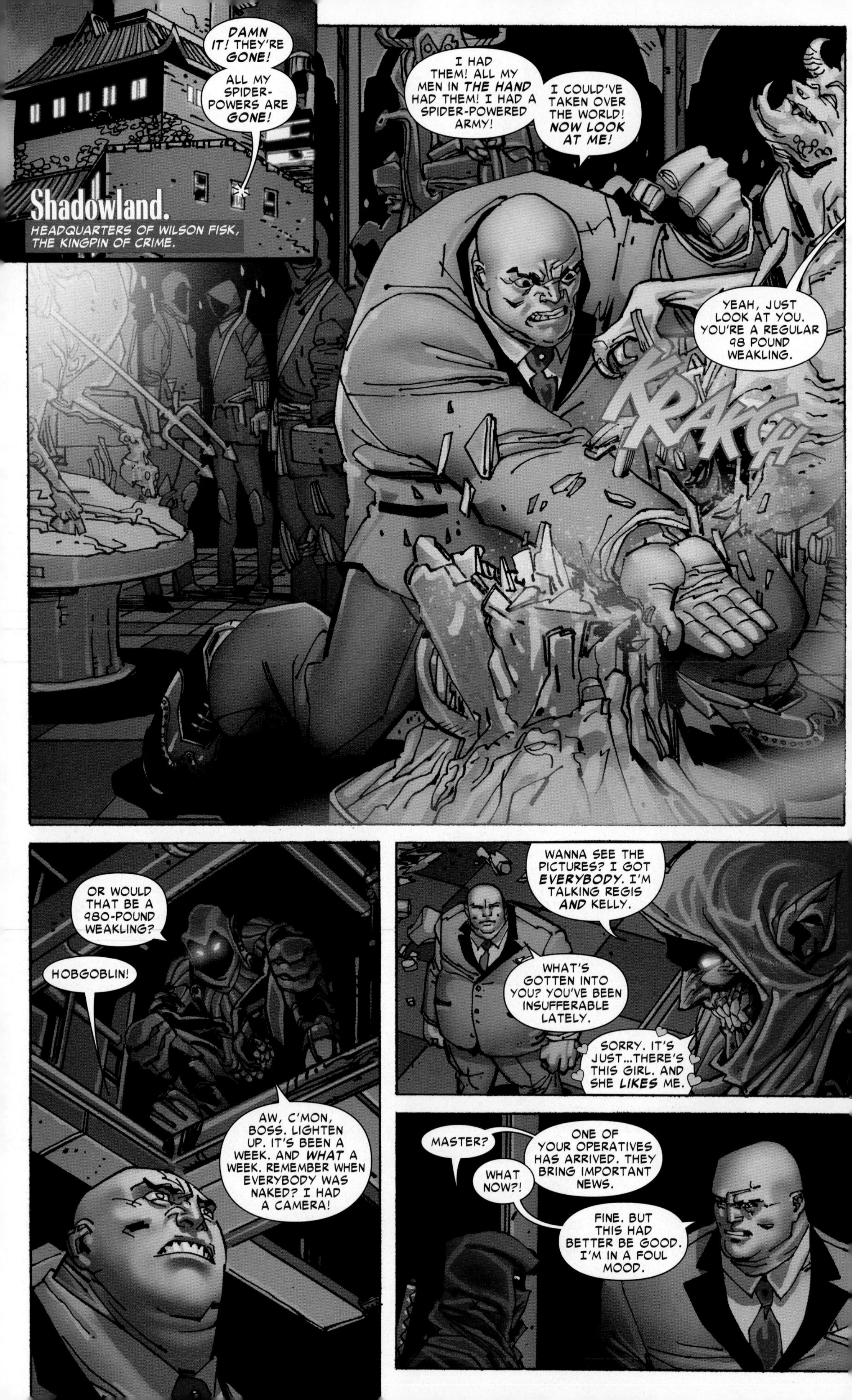

Shadowland.
HEADQUARTERS OF WILSON FISK, THE KINGPIN OF CRIME.
DAMN IT! THEY'RE GONE!
ALL MY SPIDER-POWERS ARE GONE!
I HAD THEM! ALL MY MEN IN THE HAND HAD THEM! I HAD A SPIDER-POWERED ARMY!
I COULD'VE TAKEN OVER THE WORLD! NOW LOOK AT ME!
YEAH, JUST LOOK AT YOU. YOU'RE A REGULAR 98 POUND WEAKLING.
KRAKCH
OR WOULD THAT BE A 980-POUND WEAKLING?
HOBGOBLIN!
AW, C'MON, BOSS. LIGHTEN UP. IT'S BEEN A WEEK. AND WHAT A WEEK. REMEMBER WHEN EVERYBODY WAS NAKED? I HAD A CAMERA!
WANNA SEE THE PICTURES? I GOT EVERYBODY. I'M TALKING REGIS AND KELLY.
WHAT'S GOTTEN INTO YOU? YOU'VE BEEN INSUFFERABLE LATELY.
SORRY. IT'S JUST...THERE'S THIS GIRL. AND SHE LIKES ME.
MASTER?
ONE OF YOUR OPERATIVES HAS ARRIVED. THEY BRING IMPORTANT NEWS.
WHAT NOW?!
FINE. BUT THIS HAD BETTER BE GOOD. I'M IN A FOUL MOOD.

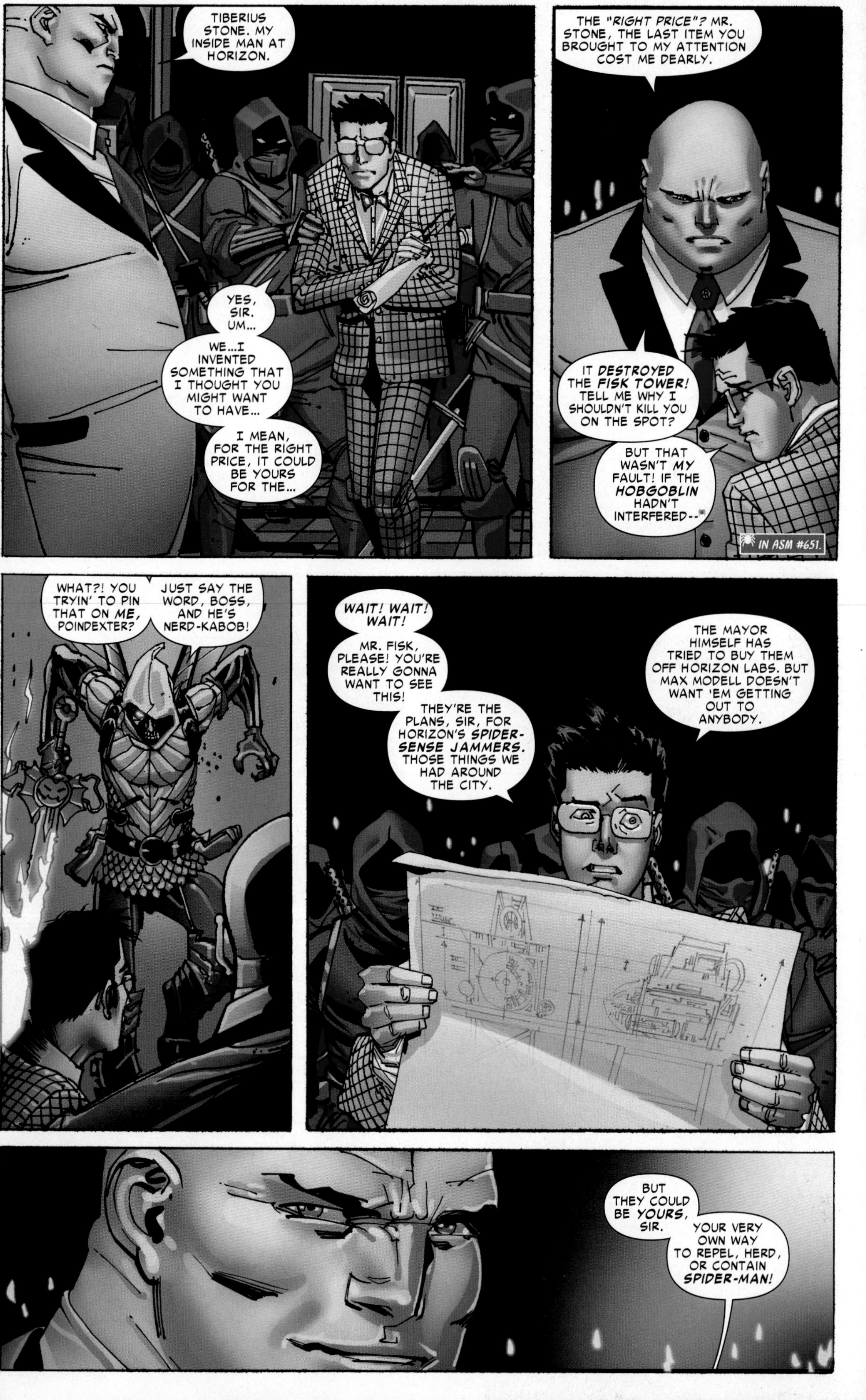
TIBERIUS STONE. MY INSIDE MAN AT HORIZON.
YES, SIR. UM...
WE...I INVENTED SOMETHING THAT I THOUGHT YOU MIGHT WANT TO HAVE...
I MEAN, FOR THE RIGHT PRICE, IT COULD BE YOURS FOR THE...
THE "RIGHT PRICE"? MR. STONE, THE LAST ITEM YOU BROUGHT TO MY ATTENTION COST ME DEARLY.
IT DESTROYED THE FISK TOWER! TELL ME WHY I SHOULDN'T KILL YOU ON THE SPOT?
BUT THAT WASN'T MY FAULT! IF THE HOBGOBLIN HADN'T INTERFERED--
IN ASM #651.
WHAT?! YOU TRYIN' TO PIN THAT ON ME, POINDEXTER?
JUST SAY THE WORD, BOSS, AND HE'S NERD-KABOB!
WAIT! WAIT! WAIT!
MR. FISK, PLEASE! YOU'RE REALLY GONNA WANT TO SEE THIS!
THEY'RE THE PLANS, SIR, FOR HORIZON'S SPIDER-SENSE JAMMERS. THOSE THINGS WE HAD AROUND THE CITY.
THE MAYOR HIMSELF HAS TRIED TO BUY THEM OFF HORIZON LABS. BUT MAX MODELL DOESN'T WANT 'EM GETTING OUT TO ANYBODY.
BUT THEY COULD BE YOURS, SIR.
YOUR VERY OWN WAY TO REPEL, HERD, OR CONTAIN SPIDER-MAN!

WHAT-- WHAT'RE YOU DOING?

WHAT'S IT LOOK LIKE? I'M VOIDING YOUR WARRANTY.

SKRRZ

THERE'S SOMETHING YOU SHOULD KNOW. THE SPIDEY IN ME REALLY DOESN'T LIKE FIGHTING NEW YORK'S FINEST...

...BUT THE PETER PARKER IN ME HAS NO PROBLEM SCRAPPING ONE OF MY OWN EXPERIMENTS.

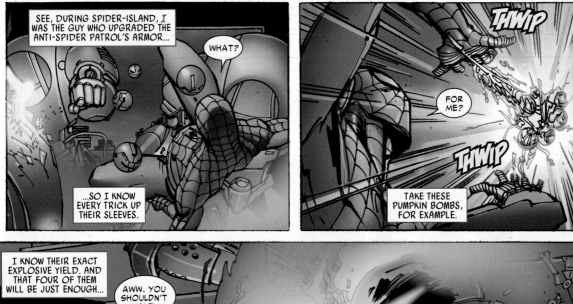

SEE, DURING SPIDER-ISLAND, I WAS THE GUY WHO UPGRADED THE ANTI-SPIDER PATROL'S ARMOR...

WHAT?

...SO I KNOW EVERY TRICK UP THEIR SLEEVES.

THWIP

FOR ME?

THWIP

TAKE THESE PUMPKIN BOMBS, FOR EXAMPLE.

I KNOW THEIR EXACT EXPLOSIVE YIELD. AND THAT FOUR OF THEM WILL BE JUST ENOUGH...

AWW. YOU SHOULDN'T HAVE.

BCHOOM

...TO KNOCK OUT THAT SUIT'S HYDRAULICS WITHOUT HURTING THE OFFICER INSIDE.

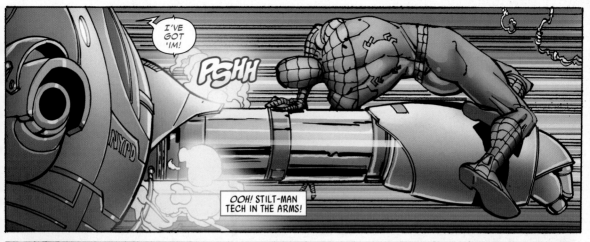

I'VE GOT 'IM!

PSHH

OOH! STILT-MAN TECH IN THE ARMS!

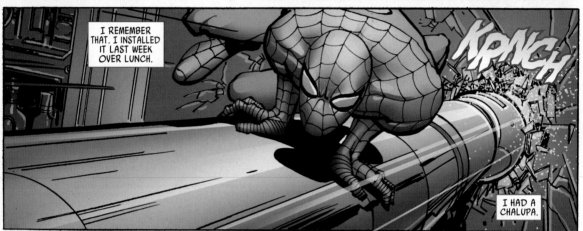

I REMEMBER THAT. I INSTALLED IT LAST WEEK OVER LUNCH.

KRNCH

I HAD A CHALUPA.

LONG ARM OF THE LAW...

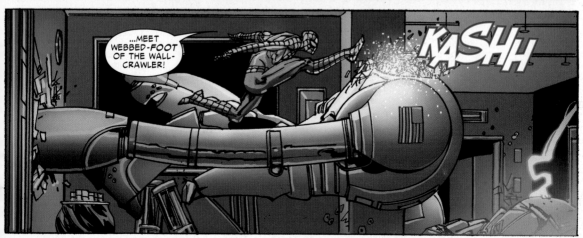

...MEET WEBBED-FOOT OF THE WALL-CRAWLER!

KASHH

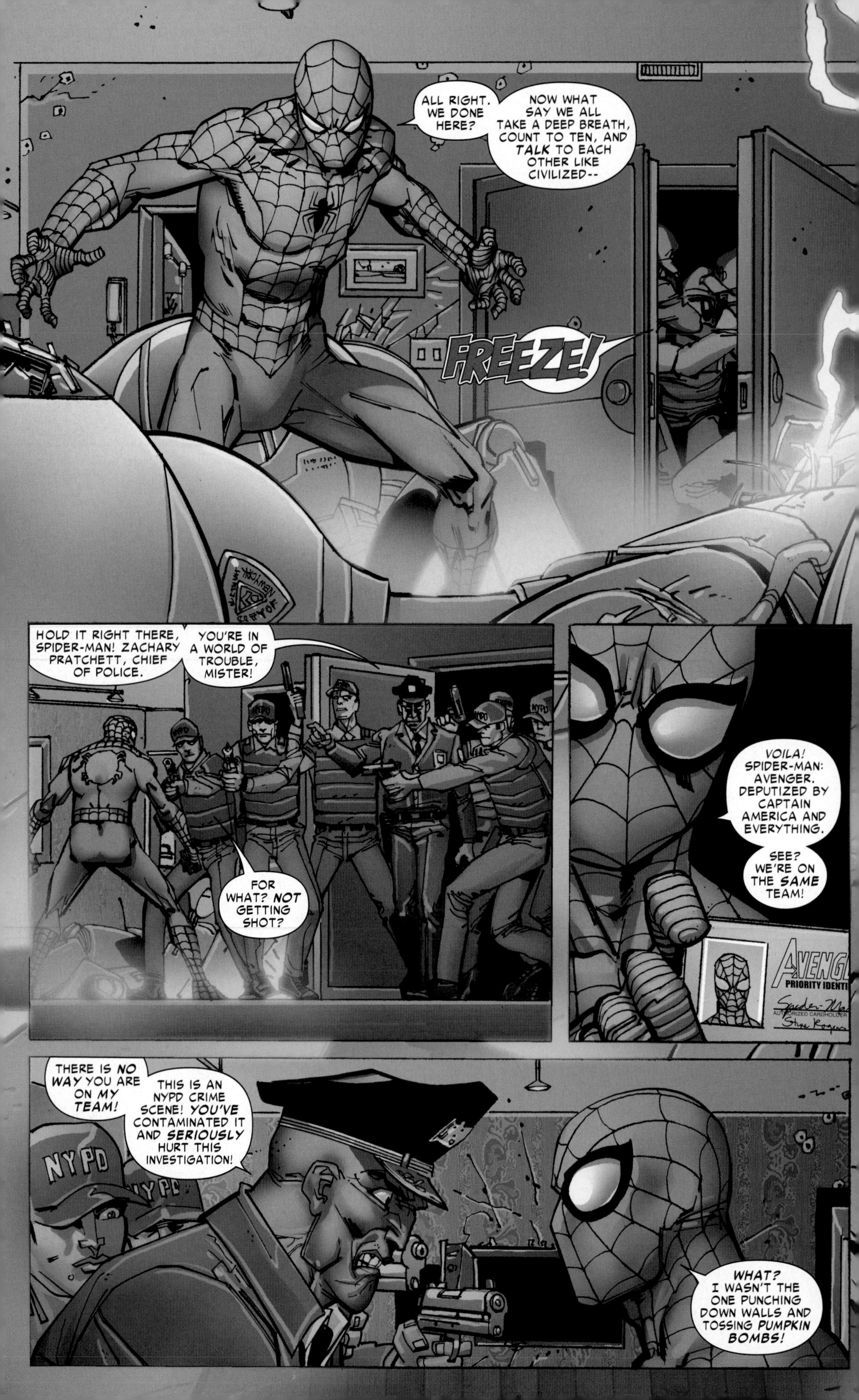
ALL RIGHT. WE DONE HERE?
NOW WHAT SAY WE ALL TAKE A DEEP BREATH, COUNT TO TEN, AND *TALK* TO EACH OTHER LIKE CIVILIZED--
FREEZE!
HOLD IT RIGHT THERE, SPIDER-MAN! ZACHARY PRATCHETT, CHIEF OF POLICE.
YOU'RE IN A WORLD OF TROUBLE, MISTER!
FOR WHAT? *NOT* GETTING SHOT?
VOILA! SPIDER-MAN: AVENGER. DEPUTIZED BY CAPTAIN AMERICA AND EVERYTHING.
SEE? WE'RE ON THE *SAME* TEAM!
THERE IS *NO WAY* YOU ARE ON *MY TEAM!*
THIS IS AN NYPD CRIME SCENE! *YOU'VE* CONTAMINATED IT AND *SERIOUSLY* HURT THIS INVESTIGATION!
NYPD
WHAT? I WASN'T THE ONE PUNCHING DOWN WALLS AND TOSSING *PUMPKIN BOMBS!*

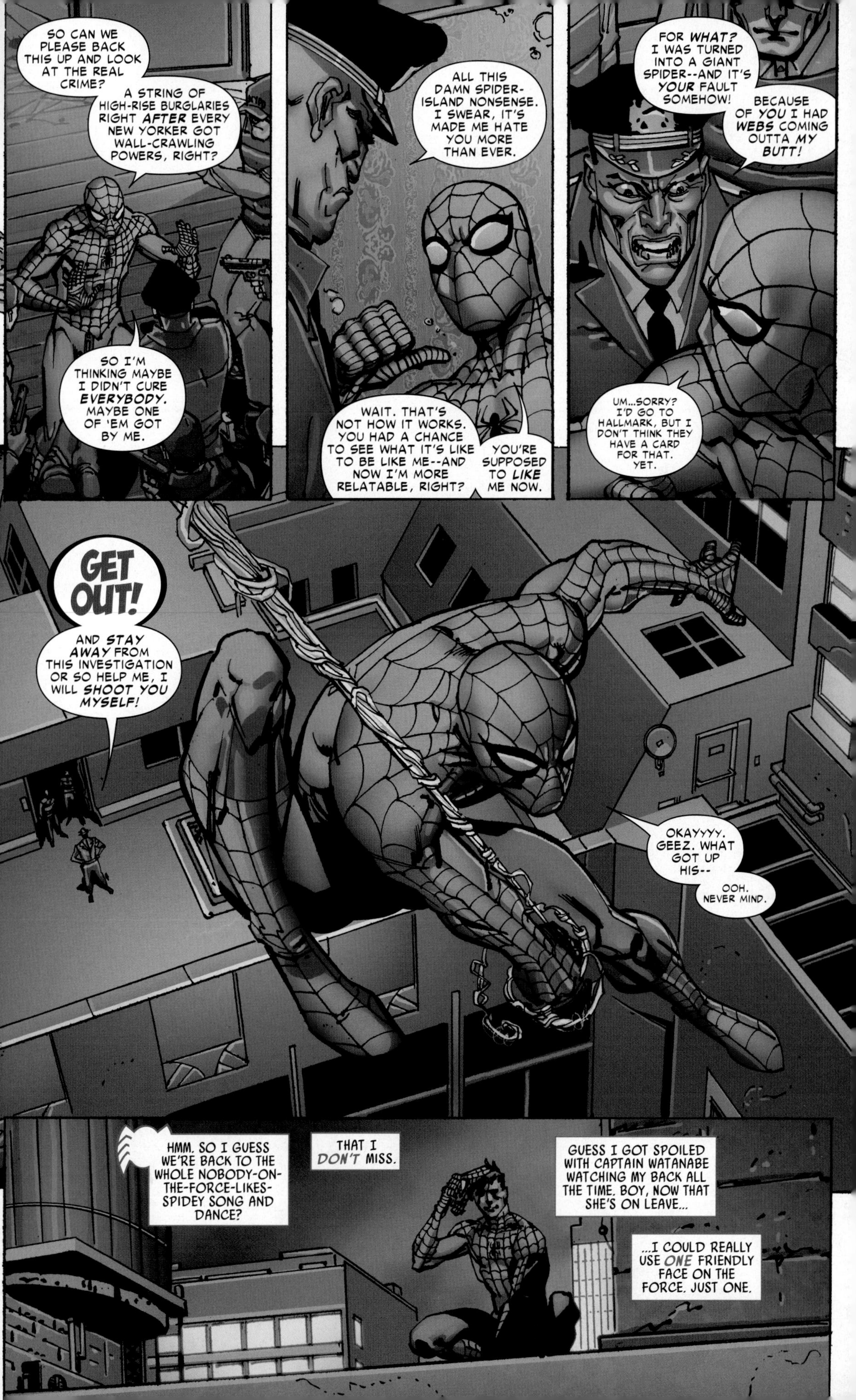
SO CAN WE PLEASE BACK THIS UP AND LOOK AT THE REAL CRIME?
A STRING OF HIGH-RISE BURGLARIES RIGHT AFTER EVERY NEW YORKER GOT WALL-CRAWLING POWERS, RIGHT?
SO I'M THINKING MAYBE I DIDN'T CURE EVERYBODY. MAYBE ONE OF 'EM GOT BY ME.
ALL THIS DAMN SPIDER-ISLAND NONSENSE. I SWEAR, IT'S MADE ME HATE YOU MORE THAN EVER.
WAIT. THAT'S NOT HOW IT WORKS. YOU HAD A CHANCE TO SEE WHAT IT'S LIKE TO BE LIKE ME--AND NOW I'M MORE RELATABLE, RIGHT?
YOU'RE SUPPOSED TO LIKE ME NOW.
FOR WHAT? I WAS TURNED INTO A GIANT SPIDER--AND IT'S YOUR FAULT SOMEHOW!
BECAUSE OF YOU I HAD WEBS COMING OUTTA MY BUTT!
UM...SORRY? I'D GO TO HALLMARK, BUT I DON'T THINK THEY HAVE A CARD FOR THAT. YET.
GET OUT!
AND STAY AWAY FROM THIS INVESTIGATION OR SO HELP ME, I WILL SHOOT YOU MYSELF!
OKAYYYY. GEEZ. WHAT GOT UP HIS--
OOH. NEVER MIND.
HMM. SO I GUESS WE'RE BACK TO THE WHOLE NOBODY-ON-THE-FORCE-LIKES-SPIDEY SONG AND DANCE?
THAT I DON'T MISS.
GUESS I GOT SPOILED WITH CAPTAIN WATANABE WATCHING MY BACK ALL THE TIME. BOY, NOW THAT SHE'S ON LEAVE...
...I COULD REALLY USE ONE FRIENDLY FACE ON THE FORCE. JUST ONE.

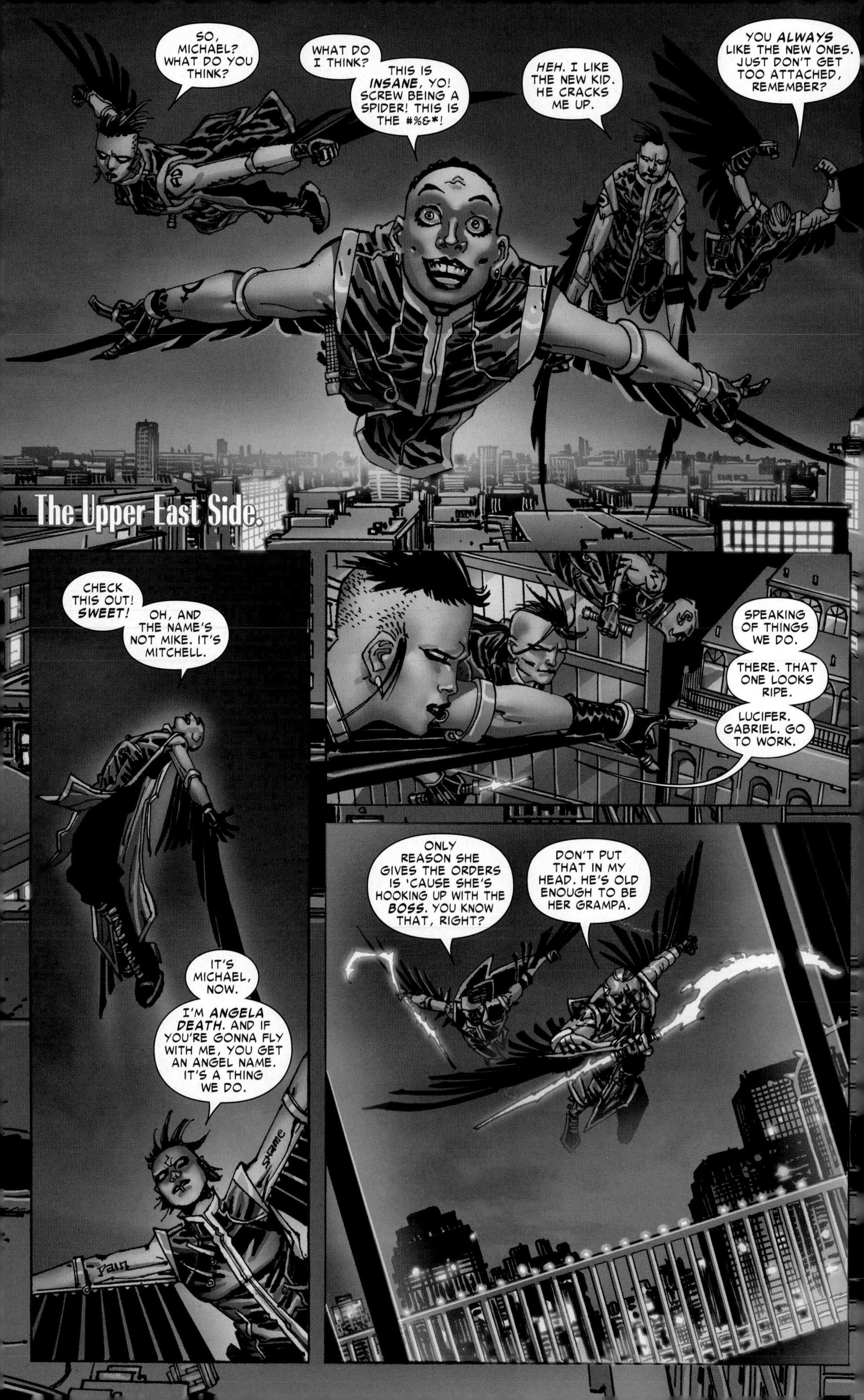
SO, MICHAEL? WHAT DO YOU THINK?
WHAT DO I THINK?
THIS IS *INSANE*, YO! SCREW BEING A SPIDER! THIS IS THE #%&*!
HEH. I LIKE THE NEW KID. HE CRACKS ME UP.
YOU *ALWAYS* LIKE THE NEW ONES. JUST DON'T GET TOO ATTACHED, REMEMBER?
The Upper East Side.
CHECK THIS OUT! *SWEET!*
OH, AND THE NAME'S NOT MIKE. IT'S MITCHELL.
IT'S MICHAEL, NOW.
I'M *ANGELA DEATH*. AND IF YOU'RE GONNA FLY WITH ME, YOU GET AN ANGEL NAME. IT'S A THING WE DO.
SPEAKING OF THINGS WE DO.
THERE. THAT ONE LOOKS RIPE.
LUCIFER. GABRIEL. GO TO WORK.
ONLY REASON SHE GIVES THE ORDERS IS 'CAUSE SHE'S HOOKING UP WITH THE *BOSS*. YOU KNOW THAT, RIGHT?
DON'T PUT THAT IN MY HEAD. HE'S OLD ENOUGH TO BE HER GRAMPA.

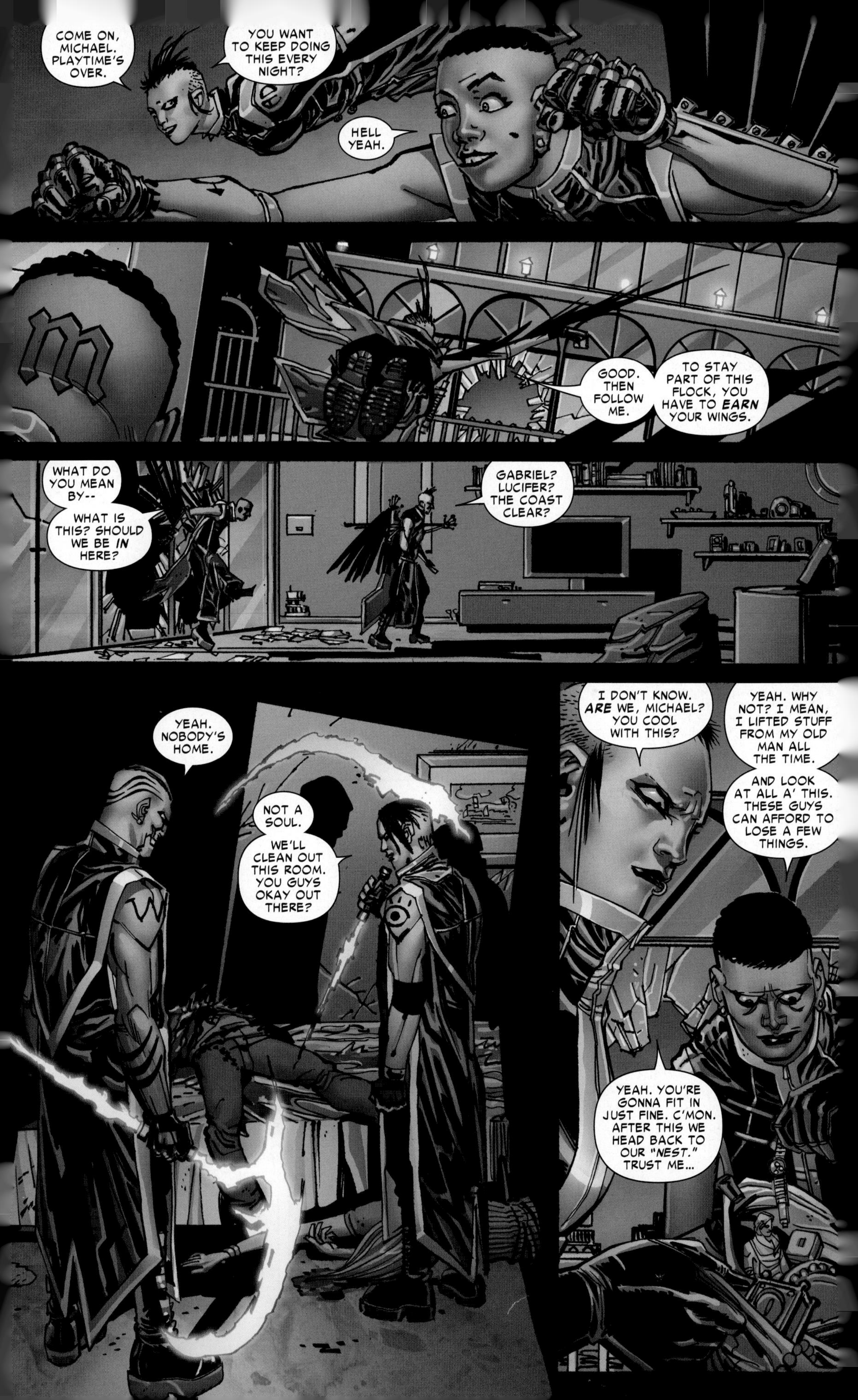

COME ON, MICHAEL. PLAYTIME'S OVER.
YOU WANT TO KEEP DOING THIS EVERY NIGHT?
HELL YEAH.
TO STAY PART OF THIS FLOCK, YOU HAVE TO EARN YOUR WINGS.
GOOD. THEN FOLLOW ME.
WHAT DO YOU MEAN BY--
WHAT IS THIS? SHOULD WE BE IN HERE?
GABRIEL? LUCIFER? THE COAST CLEAR?
YEAH. NOBODY'S HOME.
NOT A SOUL.
WE'LL CLEAN OUT THIS ROOM. YOU GUYS OKAY OUT THERE?
I DON'T KNOW. ARE WE, MICHAEL? YOU COOL WITH THIS?
YEAH. WHY NOT? I MEAN, I LIFTED STUFF FROM MY OLD MAN ALL THE TIME.
AND LOOK AT ALL A' THIS. THESE GUYS CAN AFFORD TO LOSE A FEW THINGS.
YEAH. YOU'RE GONNA FIT IN JUST FINE. C'MON. AFTER THIS WE HEAD BACK TO OUR "NEST." TRUST ME...

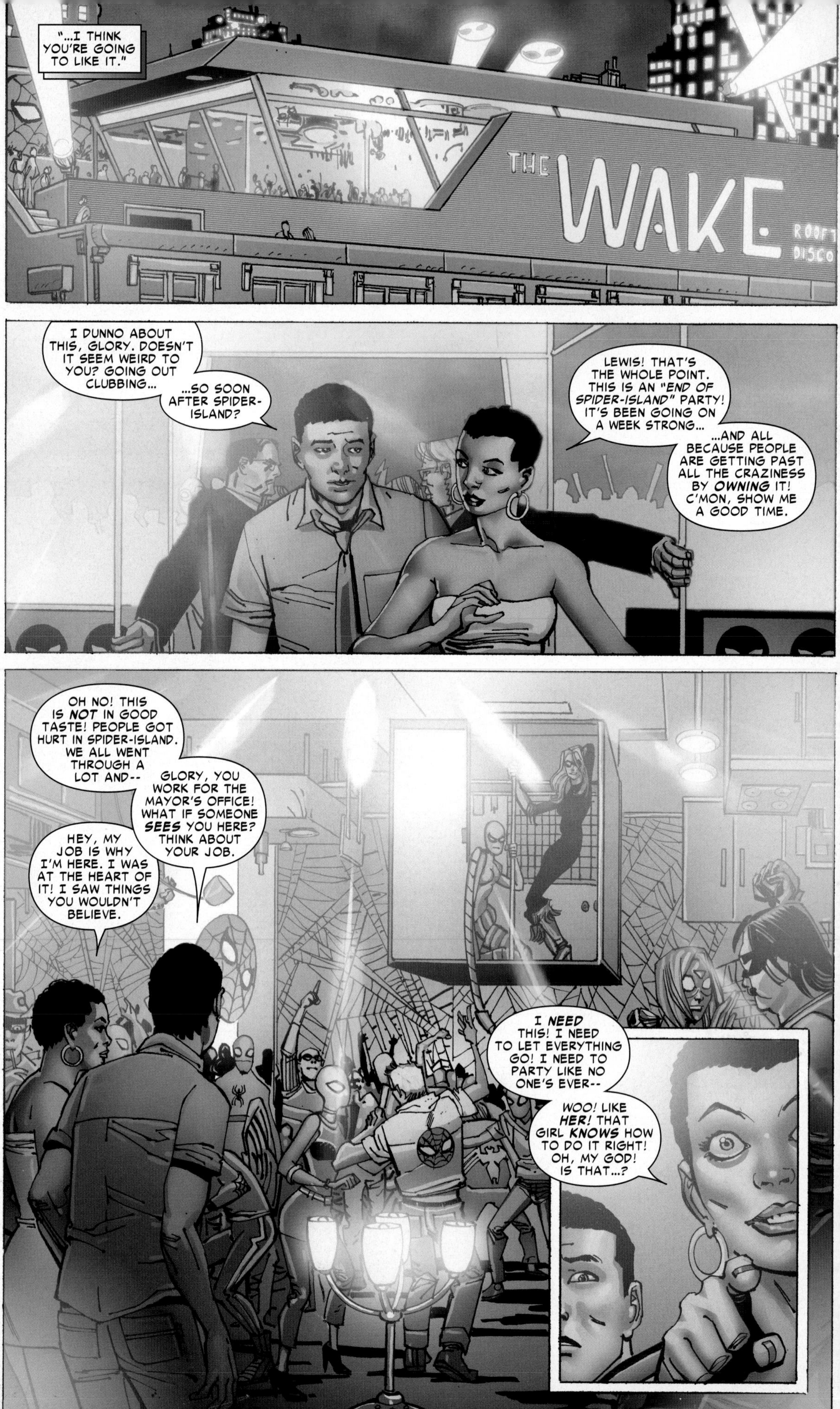
"...I THINK YOU'RE GOING TO LIKE IT."
THE WAKE ROOFT DISCO
I DUNNO ABOUT THIS, GLORY. DOESN'T IT SEEM WEIRD TO YOU? GOING OUT CLUBBING...
...SO SOON AFTER SPIDER-ISLAND?
LEWIS! THAT'S THE WHOLE POINT. THIS IS AN "END OF SPIDER-ISLAND" PARTY! IT'S BEEN GOING ON A WEEK STRONG...
...AND ALL BECAUSE PEOPLE ARE GETTING PAST ALL THE CRAZINESS BY OWNING IT! C'MON, SHOW ME A GOOD TIME.
OH NO! THIS IS NOT IN GOOD TASTE! PEOPLE GOT HURT IN SPIDER-ISLAND. WE ALL WENT THROUGH A LOT AND--
GLORY, YOU WORK FOR THE MAYOR'S OFFICE! WHAT IF SOMEONE SEES YOU HERE? THINK ABOUT YOUR JOB.
HEY, MY JOB IS WHY I'M HERE. I WAS AT THE HEART OF IT! I SAW THINGS YOU WOULDN'T BELIEVE.
I NEED THIS! I NEED TO LET EVERYTHING GO! I NEED TO PARTY LIKE NO ONE'S EVER--
WOO! LIKE HER! THAT GIRL KNOWS HOW TO DO IT RIGHT! OH, MY GOD! IS THAT...?

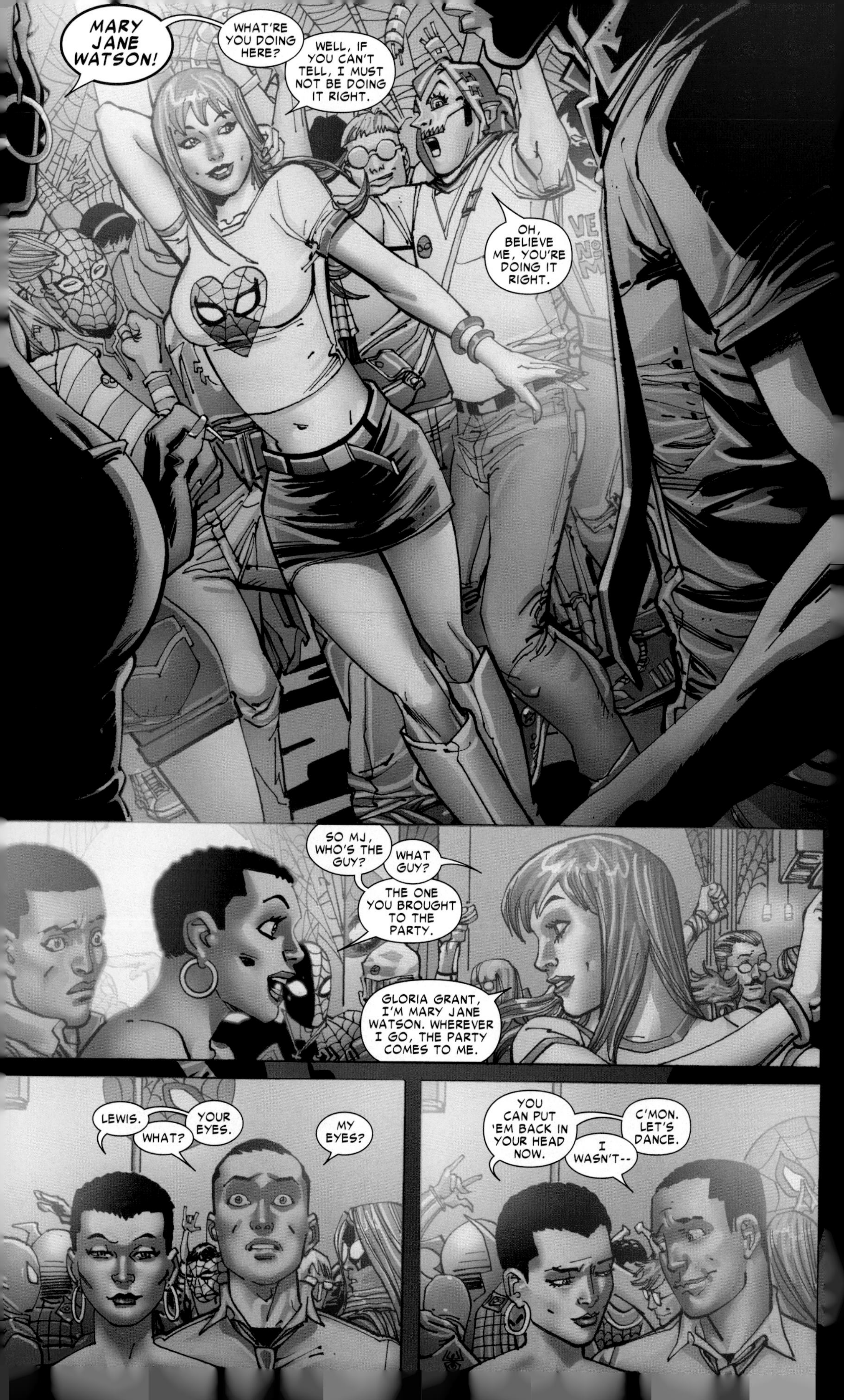
MARY JANE WATSON!
WHAT'RE YOU DOING HERE?
WELL, IF YOU CAN'T TELL, I MUST NOT BE DOING IT RIGHT.
OH, BELIEVE ME, YOU'RE DOING IT RIGHT.
SO MJ, WHO'S THE GUY?
WHAT GUY?
THE ONE YOU BROUGHT TO THE PARTY.
GLORIA GRANT, I'M MARY JANE WATSON. WHEREVER I GO, THE PARTY COMES TO ME.
LEWIS.
WHAT?
YOUR EYES.
MY EYES?
YOU CAN PUT 'EM BACK IN YOUR HEAD NOW.
I WASN'T--
C'MON. LET'S DANCE.

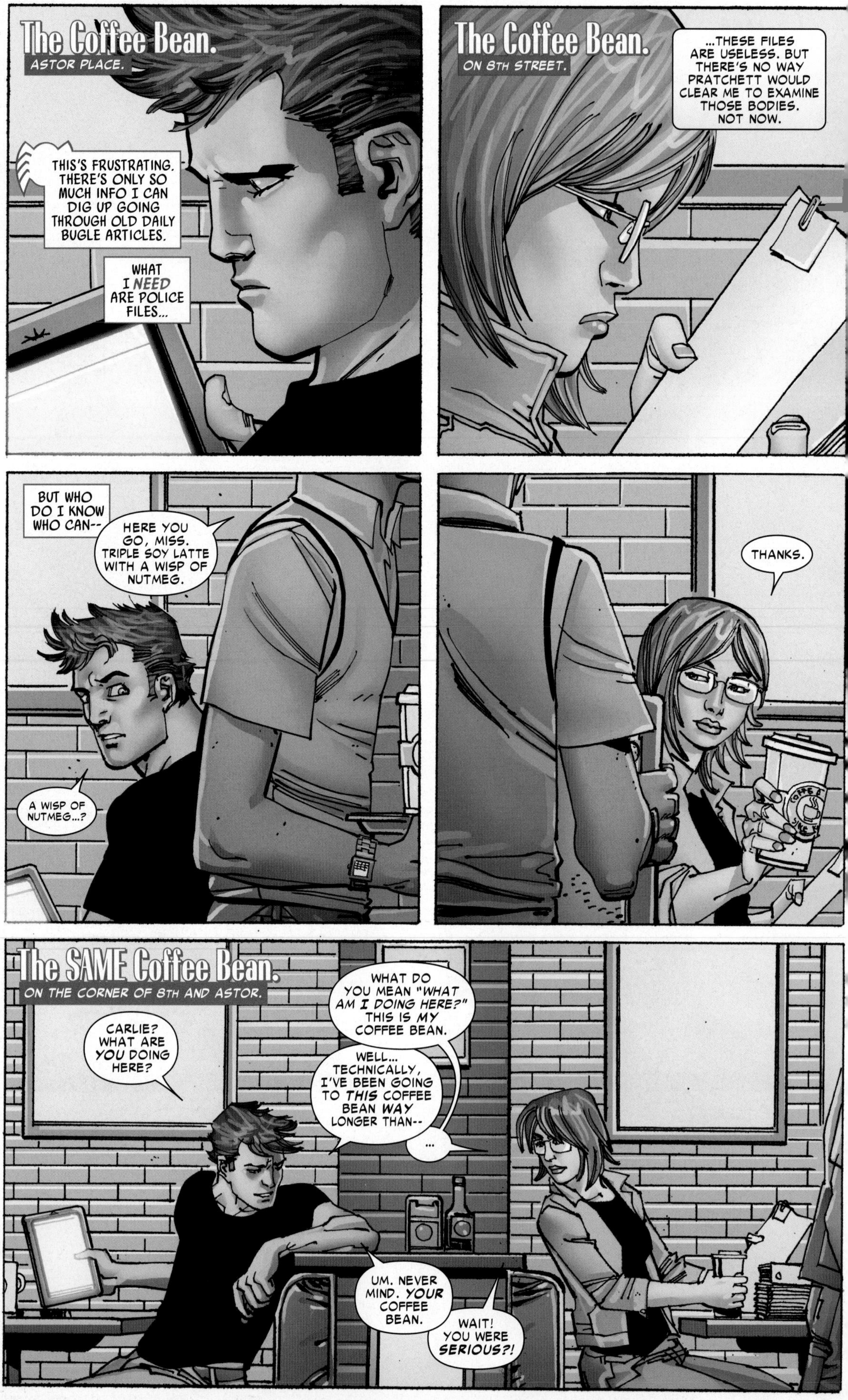
The Coffee Bean.
ASTOR PLACE.
THIS'S FRUSTRATING. THERE'S ONLY SO MUCH INFO I CAN DIG UP GOING THROUGH OLD DAILY BUGLE ARTICLES.
WHAT I NEED ARE POLICE FILES...
The Coffee Bean.
ON 8TH STREET.
...THESE FILES ARE USELESS. BUT THERE'S NO WAY PRATCHETT WOULD CLEAR ME TO EXAMINE THOSE BODIES. NOT NOW.
BUT WHO DO I KNOW WHO CAN--
HERE YOU GO, MISS. TRIPLE SOY LATTE WITH A WISP OF NUTMEG.
A WISP OF NUTMEG...?
THANKS.
The SAME Coffee Bean.
ON THE CORNER OF 8TH AND ASTOR.
CARLIE? WHAT ARE YOU DOING HERE?
WHAT DO YOU MEAN "WHAT AM I DOING HERE?" THIS IS MY COFFEE BEAN.
WELL... TECHNICALLY, I'VE BEEN GOING TO THIS COFFEE BEAN WAY LONGER THAN--
...
UM. NEVER MIND. YOUR COFFEE BEAN.
WAIT! YOU WERE SERIOUS?!

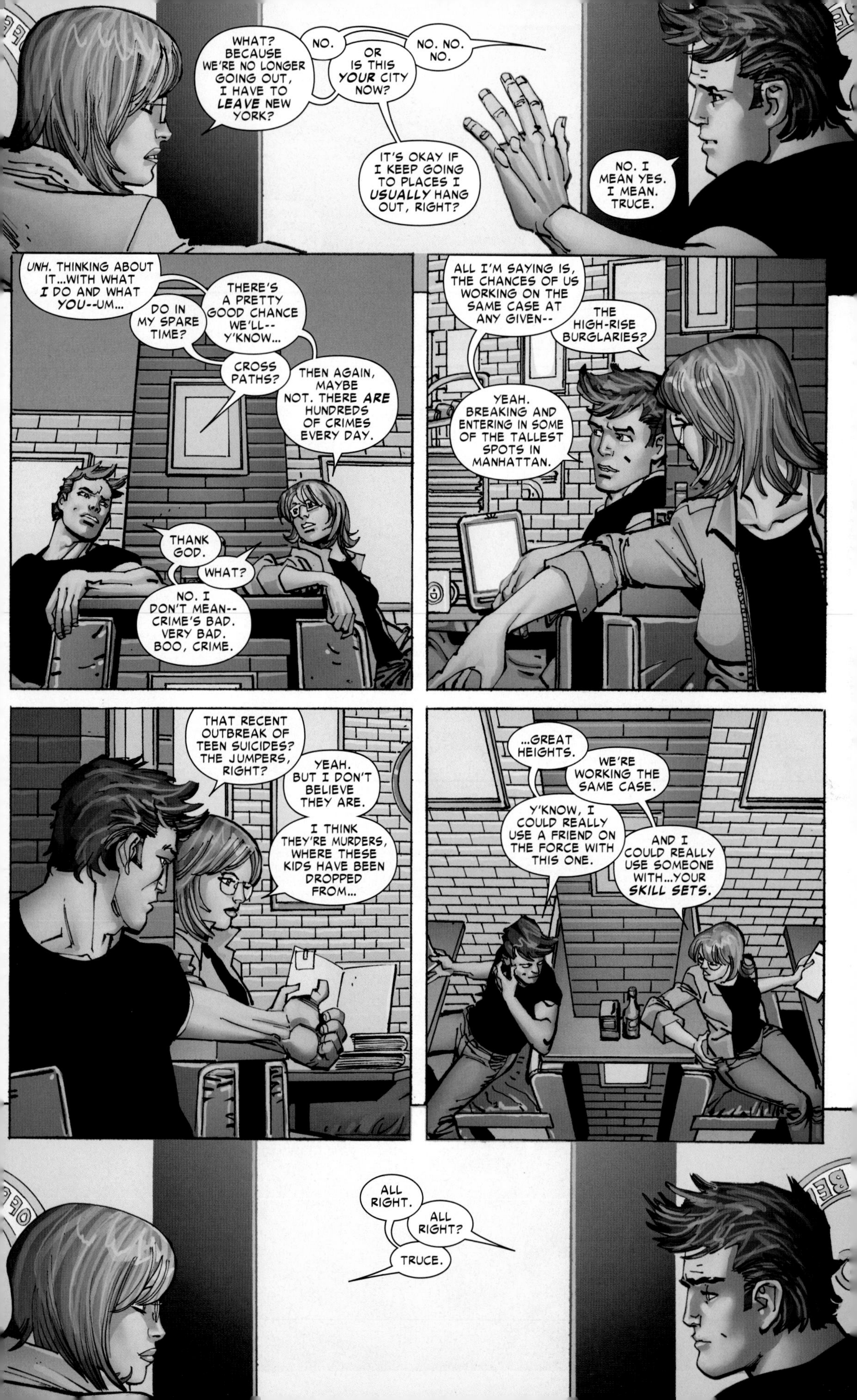
WHAT? BECAUSE WE'RE NO LONGER GOING OUT, I HAVE TO *LEAVE* NEW YORK?
NO.
OR IS THIS *YOUR* CITY NOW?
NO. NO. NO.
IT'S OKAY IF I KEEP GOING TO PLACES I *USUALLY* HANG OUT, RIGHT?
NO. I MEAN YES. I MEAN. TRUCE.
UNH. THINKING ABOUT IT...WITH WHAT *I* DO AND WHAT *YOU*--UM...
DO IN MY SPARE TIME?
THERE'S A PRETTY GOOD CHANCE WE'LL-- Y'KNOW...
CROSS PATHS?
THEN AGAIN, MAYBE NOT. THERE *ARE* HUNDREDS OF CRIMES EVERY DAY.
THANK GOD.
WHAT?
NO. I DON'T MEAN-- CRIME'S BAD. VERY BAD. BOO, CRIME.
ALL I'M SAYING IS, THE CHANCES OF US WORKING ON THE SAME CASE AT ANY GIVEN--
THE HIGH-RISE BURGLARIES?
YEAH. BREAKING AND ENTERING IN SOME OF THE TALLEST SPOTS IN MANHATTAN.
THAT RECENT OUTBREAK OF TEEN SUICIDES? THE JUMPERS, RIGHT?
YEAH. BUT I DON'T BELIEVE THEY ARE.
I THINK THEY'RE MURDERS, WHERE THESE KIDS HAVE BEEN DROPPED FROM...
...GREAT HEIGHTS.
WE'RE WORKING THE SAME CASE.
Y'KNOW, I COULD REALLY USE A FRIEND ON THE FORCE WITH THIS ONE.
AND I COULD REALLY USE SOMEONE WITH...YOUR *SKILL SETS*.
ALL RIGHT.
ALL RIGHT?
TRUCE.

Chelsea.

WE'RE HERE. NOW DO LIKE US, MICHAEL.

TIGHT FORMATION. COME IN FAST, STEEP...

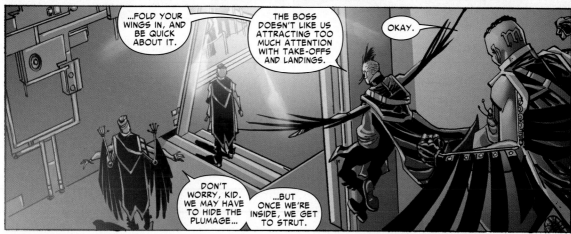

...FOLD YOUR WINGS IN, AND BE QUICK ABOUT IT.

THE BOSS DOESN'T LIKE US ATTRACTING TOO MUCH ATTENTION WITH TAKE-OFFS AND LANDINGS.

OKAY.

DON'T WORRY, KID. WE MAY HAVE TO HIDE THE PLUMAGE...

...BUT ONCE WE'RE INSIDE, WE GET TO STRUT.

REMEMBER, YOU'RE PART OF OUR FLOCK NOW. AND THIS IS OUR ROOST.

SEE ANYTHING YOU LIKE IN HERE, MICHAEL, IT'S YOURS.

UM... ANYTHING?

WHAT'RE YOU LOOKING AT, KID? SHE'S WITH ME.

SEE? THAT'S MORE LIKE IT.

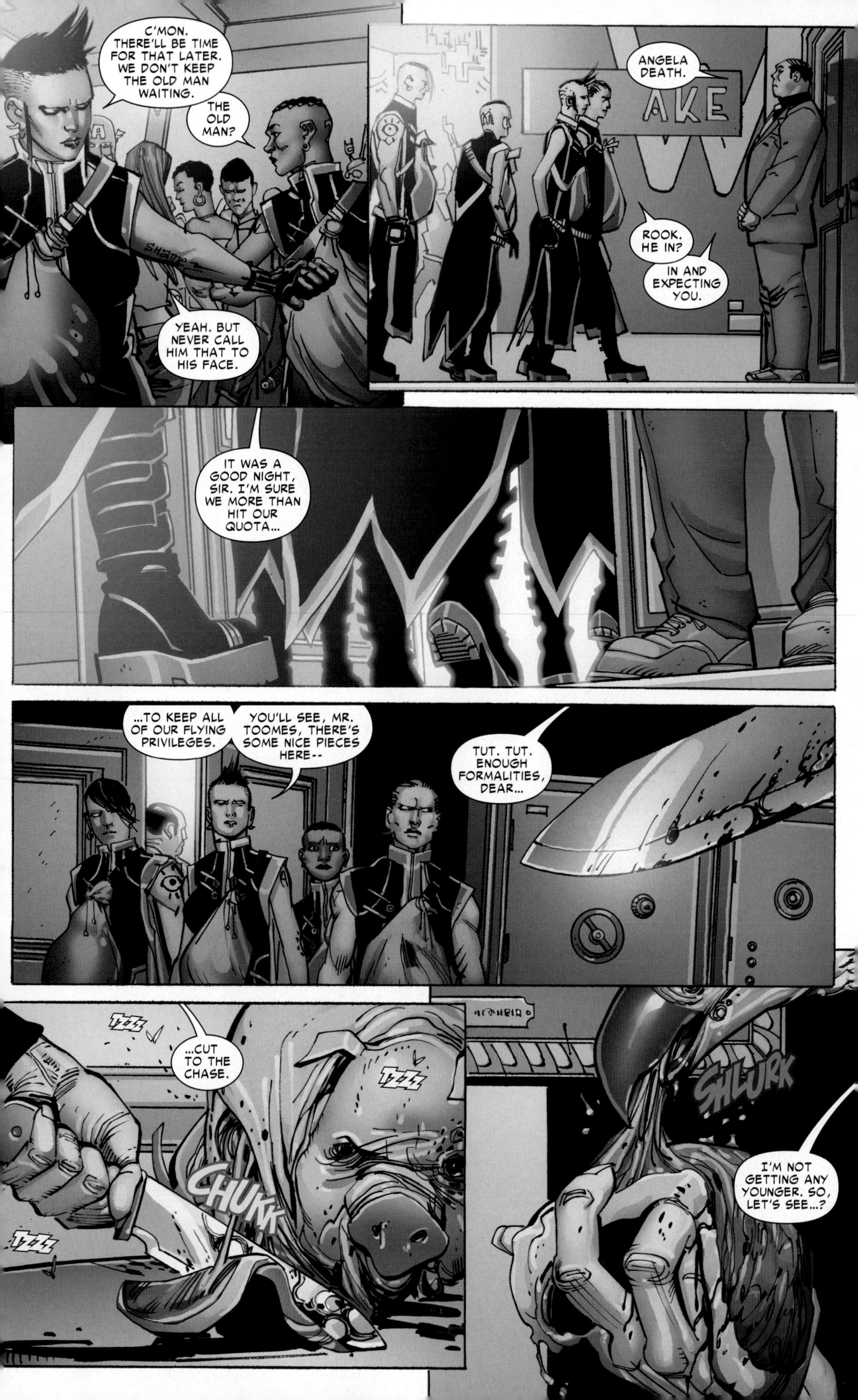
C'MON. THERE'LL BE TIME FOR THAT LATER. WE DON'T KEEP THE OLD MAN WAITING.
THE OLD MAN?
YEAH. BUT NEVER CALL HIM THAT TO HIS FACE.
ANGELA DEATH.
ROOK. HE IN?
IN AND EXPECTING YOU.
IT WAS A GOOD NIGHT, SIR. I'M SURE WE MORE THAN HIT OUR QUOTA...
...TO KEEP ALL OF OUR FLYING PRIVILEGES.
YOU'LL SEE, MR. TOOMES, THERE'S SOME NICE PIECES HERE--
TUT. TUT. ENOUGH FORMALITIES, DEAR...
TZZZ
...CUT TO THE CHASE.
TZZZ
CHUKK
TZZZ
SHLURK
I'M NOT GETTING ANY YOUNGER. SO, LET'S SEE...?

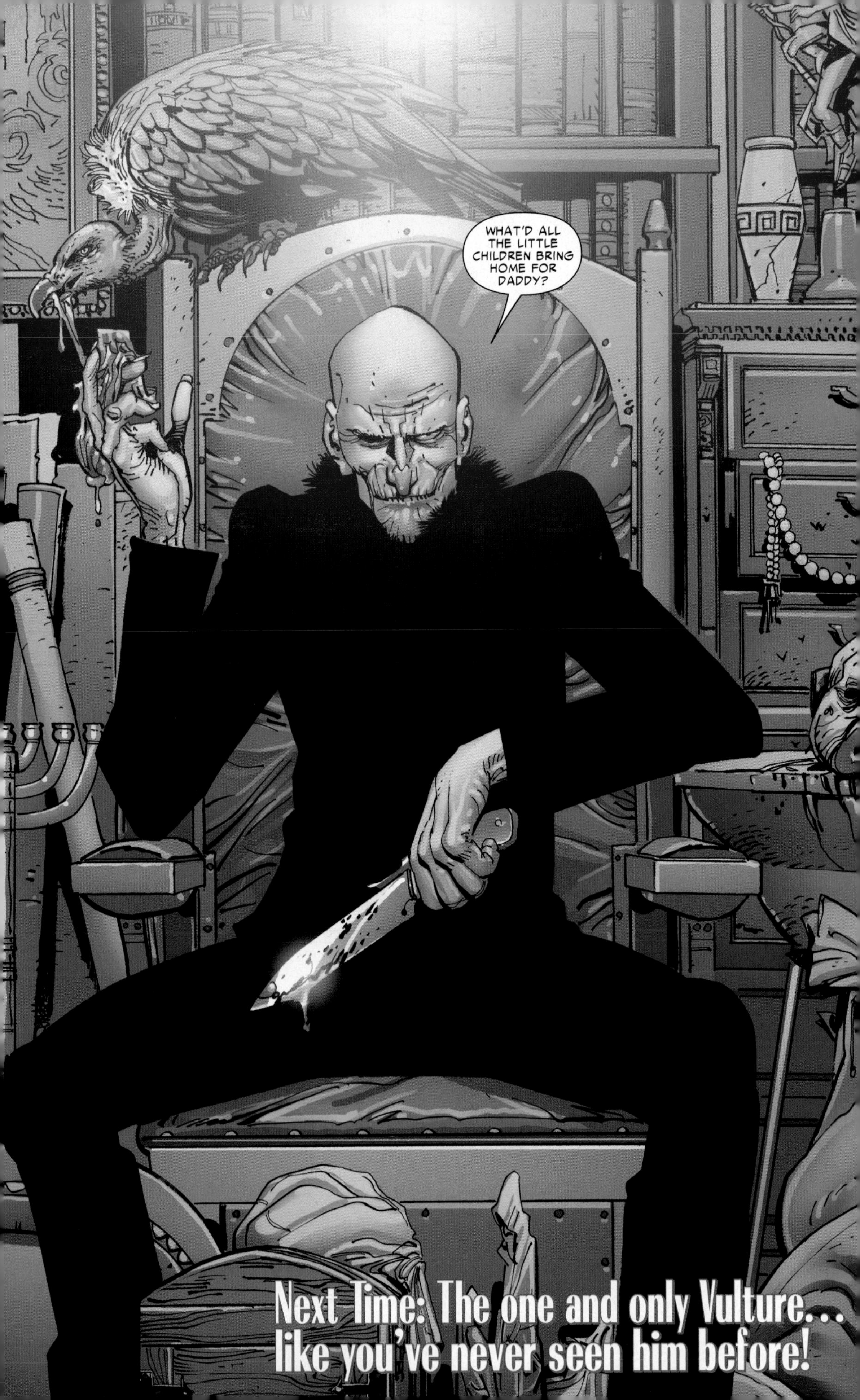
WHAT'D ALL THE LITTLE CHILDREN BRING HOME FOR DADDY?
Next Time: The one and only Vulture... like you've never seen him before!

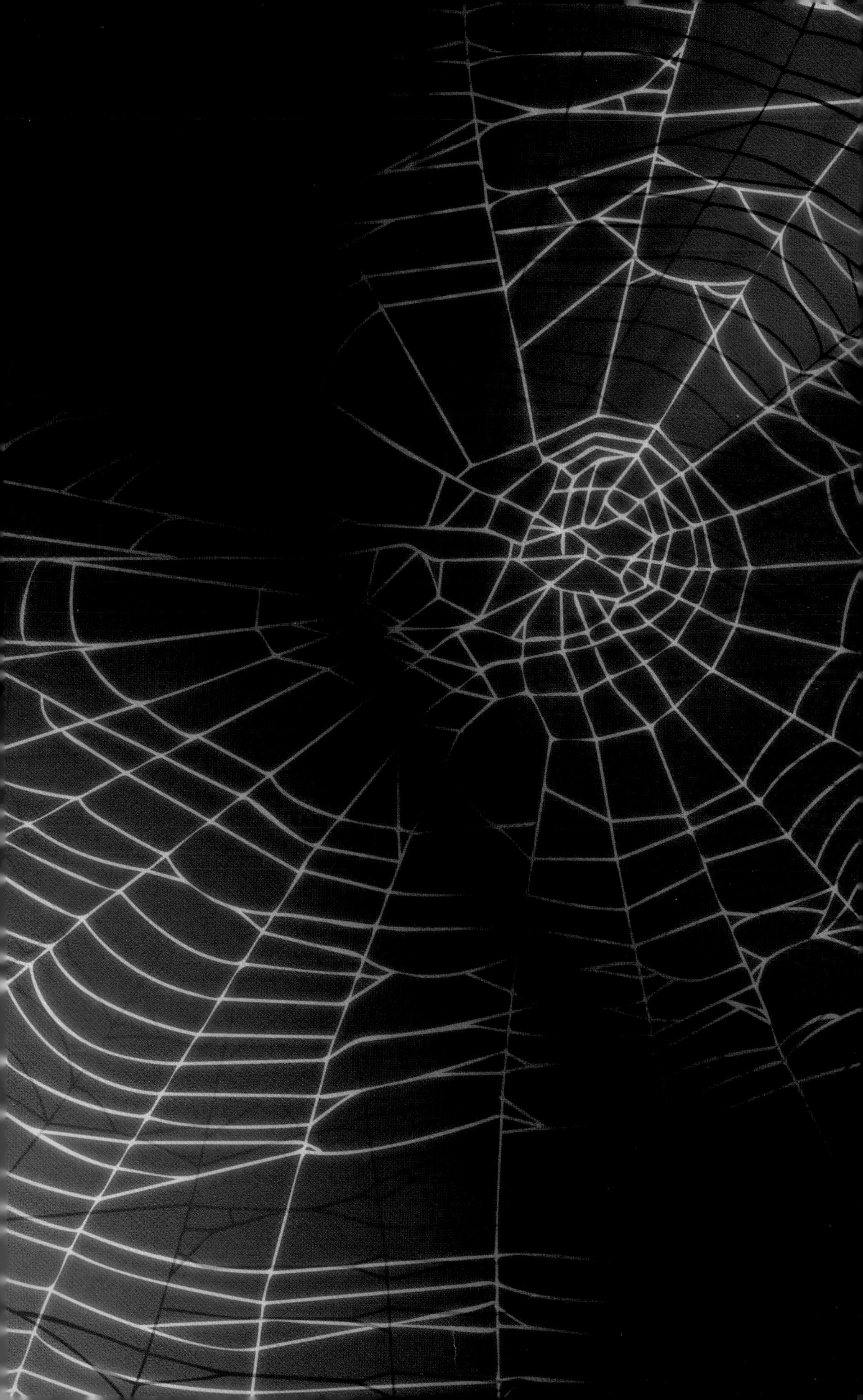

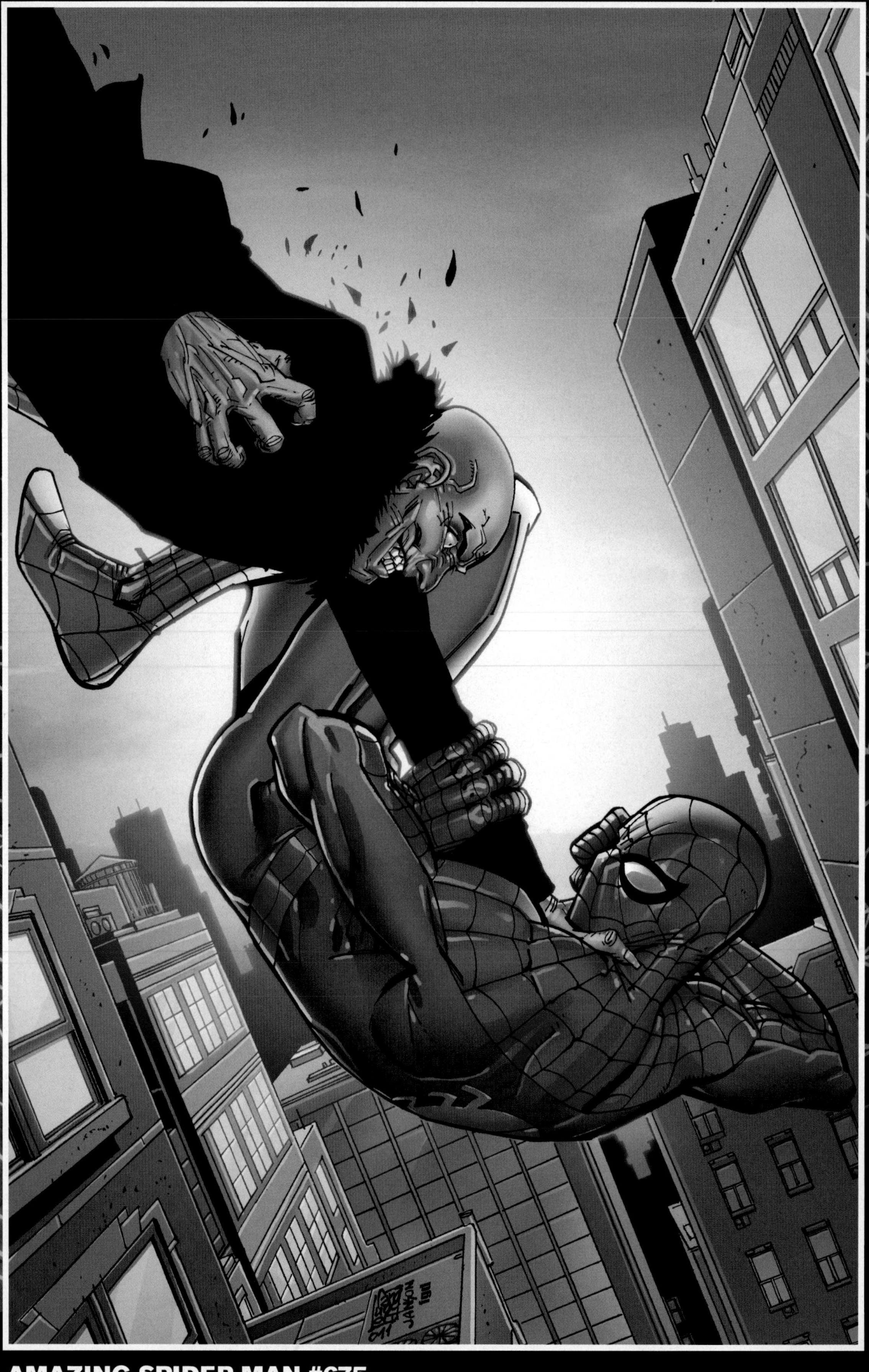

AMAZING SPIDER-MAN #675
COVER BY GIUSEPPE CAMUNCOLI, KLAUS JANSON & FRANK D'ARMATA

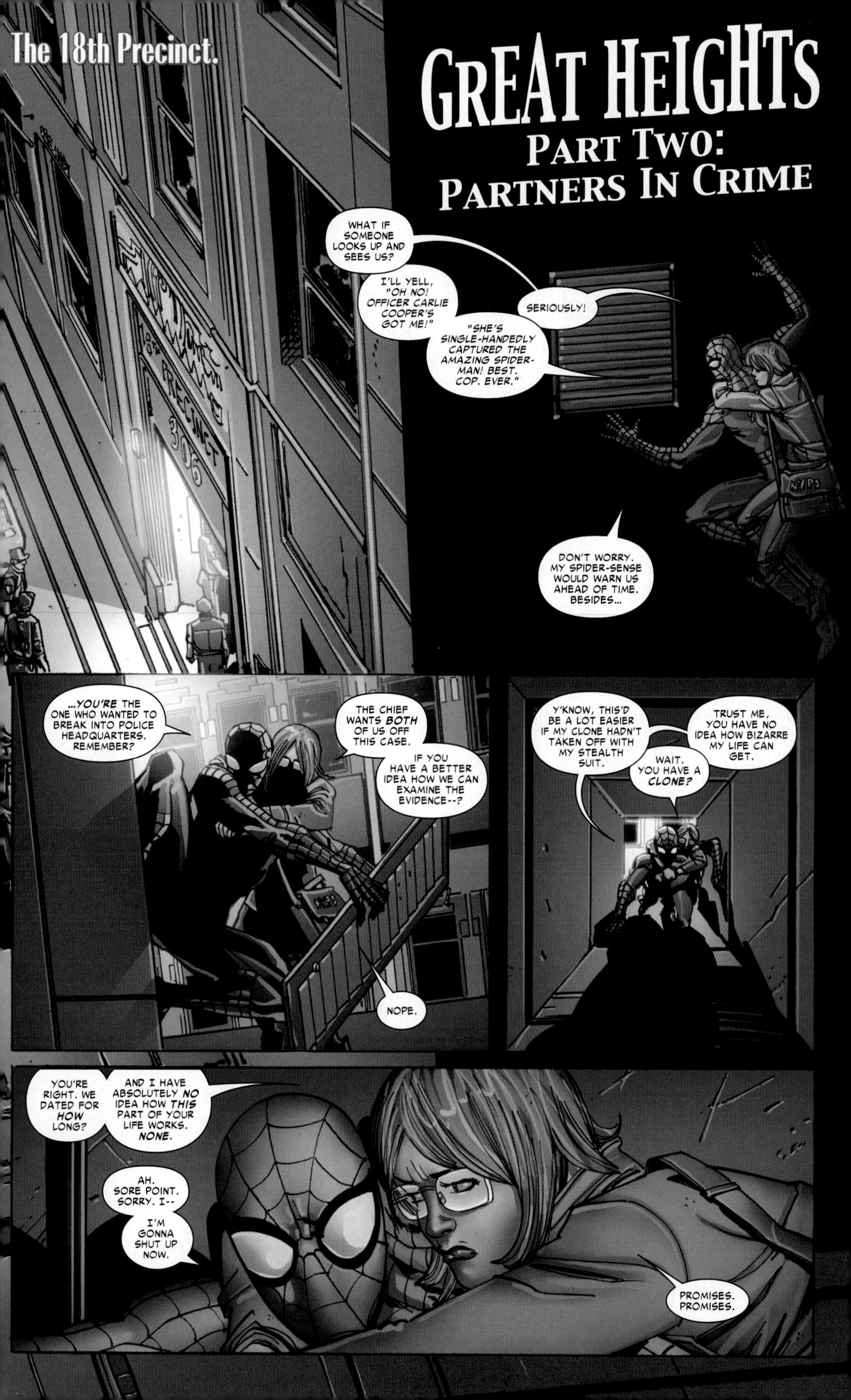
The 18th Precinct.
GREAT HEIGHTS
PART TWO:
PARTNERS IN CRIME
WHAT IF SOMEONE LOOKS UP AND SEES US?
I'LL YELL, "OH NO! OFFICER CARLIE COOPER'S GOT ME!"
"SHE'S SINGLE-HANDEDLY CAPTURED THE AMAZING SPIDER-MAN! BEST. COP. EVER."
SERIOUSLY!
DON'T WORRY. MY SPIDER-SENSE WOULD WARN US AHEAD OF TIME. BESIDES...
...YOU'RE THE ONE WHO WANTED TO BREAK INTO POLICE HEADQUARTERS. REMEMBER?
THE CHIEF WANTS BOTH OF US OFF THIS CASE.
IF YOU HAVE A BETTER IDEA HOW WE CAN EXAMINE THE EVIDENCE--?
NOPE.
Y'KNOW, THIS'D BE A LOT EASIER IF MY CLONE HADN'T TAKEN OFF WITH MY STEALTH SUIT.
WAIT. YOU HAVE A CLONE?
TRUST ME, YOU HAVE NO IDEA HOW BIZARRE MY LIFE CAN GET.
YOU'RE RIGHT. WE DATED FOR HOW LONG?
AND I HAVE ABSOLUTELY NO IDEA HOW THIS PART OF YOUR LIFE WORKS. NONE.
AH. SORE POINT. SORRY. I--
I'M GONNA SHUT UP NOW.
PROMISES. PROMISES.

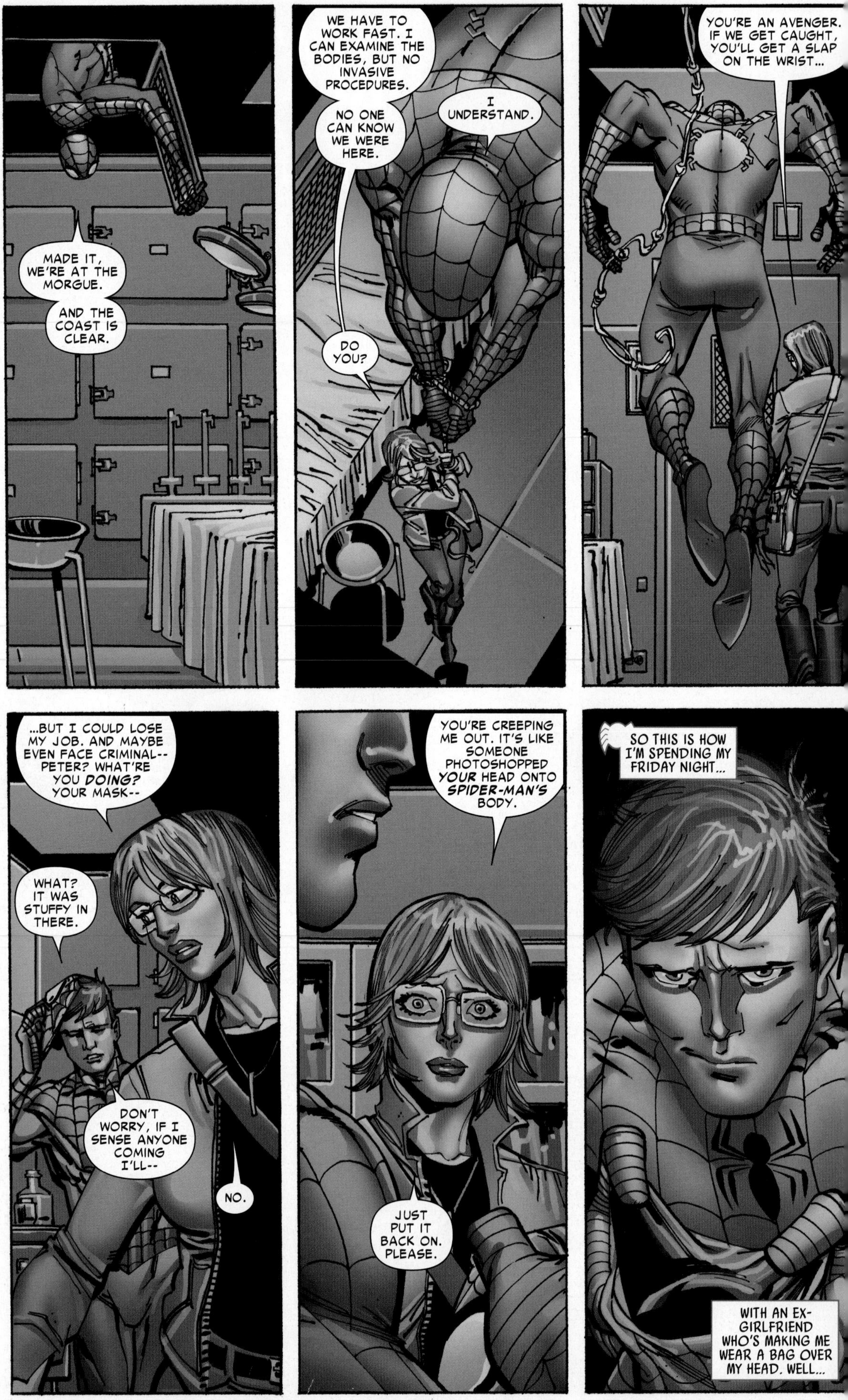
MADE IT, WE'RE AT THE MORGUE.
AND THE COAST IS CLEAR.
WE HAVE TO WORK FAST. I CAN EXAMINE THE BODIES, BUT NO INVASIVE PROCEDURES.
NO ONE CAN KNOW WE WERE HERE.
I UNDERSTAND.
DO YOU?
YOU'RE AN AVENGER. IF WE GET CAUGHT, YOU'LL GET A SLAP ON THE WRIST...
...BUT I COULD LOSE MY JOB. AND MAYBE EVEN FACE CRIMINAL-- PETER? WHAT'RE YOU *DOING?* YOUR MASK--
WHAT? IT WAS STUFFY IN THERE.
DON'T WORRY, IF I SENSE ANYONE COMING I'LL--
NO.
YOU'RE CREEPING ME OUT. IT'S LIKE SOMEONE PHOTOSHOPPED *YOUR* HEAD ONTO *SPIDER-MAN'S* BODY.
JUST PUT IT BACK ON. PLEASE.
SO THIS IS HOW I'M SPENDING MY FRIDAY NIGHT...
WITH AN EX-GIRLFRIEND WHO'S MAKING ME WEAR A BAG OVER MY HEAD. WELL...

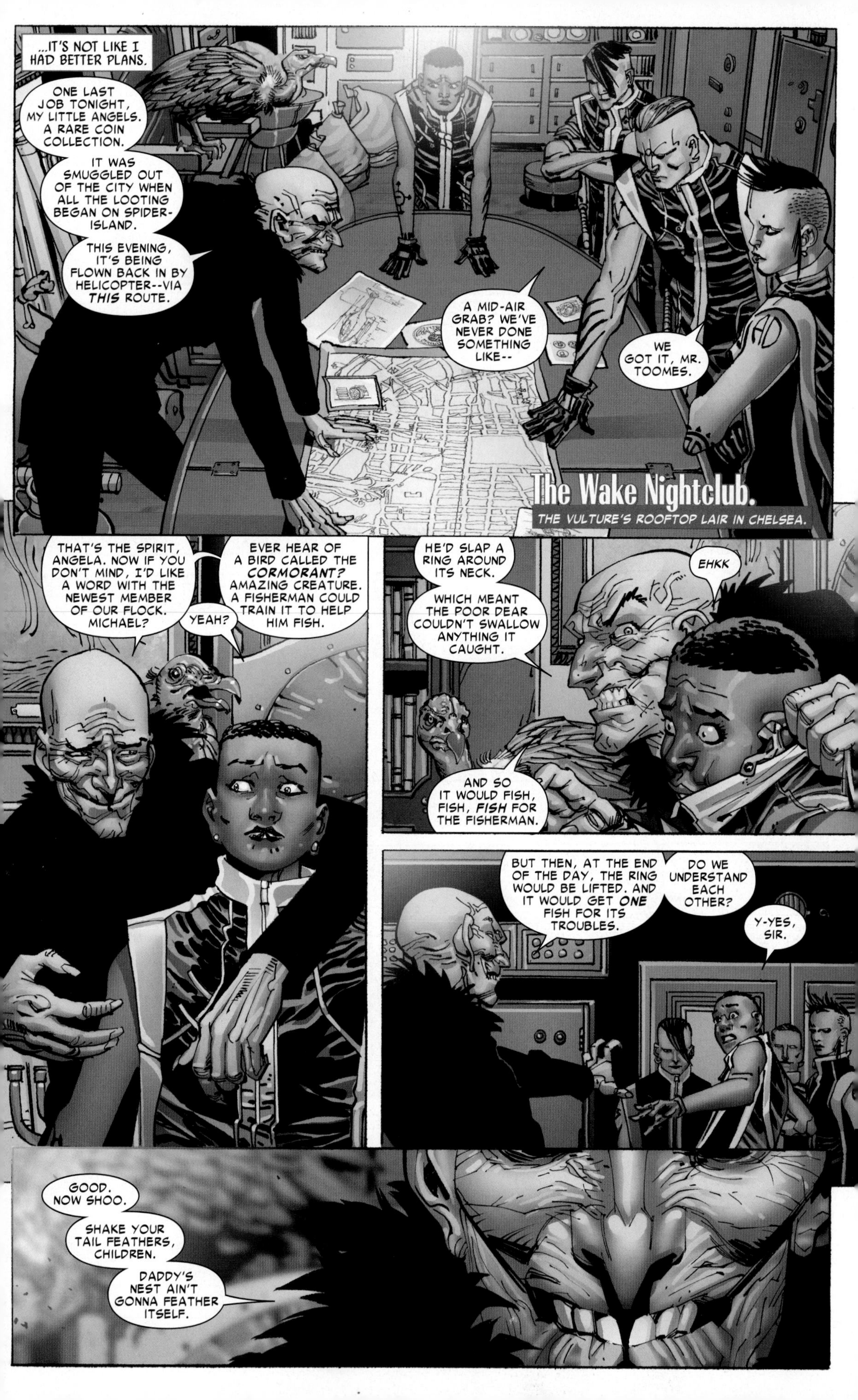
...IT'S NOT LIKE I HAD BETTER PLANS.
ONE LAST JOB TONIGHT, MY LITTLE ANGELS. A RARE COIN COLLECTION.
IT WAS SMUGGLED OUT OF THE CITY WHEN ALL THE LOOTING BEGAN ON SPIDER-ISLAND.
THIS EVENING, IT'S BEING FLOWN BACK IN BY HELICOPTER--VIA *THIS* ROUTE.
A MID-AIR GRAB? WE'VE NEVER DONE SOMETHING LIKE--
WE GOT IT, MR. TOOMES.
The Wake Nightclub.
THE VULTURE'S ROOFTOP LAIR IN CHELSEA.
THAT'S THE SPIRIT, ANGELA. NOW IF YOU DON'T MIND, I'D LIKE A WORD WITH THE NEWEST MEMBER OF OUR FLOCK. MICHAEL?
YEAH?
EVER HEAR OF A BIRD CALLED THE *CORMORANT?* AMAZING CREATURE. A FISHERMAN COULD TRAIN IT TO HELP HIM FISH.
HE'D SLAP A RING AROUND ITS NECK.
WHICH MEANT THE POOR DEAR COULDN'T SWALLOW ANYTHING IT CAUGHT.
EHKK
AND SO IT WOULD FISH, FISH, *FISH* FOR THE FISHERMAN.
BUT THEN, AT THE END OF THE DAY, THE RING WOULD BE LIFTED. AND IT WOULD GET *ONE* FISH FOR ITS TROUBLES.
DO WE UNDERSTAND EACH OTHER?
Y-YES, SIR.
GOOD. NOW SHOO.
SHAKE YOUR TAIL FEATHERS, CHILDREN.
DADDY'S NEST AIN'T GONNA FEATHER ITSELF.

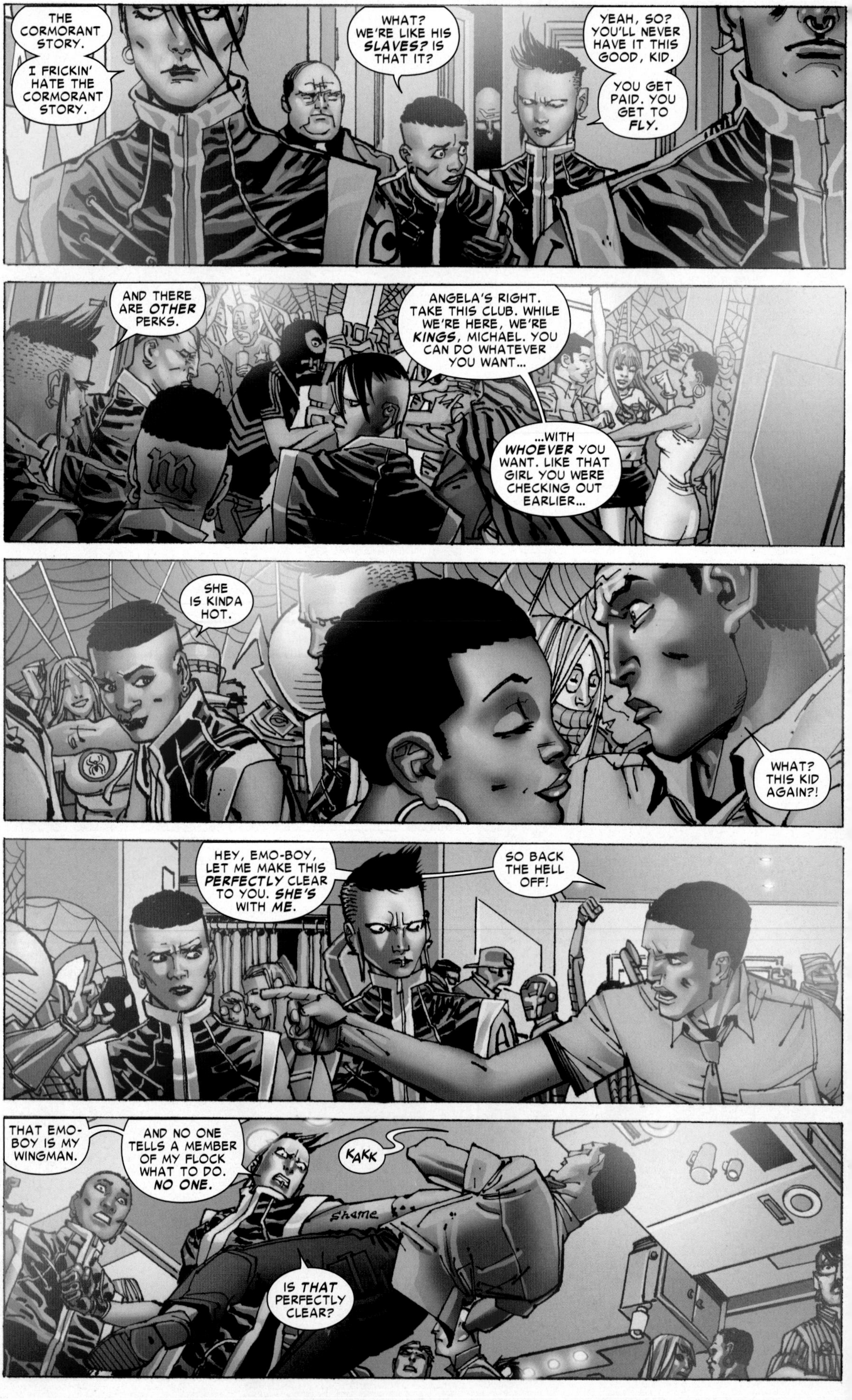
THE CORMORANT STORY.
I FRICKIN' HATE THE CORMORANT STORY.
WHAT? WE'RE LIKE HIS SLAVES? IS THAT IT?
YEAH, SO? YOU'LL NEVER HAVE IT THIS GOOD, KID.
YOU GET PAID. YOU GET TO FLY.
AND THERE ARE OTHER PERKS.
ANGELA'S RIGHT. TAKE THIS CLUB. WHILE WE'RE HERE, WE'RE KINGS, MICHAEL. YOU CAN DO WHATEVER YOU WANT...
...WITH WHOEVER YOU WANT. LIKE THAT GIRL YOU WERE CHECKING OUT EARLIER...
SHE IS KINDA HOT.
WHAT? THIS KID AGAIN?!
HEY, EMO-BOY, LET ME MAKE THIS PERFECTLY CLEAR TO YOU. SHE'S WITH ME.
SO BACK THE HELL OFF!
THAT EMO-BOY IS MY WINGMAN.
AND NO ONE TELLS A MEMBER OF MY FLOCK WHAT TO DO. NO ONE.
KAKK
IS THAT PERFECTLY CLEAR?

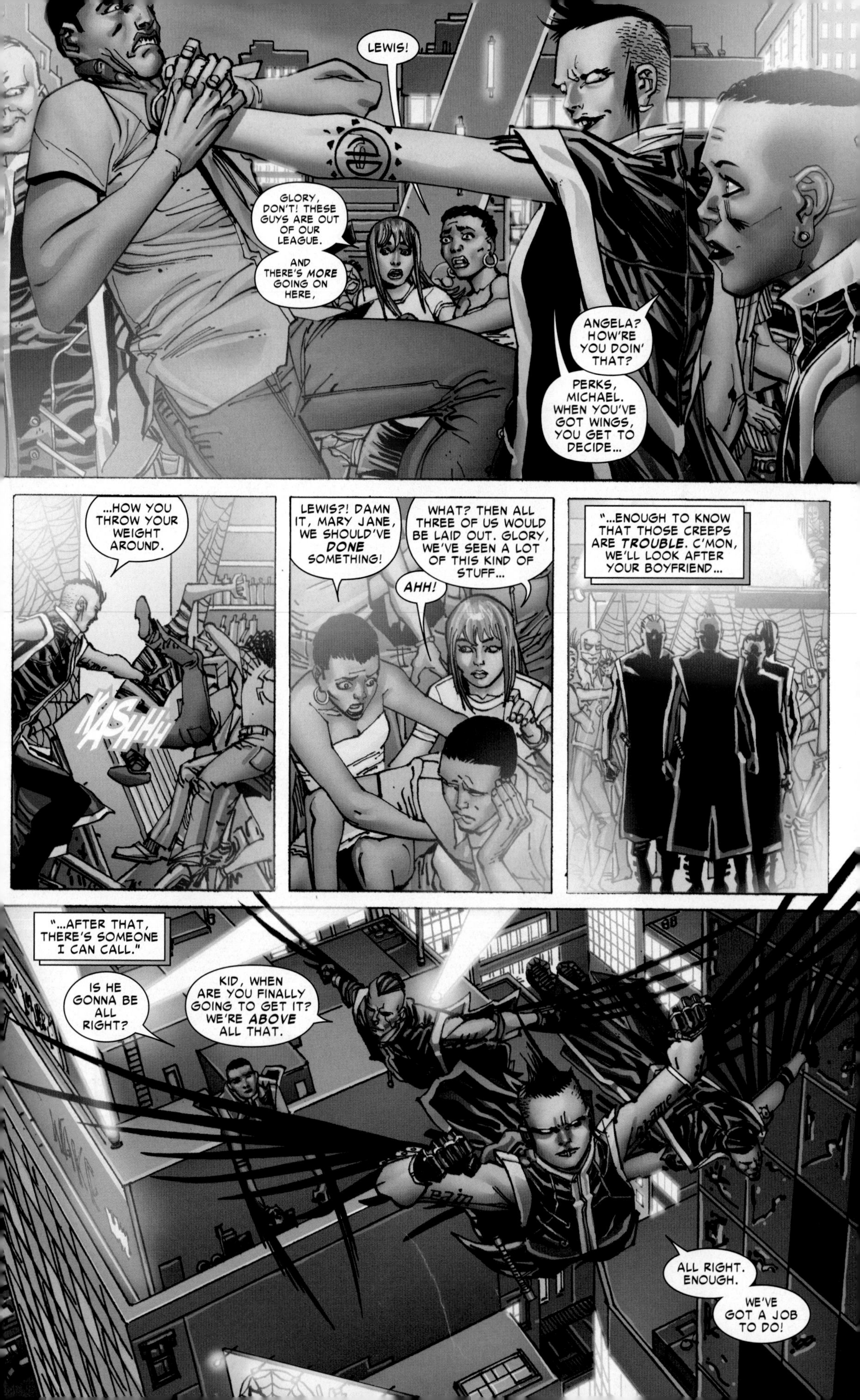
LEWIS!
GLORY, DON'T! THESE GUYS ARE OUT OF OUR LEAGUE.
AND THERE'S MORE GOING ON HERE,
ANGELA? HOW'RE YOU DOIN' THAT?
PERKS, MICHAEL. WHEN YOU'VE GOT WINGS, YOU GET TO DECIDE...
...HOW YOU THROW YOUR WEIGHT AROUND.
KASHHH
LEWIS?! DAMN IT, MARY JANE, WE SHOULD'VE DONE SOMETHING!
WHAT? THEN ALL THREE OF US WOULD BE LAID OUT. GLORY, WE'VE SEEN A LOT OF THIS KIND OF STUFF...
AHH!
"...ENOUGH TO KNOW THAT THOSE CREEPS ARE TROUBLE. C'MON, WE'LL LOOK AFTER YOUR BOYFRIEND...
"...AFTER THAT, THERE'S SOMEONE I CAN CALL."
IS HE GONNA BE ALL RIGHT?
KID, WHEN ARE YOU FINALLY GOING TO GET IT? WE'RE ABOVE ALL THAT.
ALL RIGHT. ENOUGH.
WE'VE GOT A JOB TO DO!

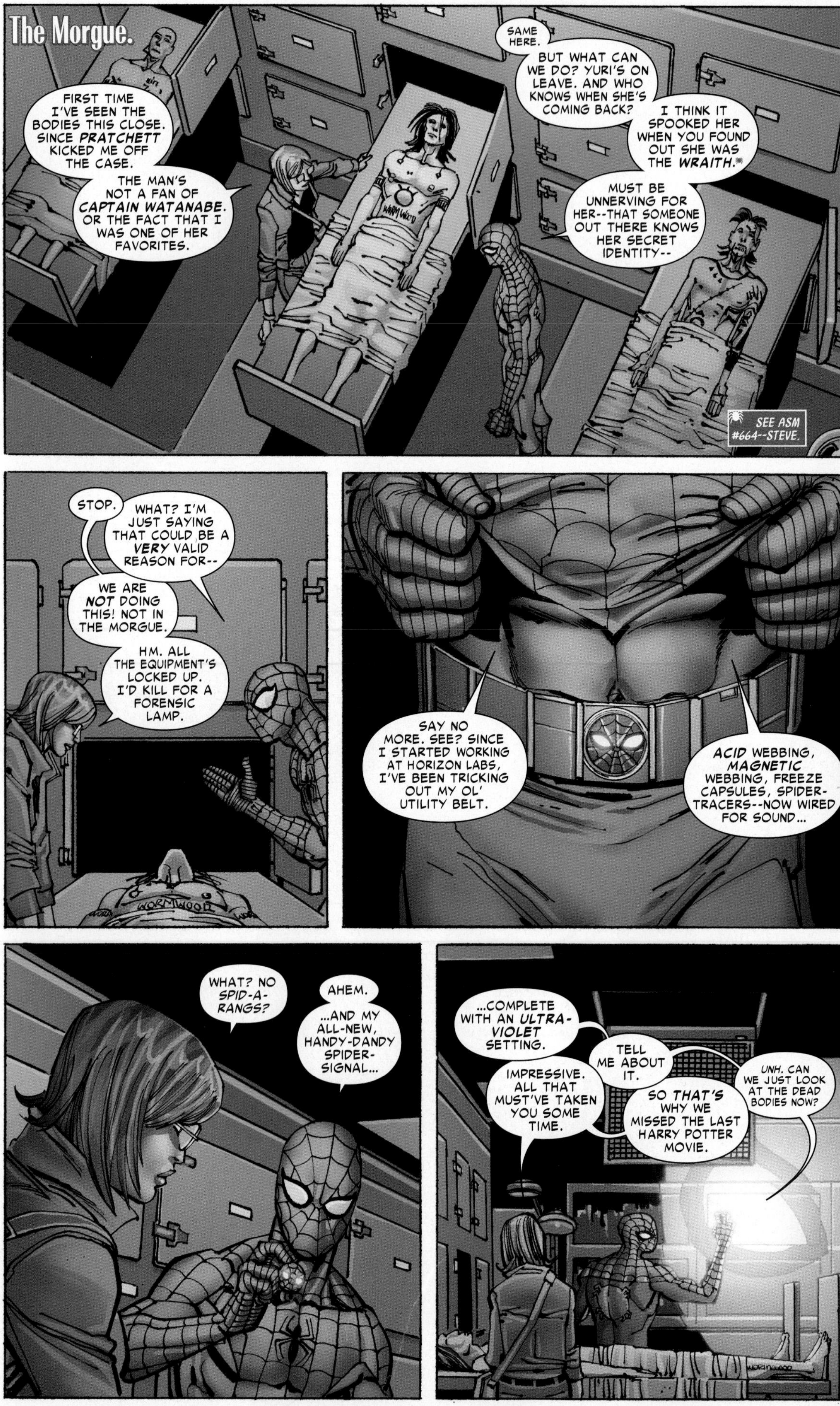
The Morgue.
FIRST TIME I'VE SEEN THE BODIES THIS CLOSE. SINCE PRATCHETT KICKED ME OFF THE CASE.
THE MAN'S NOT A FAN OF CAPTAIN WATANABE. OR THE FACT THAT I WAS ONE OF HER FAVORITES.
SAME HERE.
BUT WHAT CAN WE DO? YURI'S ON LEAVE. AND WHO KNOWS WHEN SHE'S COMING BACK?
I THINK IT SPOOKED HER WHEN YOU FOUND OUT SHE WAS THE WRAITH.
MUST BE UNNERVING FOR HER--THAT SOMEONE OUT THERE KNOWS HER SECRET IDENTITY--
SEE ASM #664--STEVE.
WORMWOOD
STOP.
WHAT? I'M JUST SAYING THAT COULD BE A VERY VALID REASON FOR--
WE ARE NOT DOING THIS! NOT IN THE MORGUE.
HM. ALL THE EQUIPMENT'S LOCKED UP. I'D KILL FOR A FORENSIC LAMP.
SAY NO MORE. SEE? SINCE I STARTED WORKING AT HORIZON LABS, I'VE BEEN TRICKING OUT MY OL' UTILITY BELT.
ACID WEBBING, MAGNETIC WEBBING, FREEZE CAPSULES, SPIDER-TRACERS--NOW WIRED FOR SOUND...
WHAT? NO SPID-A-RANGS?
AHEM.
...AND MY ALL-NEW, HANDY-DANDY SPIDER-SIGNAL...
...COMPLETE WITH AN ULTRA-VIOLET SETTING.
TELL ME ABOUT IT.
IMPRESSIVE. ALL THAT MUST'VE TAKEN YOU SOME TIME.
SO THAT'S WHY WE MISSED THE LAST HARRY POTTER MOVIE.
UNH. CAN WE JUST LOOK AT THE DEAD BODIES NOW?

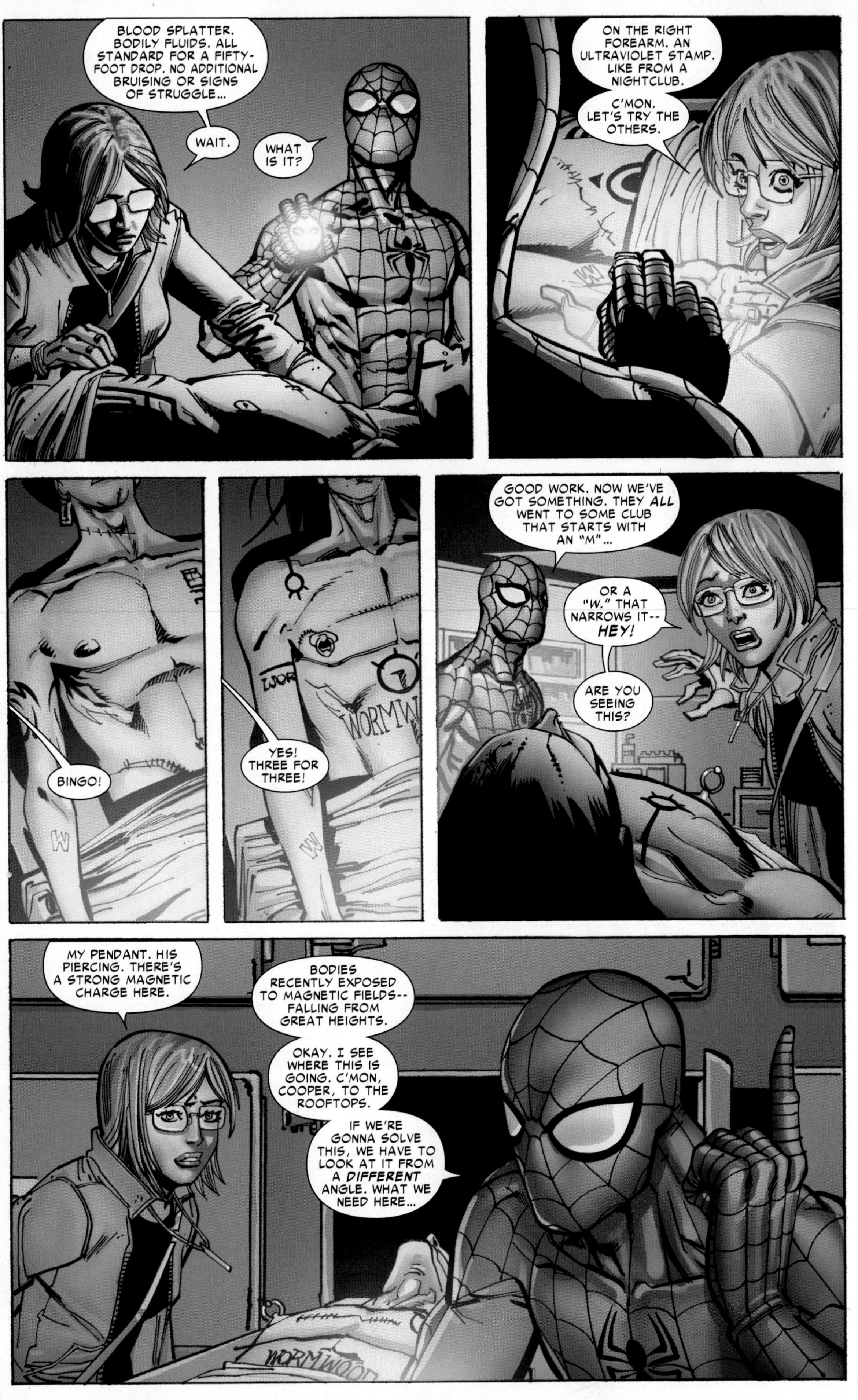
BLOOD SPLATTER. BODILY FLUIDS. ALL STANDARD FOR A FIFTY-FOOT DROP. NO ADDITIONAL BRUISING OR SIGNS OF STRUGGLE...
WAIT.
WHAT IS IT?
ON THE RIGHT FOREARM. AN ULTRAVIOLET STAMP. LIKE FROM A NIGHTCLUB.
C'MON. LET'S TRY THE OTHERS.
BINGO!
YES! THREE FOR THREE!
GOOD WORK. NOW WE'VE GOT SOMETHING. THEY ALL WENT TO SOME CLUB THAT STARTS WITH AN "M"...
OR A "W." THAT NARROWS IT-- HEY!
ARE YOU SEEING THIS?
MY PENDANT. HIS PIERCING. THERE'S A STRONG MAGNETIC CHARGE HERE.
BODIES RECENTLY EXPOSED TO MAGNETIC FIELDS-- FALLING FROM GREAT HEIGHTS.
OKAY. I SEE WHERE THIS IS GOING. C'MON, COOPER, TO THE ROOFTOPS.
IF WE'RE GONNA SOLVE THIS, WE HAVE TO LOOK AT IT FROM A DIFFERENT ANGLE. WHAT WE NEED HERE...
WORMWOOD

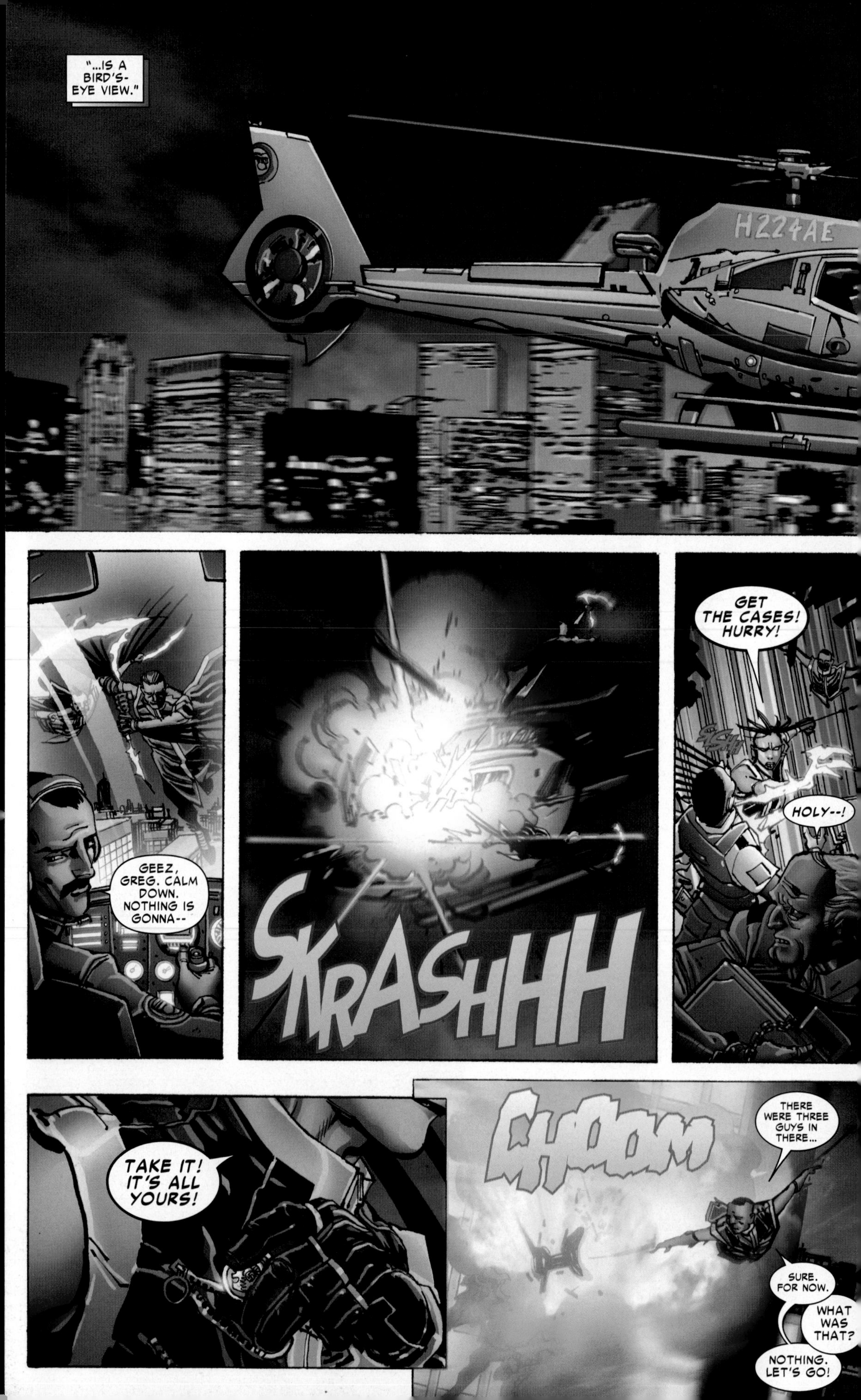
"...IS A BIRD'S-EYE VIEW."
H224AE
GEEZ, GREG. CALM DOWN. NOTHING IS GONNA--
SKRASHHH
GET THE CASES! HURRY!
HOLY--!
TAKE IT! IT'S ALL YOURS!
CHOOM
THERE WERE THREE GUYS IN THERE...
SURE. FOR NOW.
WHAT WAS THAT?
NOTHING. LET'S GO!

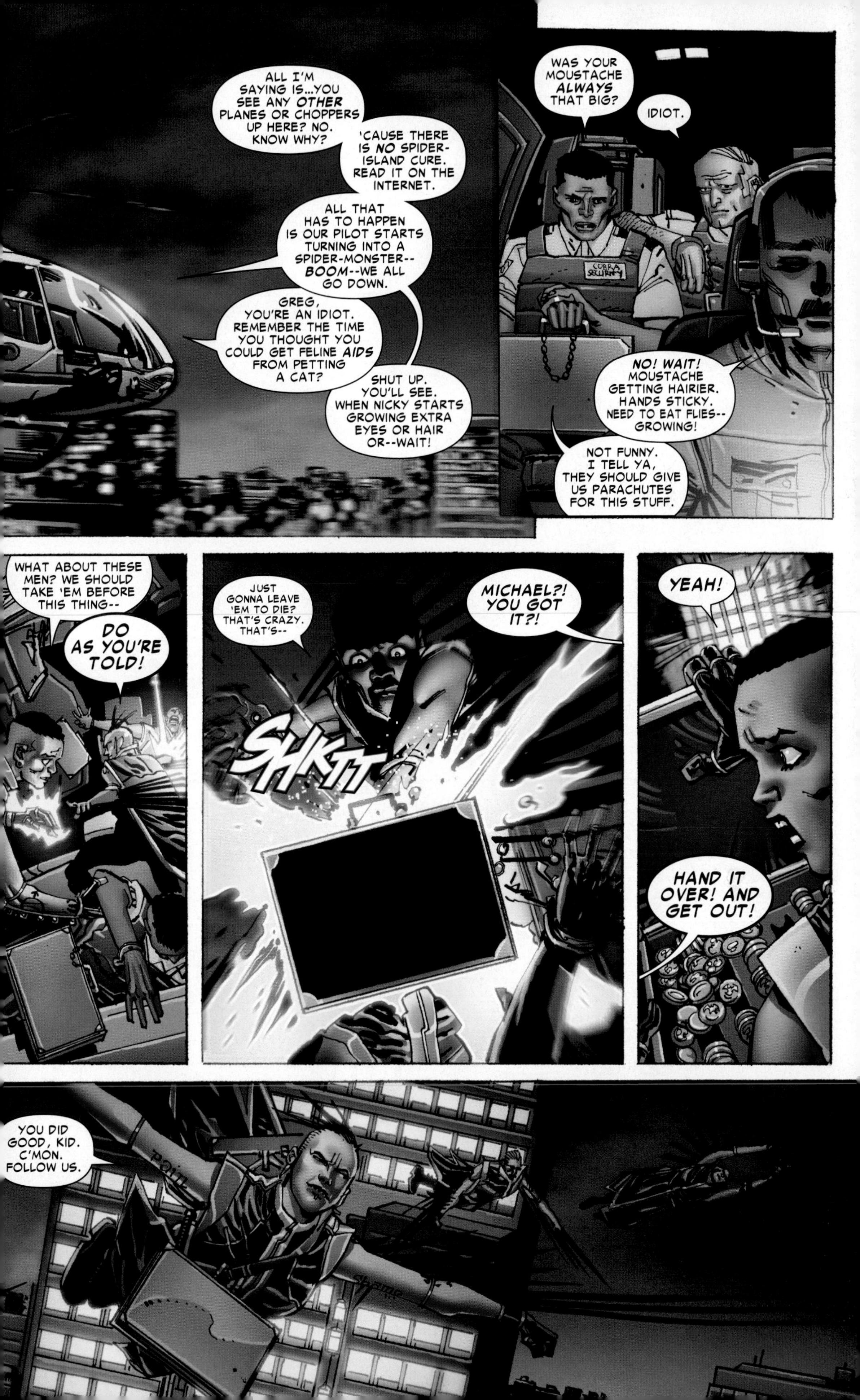
ALL I'M SAYING IS...YOU SEE ANY OTHER PLANES OR CHOPPERS UP HERE? NO. KNOW WHY?
'CAUSE THERE IS NO SPIDER-ISLAND CURE. READ IT ON THE INTERNET.
ALL THAT HAS TO HAPPEN IS OUR PILOT STARTS TURNING INTO A SPIDER-MONSTER--BOOM--WE ALL GO DOWN.
GREG, YOU'RE AN IDIOT. REMEMBER THE TIME YOU THOUGHT YOU COULD GET FELINE AIDS FROM PETTING A CAT?
SHUT UP. YOU'LL SEE. WHEN NICKY STARTS GROWING EXTRA EYES OR HAIR OR--WAIT!
WAS YOUR MOUSTACHE ALWAYS THAT BIG?
IDIOT.
NO! WAIT! MOUSTACHE GETTING HAIRIER. HANDS STICKY. NEED TO EAT FLIES--GROWING!
NOT FUNNY. I TELL YA, THEY SHOULD GIVE US PARACHUTES FOR THIS STUFF.
WHAT ABOUT THESE MEN? WE SHOULD TAKE 'EM BEFORE THIS THING--
DO AS YOU'RE TOLD!
JUST GONNA LEAVE 'EM TO DIE? THAT'S CRAZY. THAT'S--
MICHAEL?! YOU GOT IT?!
SHKTT
YEAH!
HAND IT OVER! AND GET OUT!
YOU DID GOOD, KID. C'MON. FOLLOW US.

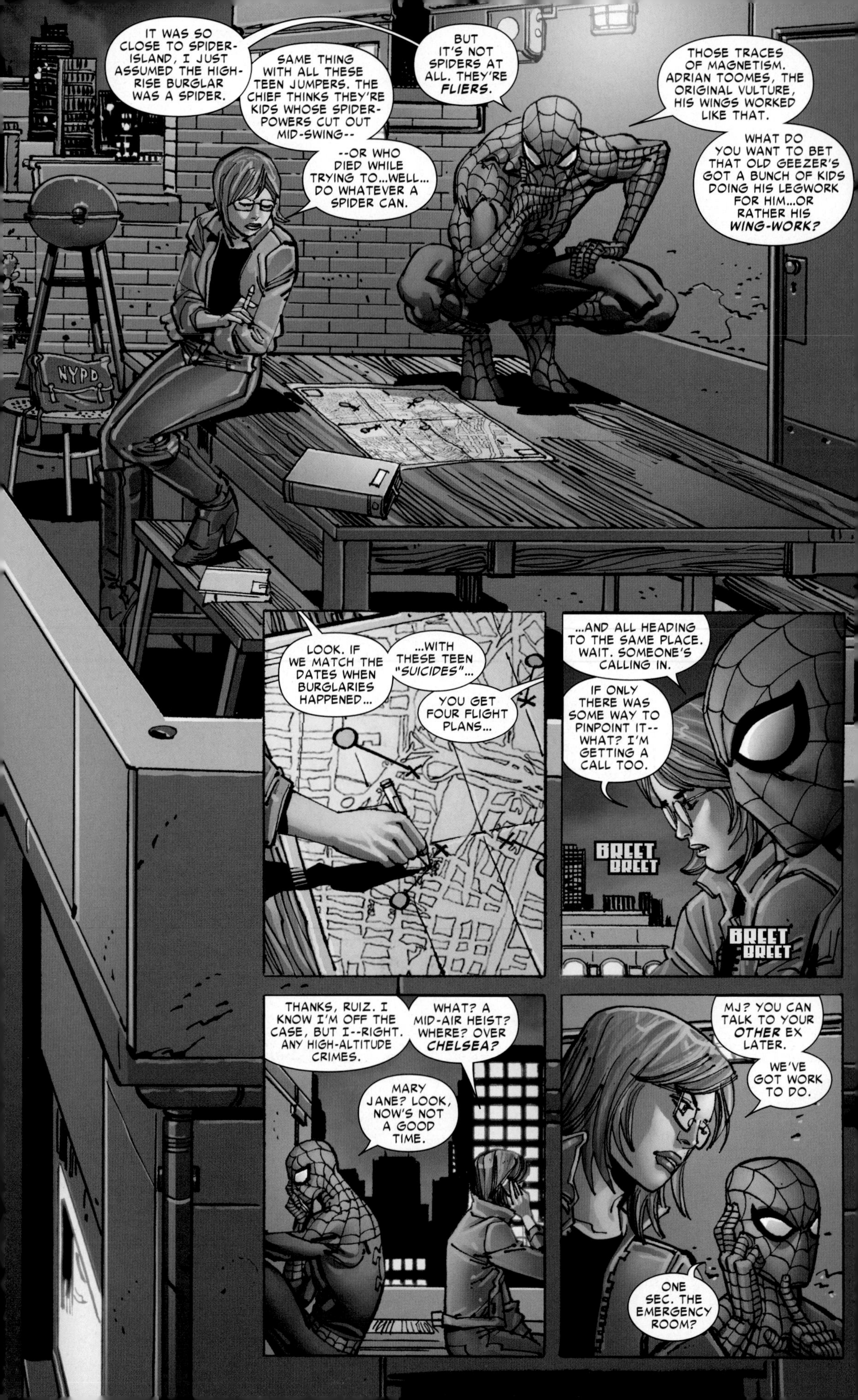
IT WAS SO CLOSE TO SPIDER-ISLAND, I JUST ASSUMED THE HIGH-RISE BURGLAR WAS A SPIDER.
BUT IT'S NOT SPIDERS AT ALL. THEY'RE FLIERS.
SAME THING WITH ALL THESE TEEN JUMPERS. THE CHIEF THINKS THEY'RE KIDS WHOSE SPIDER-POWERS CUT OUT MID-SWING--
--OR WHO DIED WHILE TRYING TO...WELL... DO WHATEVER A SPIDER CAN.
THOSE TRACES OF MAGNETISM. ADRIAN TOOMES, THE ORIGINAL VULTURE, HIS WINGS WORKED LIKE THAT.
WHAT DO YOU WANT TO BET THAT OLD GEEZER'S GOT A BUNCH OF KIDS DOING HIS LEGWORK FOR HIM...OR RATHER HIS WING-WORK?
NYPD
LOOK. IF WE MATCH THE DATES WHEN BURGLARIES HAPPENED...
...WITH THESE TEEN "SUICIDES"...
YOU GET FOUR FLIGHT PLANS...
...AND ALL HEADING TO THE SAME PLACE. WAIT. SOMEONE'S CALLING IN.
IF ONLY THERE WAS SOME WAY TO PINPOINT IT-- WHAT? I'M GETTING A CALL TOO.
BREET BREET
BREET BREET
THANKS, RUIZ. I KNOW I'M OFF THE CASE, BUT I--RIGHT. ANY HIGH-ALTITUDE CRIMES.
WHAT? A MID-AIR HEIST? WHERE? OVER CHELSEA?
MARY JANE? LOOK, NOW'S NOT A GOOD TIME.
MJ? YOU CAN TALK TO YOUR OTHER EX LATER.
WE'VE GOT WORK TO DO.
ONE SEC. THE EMERGENCY ROOM?

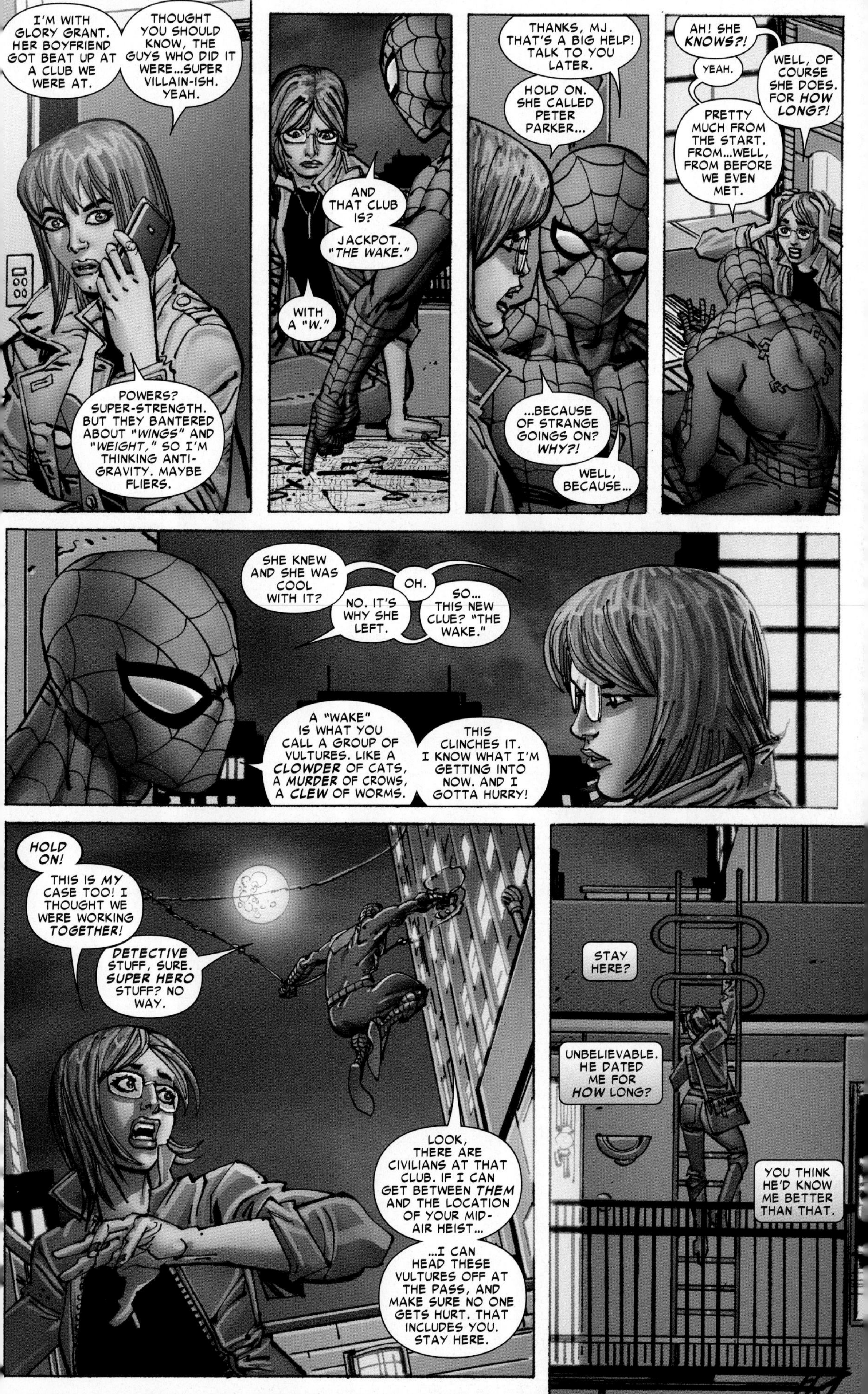
I'M WITH GLORY GRANT. HER BOYFRIEND GOT BEAT UP AT A CLUB WE WERE AT.
THOUGHT YOU SHOULD KNOW, THE GUYS WHO DID IT WERE...SUPER VILLAIN-ISH. YEAH.
POWERS? SUPER-STRENGTH. BUT THEY BANTERED ABOUT "WINGS" AND "WEIGHT," SO I'M THINKING ANTI-GRAVITY. MAYBE FLIERS.
AND THAT CLUB IS?
JACKPOT. "THE WAKE."
WITH A "W."
THANKS, MJ. THAT'S A BIG HELP! TALK TO YOU LATER.
HOLD ON. SHE CALLED PETER PARKER...
...BECAUSE OF STRANGE GOINGS ON? WHY?!
WELL, BECAUSE...
AH! SHE KNOWS?!
YEAH.
WELL, OF COURSE SHE DOES. FOR HOW LONG?!
PRETTY MUCH FROM THE START. FROM...WELL, FROM BEFORE WE EVEN MET.
SHE KNEW AND SHE WAS COOL WITH IT?
NO. IT'S WHY SHE LEFT.
OH.
SO... THIS NEW CLUE? "THE WAKE."
A "WAKE" IS WHAT YOU CALL A GROUP OF VULTURES. LIKE A CLOWDER OF CATS, A MURDER OF CROWS, A CLEW OF WORMS.
THIS CLINCHES IT. I KNOW WHAT I'M GETTING INTO NOW. AND I GOTTA HURRY!
HOLD ON!
THIS IS MY CASE TOO! I THOUGHT WE WERE WORKING TOGETHER!
DETECTIVE STUFF, SURE. SUPER HERO STUFF? NO WAY.
LOOK, THERE ARE CIVILIANS AT THAT CLUB. IF I CAN GET BETWEEN THEM AND THE LOCATION OF YOUR MID-AIR HEIST...
...I CAN HEAD THESE VULTURES OFF AT THE PASS, AND MAKE SURE NO ONE GETS HURT. THAT INCLUDES YOU. STAY HERE.
STAY HERE?
UNBELIEVABLE. HE DATED ME FOR HOW LONG?
YOU THINK HE'D KNOW ME BETTER THAN THAT.

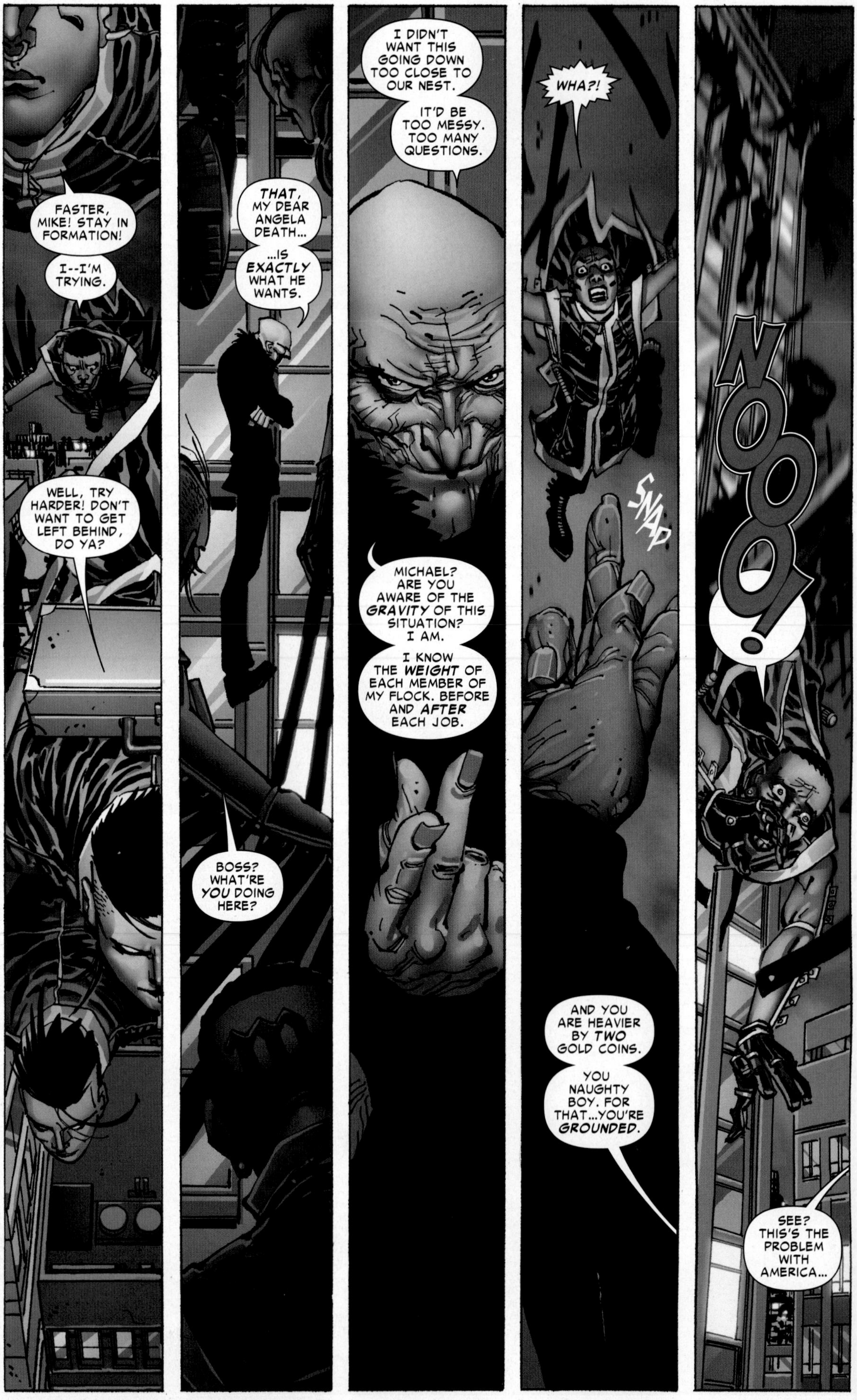
FASTER, MIKE! STAY IN FORMATION!
I--I'M TRYING.
WELL, TRY HARDER! DON'T WANT TO GET LEFT BEHIND, DO YA?
THAT, MY DEAR ANGELA DEATH...
...IS EXACTLY WHAT HE WANTS.
BOSS? WHAT'RE YOU DOING HERE?
I DIDN'T WANT THIS GOING DOWN TOO CLOSE TO OUR NEST.
IT'D BE TOO MESSY. TOO MANY QUESTIONS.
MICHAEL? ARE YOU AWARE OF THE GRAVITY OF THIS SITUATION? I AM.
I KNOW THE WEIGHT OF EACH MEMBER OF MY FLOCK. BEFORE AND AFTER EACH JOB.
WHA?!
SNAP
AND YOU ARE HEAVIER BY TWO GOLD COINS.
YOU NAUGHTY BOY. FOR THAT...YOU'RE GROUNDED.
NOOO!
SEE? THIS'S THE PROBLEM WITH AMERICA...

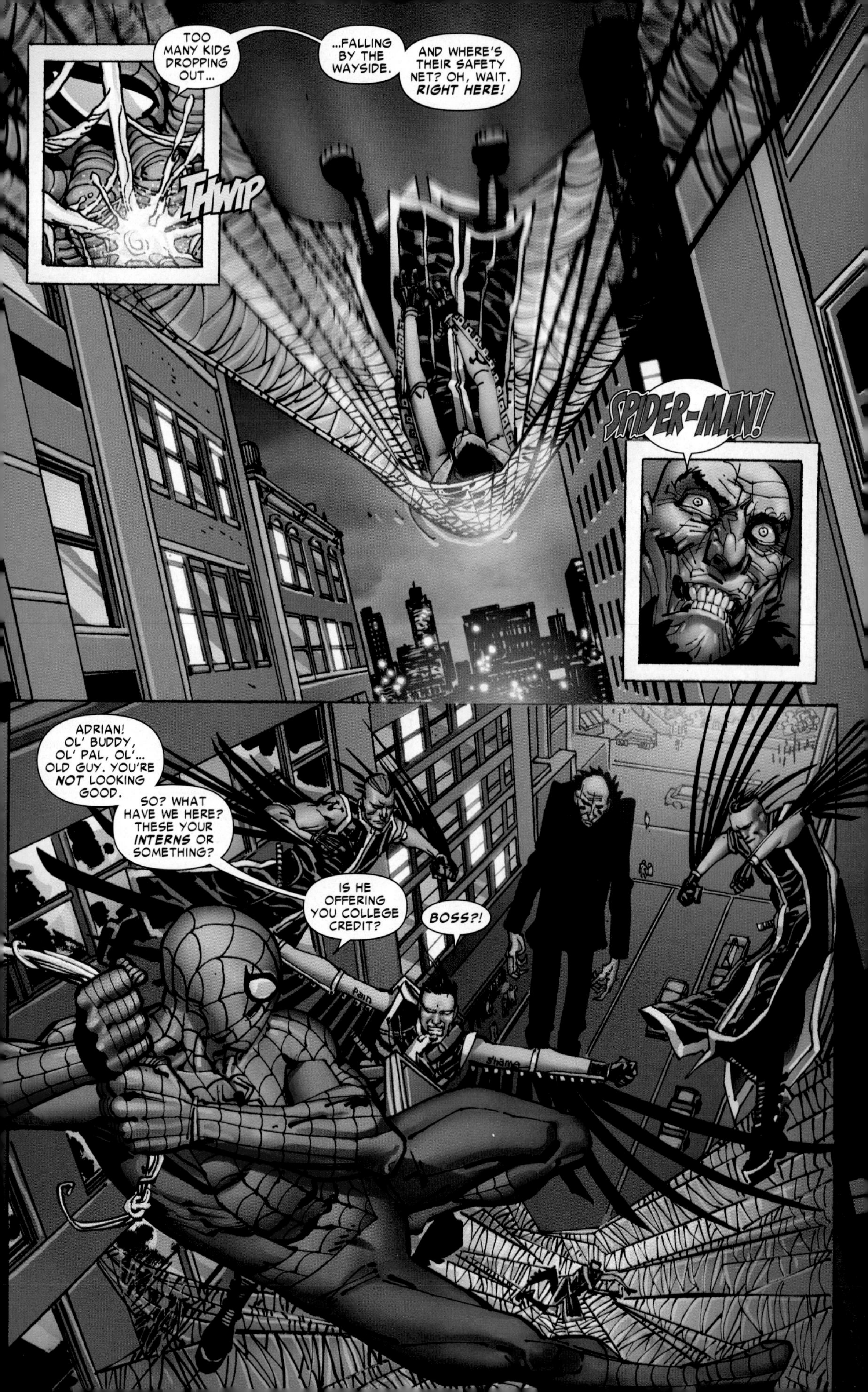
TOO MANY KIDS DROPPING OUT...
...FALLING BY THE WAYSIDE.
AND WHERE'S THEIR SAFETY NET? OH, WAIT. *RIGHT HERE!*
THWIP
SPIDER-MAN!
ADRIAN! OL' BUDDY, OL' PAL, OL'... OLD GUY. YOU'RE **NOT** LOOKING GOOD.
SO? WHAT HAVE WE HERE? THESE YOUR *INTERNS* OR SOMETHING?
IS HE OFFERING YOU COLLEGE CREDIT?
BOSS?!
pain
shame

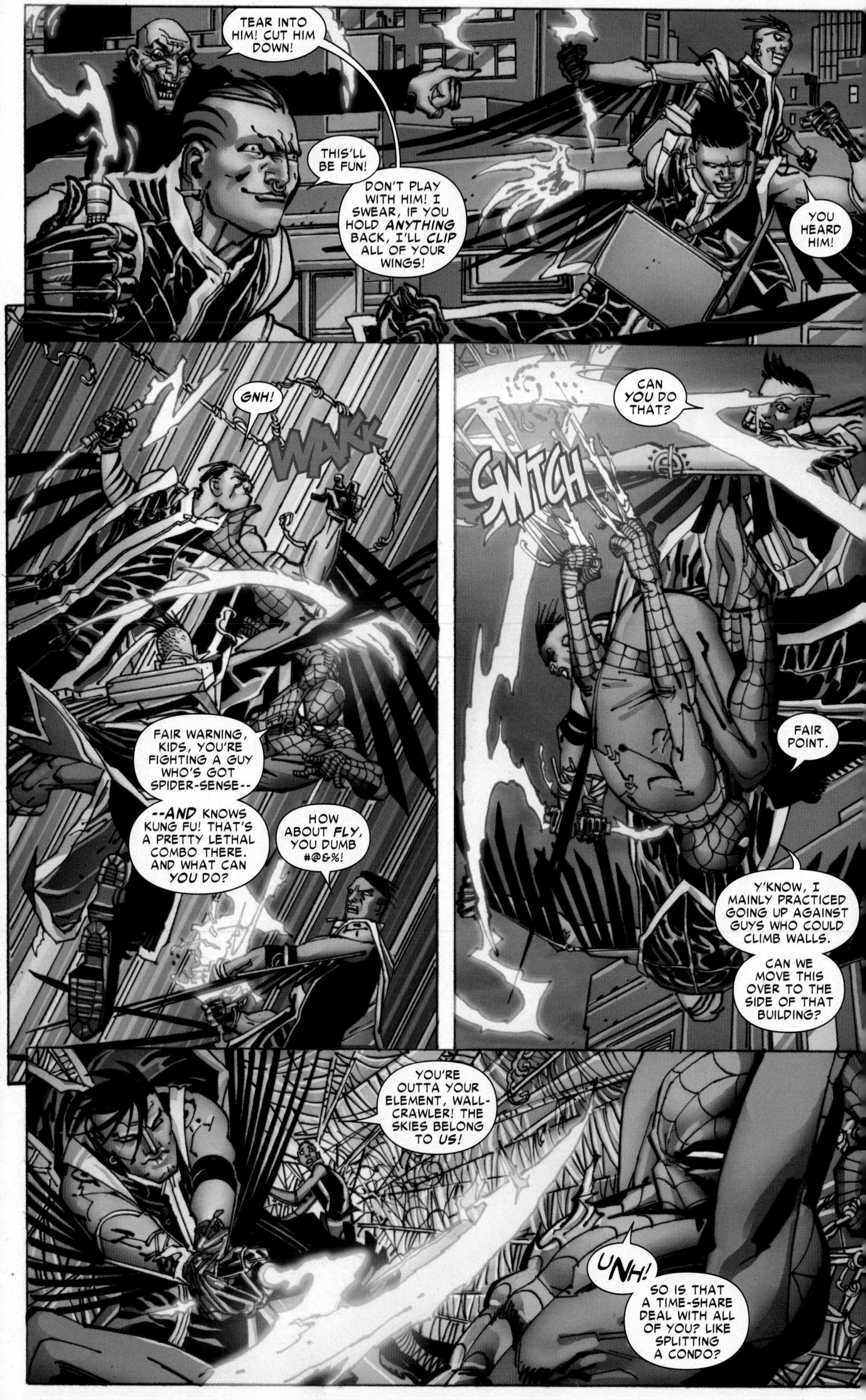
TEAR INTO HIM! CUT HIM DOWN!
THIS'LL BE FUN!
DON'T PLAY WITH HIM! I SWEAR, IF YOU HOLD ANYTHING BACK, I'LL CLIP ALL OF YOUR WINGS!
YOU HEARD HIM!
GNH!
WAKK
FAIR WARNING, KIDS, YOU'RE FIGHTING A GUY WHO'S GOT SPIDER-SENSE--
--AND KNOWS KUNG FU! THAT'S A PRETTY LETHAL COMBO THERE. AND WHAT CAN YOU DO?
HOW ABOUT FLY, YOU DUMB #@&%!
CAN YOU DO THAT?
SWTCH
FAIR POINT.
Y'KNOW, I MAINLY PRACTICED GOING UP AGAINST GUYS WHO COULD CLIMB WALLS.
CAN WE MOVE THIS OVER TO THE SIDE OF THAT BUILDING?
YOU'RE OUTTA YOUR ELEMENT, WALL-CRAWLER! THE SKIES BELONG TO US!
UNH!
SO IS THAT A TIME-SHARE DEAL WITH ALL OF YOU? LIKE SPLITTING A CONDO?

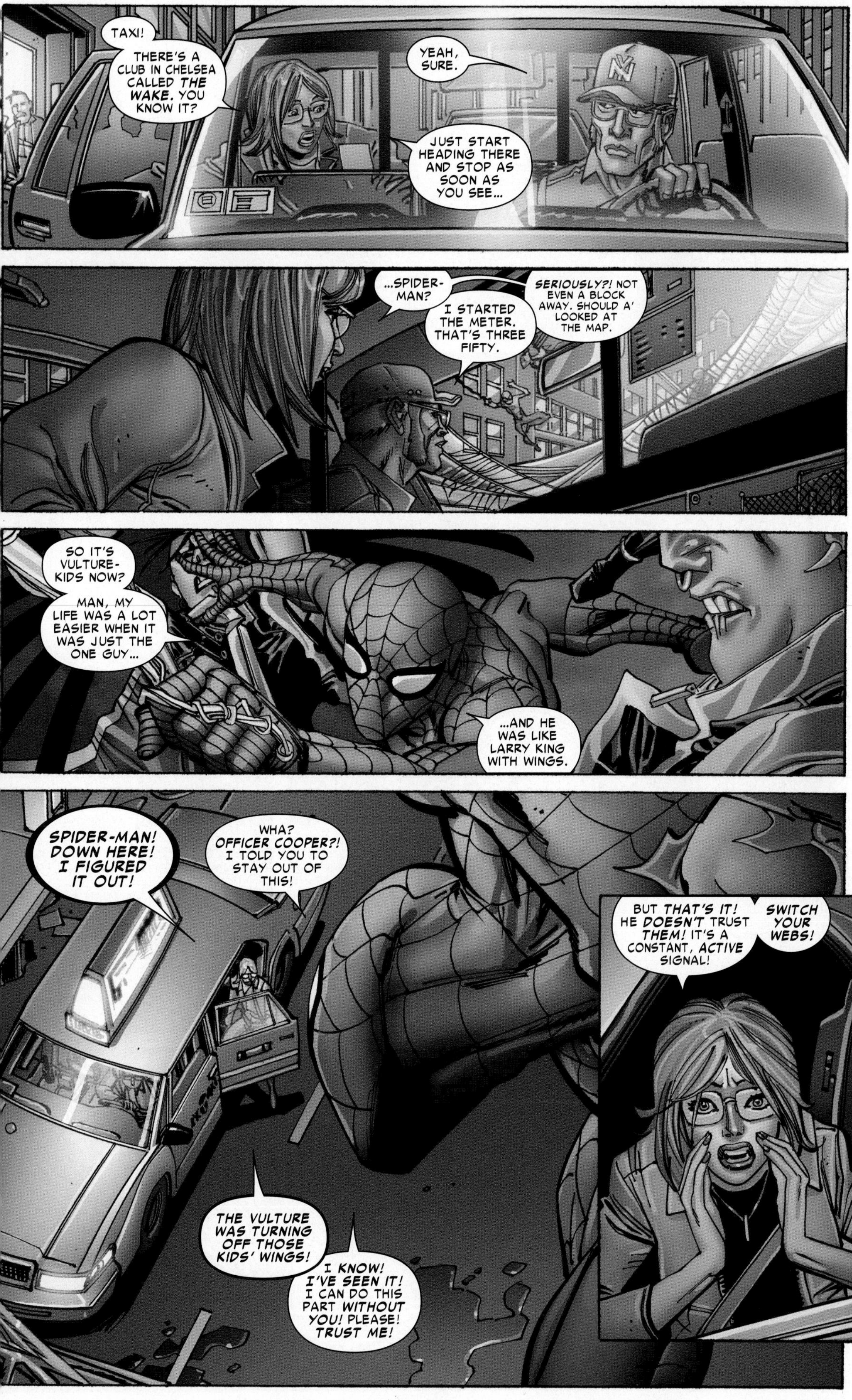
TAXI!
THERE'S A CLUB IN CHELSEA CALLED THE WAKE. YOU KNOW IT?
YEAH, SURE.
JUST START HEADING THERE AND STOP AS SOON AS YOU SEE...
...SPIDER-MAN?
I STARTED THE METER. THAT'S THREE FIFTY.
SERIOUSLY?! NOT EVEN A BLOCK AWAY. SHOULD A' LOOKED AT THE MAP.
SO IT'S VULTURE-KIDS NOW?
MAN, MY LIFE WAS A LOT EASIER WHEN IT WAS JUST THE ONE GUY...
...AND HE WAS LIKE LARRY KING WITH WINGS.
SPIDER-MAN! DOWN HERE! I FIGURED IT OUT!
WHA? OFFICER COOPER?! I TOLD YOU TO STAY OUT OF THIS!
BUT THAT'S IT! HE DOESN'T TRUST THEM! IT'S A CONSTANT, ACTIVE SIGNAL!
SWITCH YOUR WEBS!
THE VULTURE WAS TURNING OFF THOSE KIDS' WINGS!
I KNOW! I'VE SEEN IT! I CAN DO THIS PART WITHOUT YOU! PLEASE! TRUST ME!

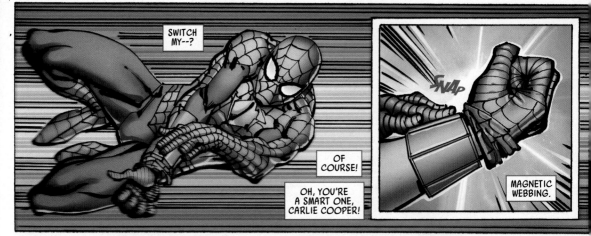

SWITCH MY--?

OF COURSE!

OH, YOU'RE A SMART ONE, CARLIE COOPER!

SNAP

MAGNETIC WEBBING.

BLOCKS ALL RADIO WAVES.

NICE AIM, LOSER. YOU'RE MISSING US BY MILES.

AND YOU'RE MISSING THE POINT. GRAMPS NEVER TRUSTED YOU FARTHER THAN HE COULD THROW YOU.

OR RATHER, FARTHER THAN YOU COULD FLY AWAY. YOU WEREN'T HIS WINGMEN...

...YOU WERE HIS KITES. AND HE KEPT YOU ON A LONG STRING...

...THAT I JUST CUT. HAPPY LANDINGS.

UNFF!

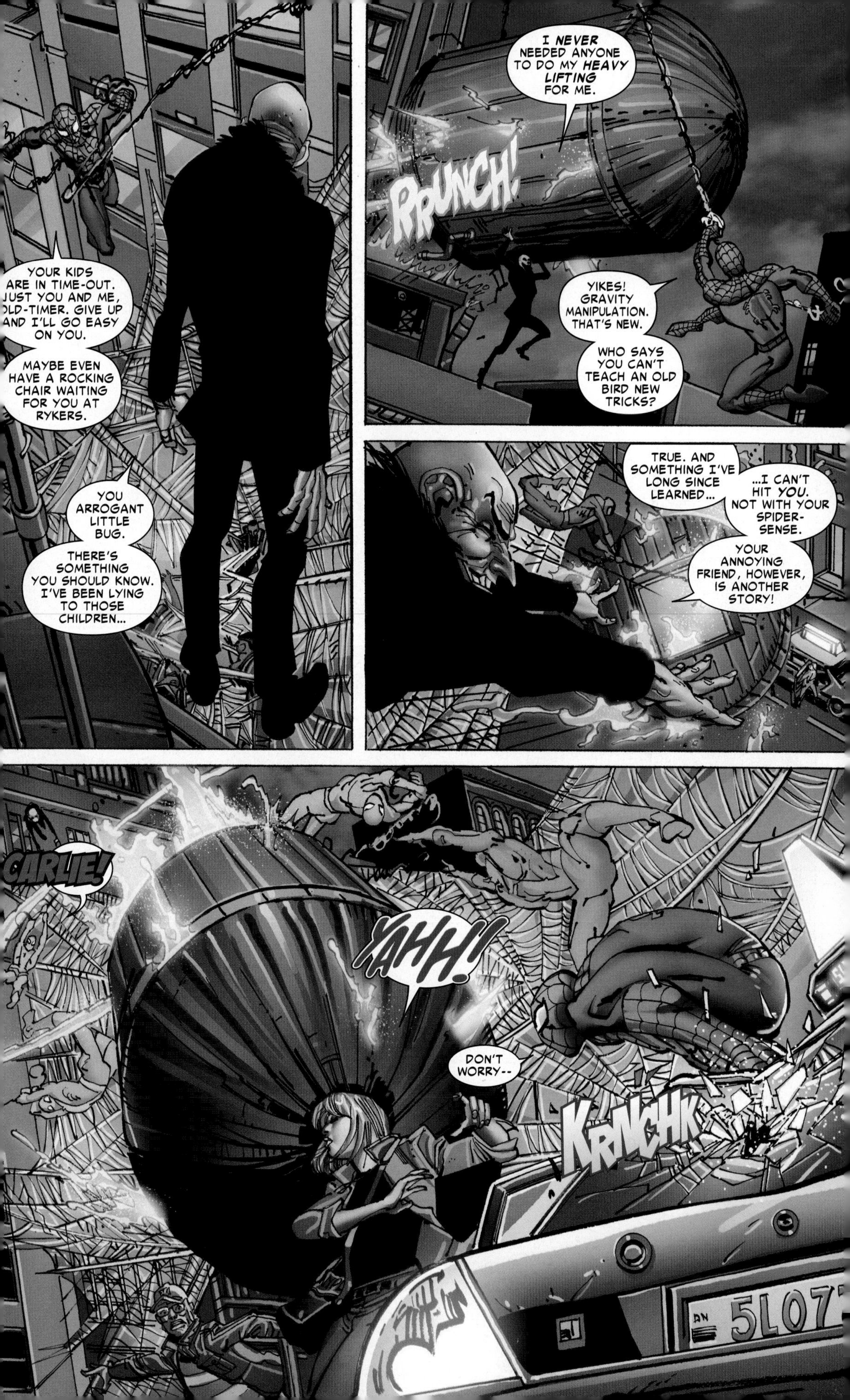

YOUR KIDS ARE IN TIME-OUT. JUST YOU AND ME, OLD-TIMER. GIVE UP AND I'LL GO EASY ON YOU.
MAYBE EVEN HAVE A ROCKING CHAIR WAITING FOR YOU AT RYKERS.
YOU ARROGANT LITTLE BUG.
THERE'S SOMETHING YOU SHOULD KNOW. I'VE BEEN LYING TO THOSE CHILDREN...
I NEVER NEEDED ANYONE TO DO MY HEAVY LIFTING FOR ME.
RRUNCH!
YIKES! GRAVITY MANIPULATION. THAT'S NEW.
WHO SAYS YOU CAN'T TEACH AN OLD BIRD NEW TRICKS?
TRUE. AND SOMETHING I'VE LONG SINCE LEARNED...
...I CAN'T HIT YOU. NOT WITH YOUR SPIDER-SENSE.
YOUR ANNOYING FRIEND, HOWEVER, IS ANOTHER STORY!
CARLIE!
YAHH!
DON'T WORRY--
KRNCHK

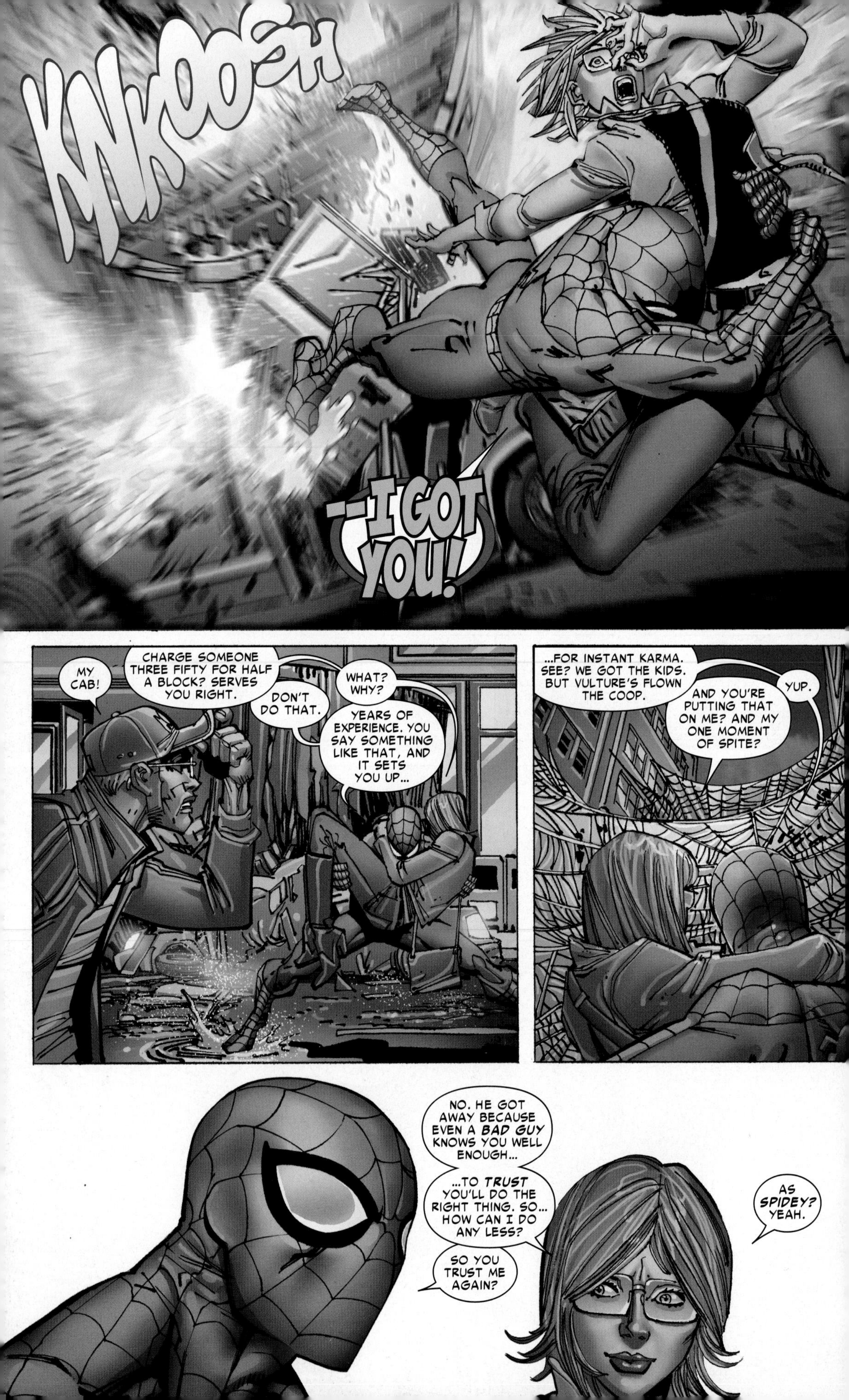
KNKOOSH
--I GOT YOU!
MY CAB!
CHARGE SOMEONE THREE FIFTY FOR HALF A BLOCK? SERVES YOU RIGHT.
DON'T DO THAT.
WHAT? WHY?
YEARS OF EXPERIENCE. YOU SAY SOMETHING LIKE THAT, AND IT SETS YOU UP...
...FOR INSTANT KARMA. SEE? WE GOT THE KIDS. BUT VULTURE'S FLOWN THE COOP.
AND YOU'RE PUTTING THAT ON ME? AND MY ONE MOMENT OF SPITE?
YUP.
NO. HE GOT AWAY BECAUSE EVEN A *BAD GUY* KNOWS YOU WELL ENOUGH...
...TO *TRUST* YOU'LL DO THE RIGHT THING. SO... HOW CAN I DO ANY LESS?
SO YOU TRUST ME AGAIN?
AS *SPIDEY?* YEAH.

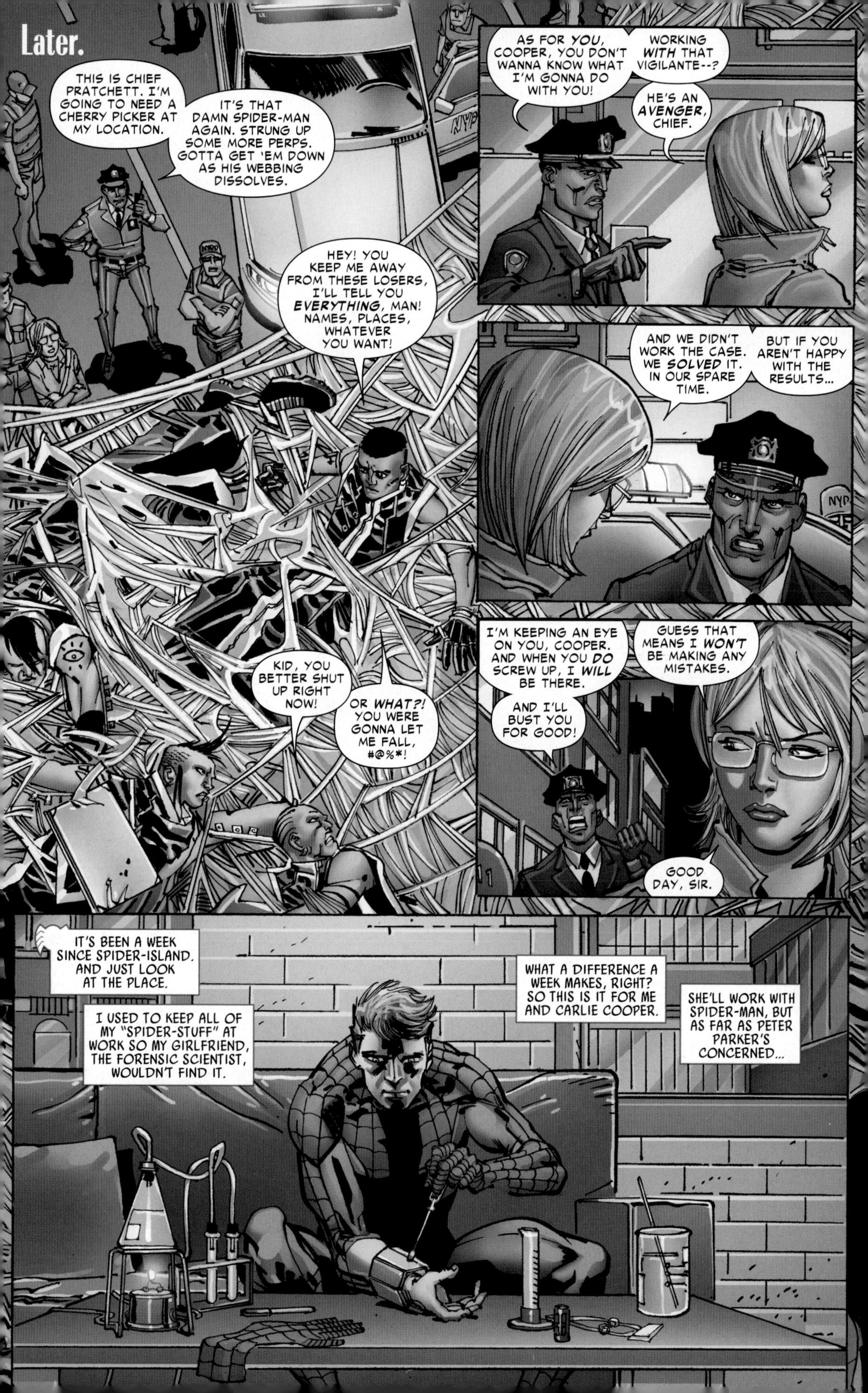

Later.
THIS IS CHIEF PRATCHETT. I'M GOING TO NEED A CHERRY PICKER AT MY LOCATION.
IT'S THAT DAMN SPIDER-MAN AGAIN. STRUNG UP SOME MORE PERPS. GOTTA GET 'EM DOWN AS HIS WEBBING DISSOLVES.
HEY! YOU KEEP ME AWAY FROM THESE LOSERS, I'LL TELL YOU EVERYTHING, MAN! NAMES, PLACES, WHATEVER YOU WANT!
KID, YOU BETTER SHUT UP RIGHT NOW!
OR WHAT?! YOU WERE GONNA LET ME FALL, #@%*!
AS FOR YOU, COOPER, YOU DON'T WANNA KNOW WHAT I'M GONNA DO WITH YOU!
WORKING WITH THAT VIGILANTE--?
HE'S AN AVENGER, CHIEF.
AND WE DIDN'T WORK THE CASE. WE SOLVED IT. IN OUR SPARE TIME.
BUT IF YOU AREN'T HAPPY WITH THE RESULTS...
I'M KEEPING AN EYE ON YOU, COOPER. AND WHEN YOU DO SCREW UP, I WILL BE THERE.
AND I'LL BUST YOU FOR GOOD!
GUESS THAT MEANS I WON'T BE MAKING ANY MISTAKES.
GOOD DAY, SIR.
IT'S BEEN A WEEK SINCE SPIDER-ISLAND. AND JUST LOOK AT THE PLACE.
I USED TO KEEP ALL OF MY "SPIDER-STUFF" AT WORK SO MY GIRLFRIEND, THE FORENSIC SCIENTIST, WOULDN'T FIND IT.
WHAT A DIFFERENCE A WEEK MAKES, RIGHT? SO THIS IS IT FOR ME AND CARLIE COOPER.
SHE'LL WORK WITH SPIDER-MAN, BUT AS FAR AS PETER PARKER'S CONCERNED...

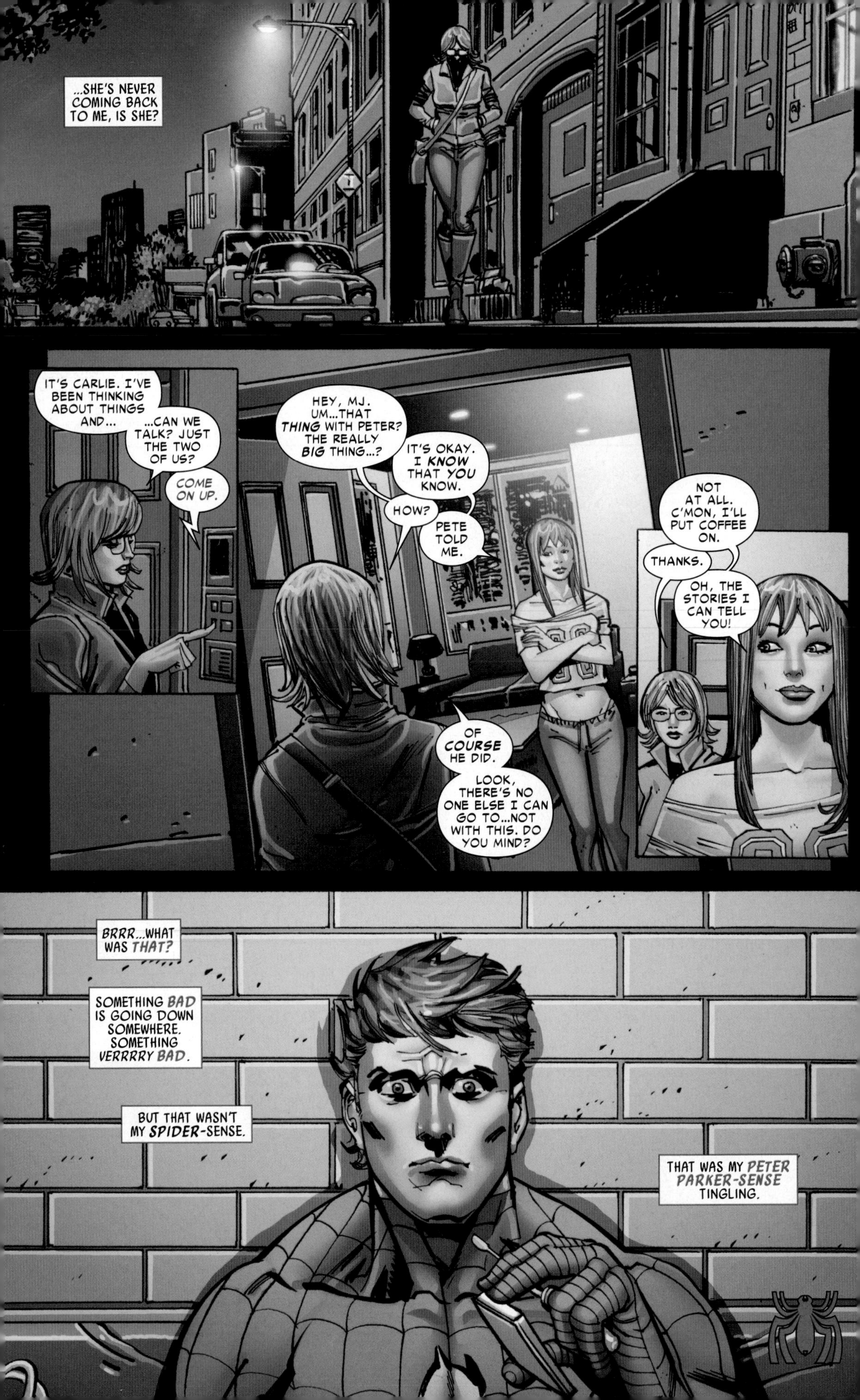
...SHE'S NEVER COMING BACK TO ME, IS SHE?
IT'S CARLIE. I'VE BEEN THINKING ABOUT THINGS AND...
...CAN WE TALK? JUST THE TWO OF US?
COME ON UP.
HEY, MJ. UM...THAT THING WITH PETER? THE REALLY BIG THING...?
IT'S OKAY. I KNOW THAT YOU KNOW.
HOW?
PETE TOLD ME.
OF COURSE HE DID.
LOOK, THERE'S NO ONE ELSE I CAN GO TO...NOT WITH THIS. DO YOU MIND?
NOT AT ALL. C'MON, I'LL PUT COFFEE ON.
THANKS.
OH, THE STORIES I CAN TELL YOU!
BRRR...WHAT WAS THAT?
SOMETHING BAD IS GOING DOWN SOMEWHERE. SOMETHING VERRRRY BAD.
BUT THAT WASN'T MY SPIDER-SENSE.
THAT WAS MY PETER PARKER-SENSE TINGLING.

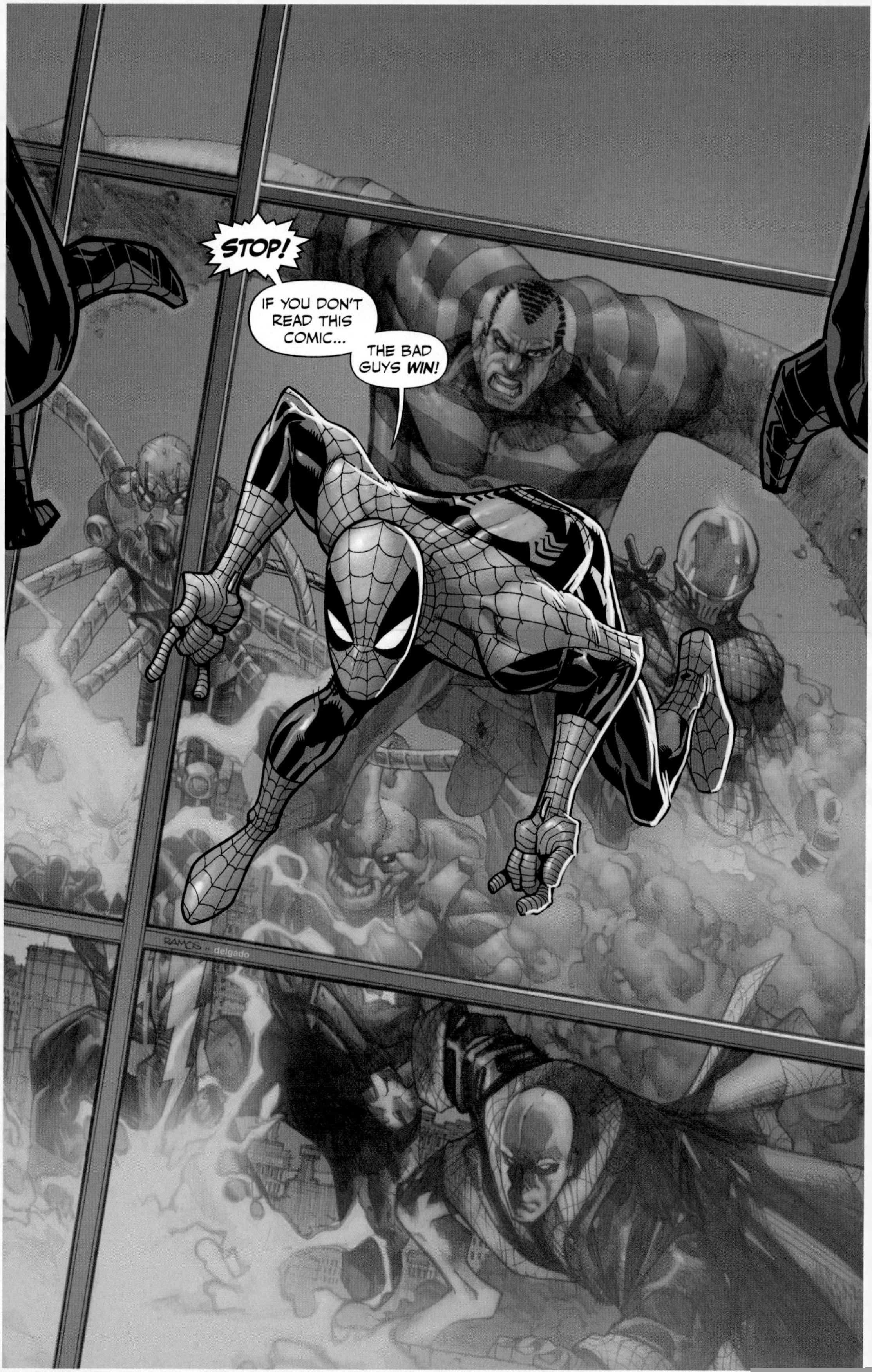
STOP!
IF YOU DON'T READ THIS COMIC...
THE BAD GUYS WIN!
RAMOS
delgado

SPIDER-M
& EDGAR

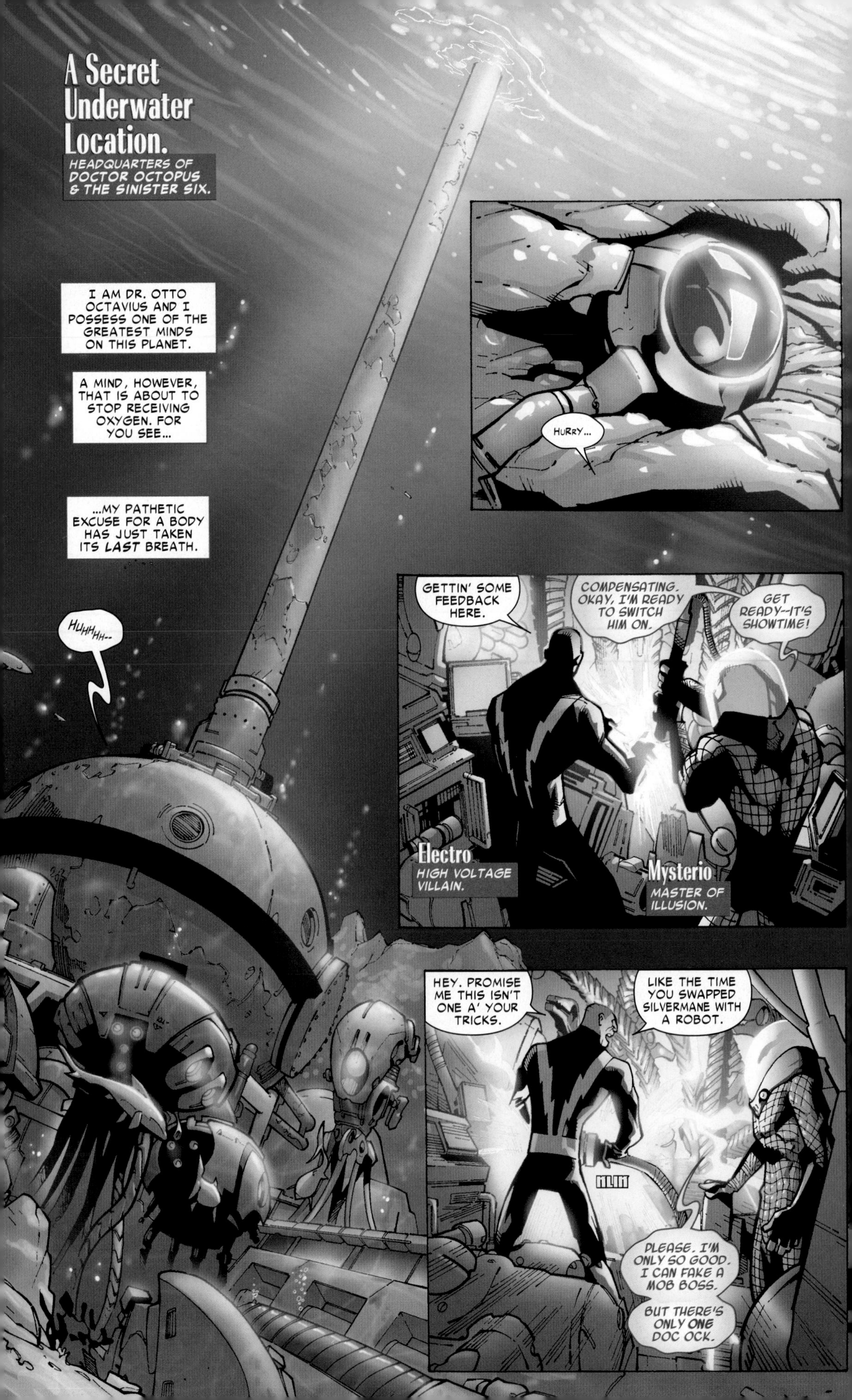
A Secret Underwater Location.
HEADQUARTERS OF DOCTOR OCTOPUS & THE SINISTER SIX.
I AM DR. OTTO OCTAVIUS AND I POSSESS ONE OF THE GREATEST MINDS ON THIS PLANET.
A MIND, HOWEVER, THAT IS ABOUT TO STOP RECEIVING OXYGEN. FOR YOU SEE...
...MY PATHETIC EXCUSE FOR A BODY HAS JUST TAKEN ITS LAST BREATH.
HUHHHH--
HURRY...
GETTIN' SOME FEEDBACK HERE.
COMPENSATING. OKAY, I'M READY TO SWITCH HIM ON.
GET READY--IT'S SHOWTIME!
Electro
HIGH VOLTAGE VILLAIN.
Mysterio
MASTER OF ILLUSION.
HEY. PROMISE ME THIS ISN'T ONE A' YOUR TRICKS.
LIKE THE TIME YOU SWAPPED SILVERMANE WITH A ROBOT.
NLIN
PLEASE. I'M ONLY SO GOOD. I CAN FAKE A MOB BOSS.
BUT THERE'S ONLY ONE DOC OCK.

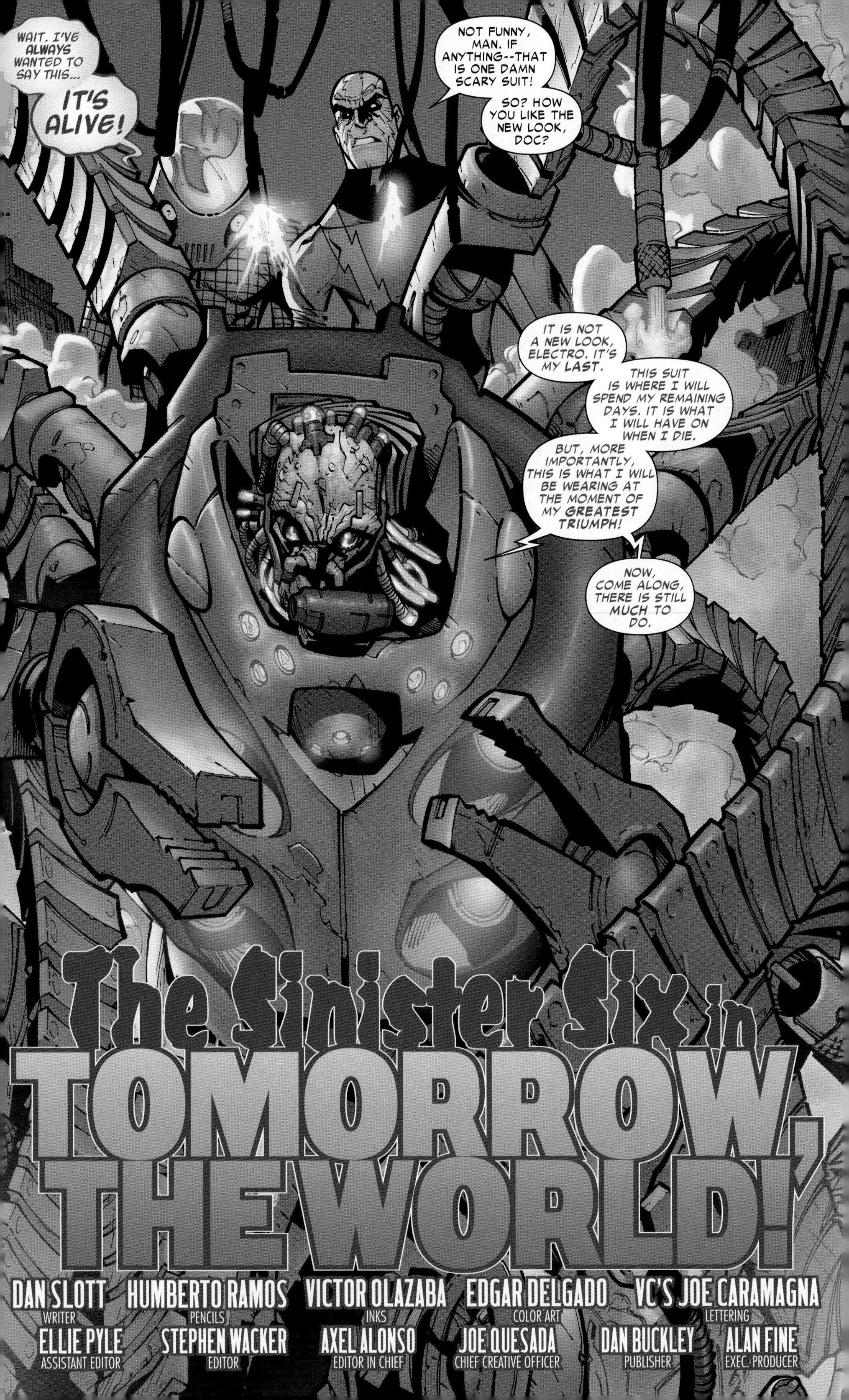
WAIT. I'VE ALWAYS WANTED TO SAY THIS...
IT'S ALIVE!
NOT FUNNY, MAN. IF ANYTHING--THAT IS ONE DAMN SCARY SUIT!
SO? HOW YOU LIKE THE NEW LOOK, DOC?
IT IS NOT A NEW LOOK, ELECTRO. IT'S MY LAST.
THIS SUIT IS WHERE I WILL SPEND MY REMAINING DAYS. IT IS WHAT I WILL HAVE ON WHEN I DIE.
BUT, MORE IMPORTANTLY, THIS IS WHAT I WILL BE WEARING AT THE MOMENT OF MY GREATEST TRIUMPH!
NOW, COME ALONG, THERE IS STILL MUCH TO DO.
The Sinister Six in
TOMORROW, THE WORLD!
DAN SLOTT WRITER
HUMBERTO RAMOS PENCILS
VICTOR OLAZABA INKS
EDGAR DELGADO COLOR ART
VC'S JOE CARAMAGNA LETTERING
ELLIE PYLE ASSISTANT EDITOR
STEPHEN WACKER EDITOR
AXEL ALONSO EDITOR IN CHIEF
JOE QUESADA CHIEF CREATIVE OFFICER
DAN BUCKLEY PUBLISHER
ALAN FINE EXEC. PRODUCER

FINAL

DAILY 🎺 BUGLE

NEW YORK'S FINEST DAILY NEWSPAPER

SINCE 1897
☆☆☆☆
$1.00 (in NYC)
$1.50 (outside city)

INSIDE: SKI LODGE SHOOTING BLOODIES HUDSON RIVER VALLEY; MAYOR MISSING AFTER MOLOID MARATHON MADNESS; NORMAN OSBORN RETURNS!

SPECIAL EDITION:
VILLAINOUS TEAMS YOU SHOULD KNOW

THE SINISTER SIX

ARE RUMORED TO BE WORKING TOWARD FULFILLMENT OF DOC OCK'S MYSTERIOUS MASTER PLAN. BE ON THE LOOKOUT FOR:

THE INTELLIGENCIA

ARE A LEAGUE OF EVIL SUPER-GENIUSES DEVOTED TO PROVING THEMSELVES THE SMARTEST SUPER VILLAINS ON EARTH. THEY INCLUDE:

 **DOCTOR OCTOPUS**

 **M.O.D.O.K.**

 **SANDMAN**

 **RED GHOST**

 **CHAMELEON**

 **MAD THINKER**

 **RHINO**

 **WIZARD**

 **ELECTRO**

 **KLAW**

 **MYSTERIO**

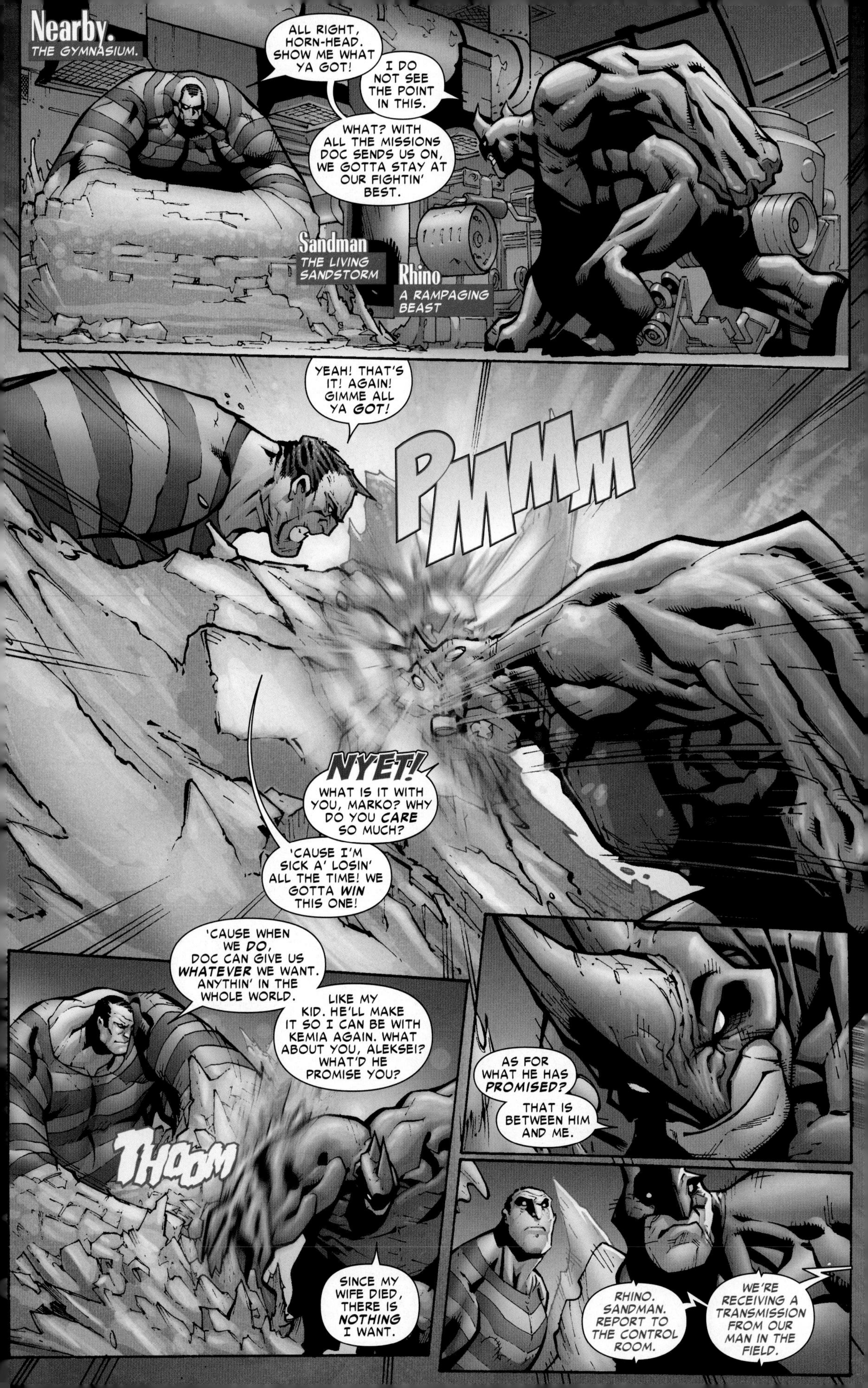
Nearby.
THE GYMNASIUM.
ALL RIGHT, HORN-HEAD. SHOW ME WHAT YA GOT!
I DO NOT SEE THE POINT IN THIS.
WHAT? WITH ALL THE MISSIONS DOC SENDS US ON, WE GOTTA STAY AT OUR FIGHTIN' BEST.
Sandman
THE LIVING SANDSTORM
Rhino
A RAMPAGING BEAST
YEAH! THAT'S IT! AGAIN! GIMME ALL YA GOT!
PMMMM
NYET!
WHAT IS IT WITH YOU, MARKO? WHY DO YOU CARE SO MUCH?
'CAUSE I'M SICK A' LOSIN' ALL THE TIME! WE GOTTA WIN THIS ONE!
'CAUSE WHEN WE DO, DOC CAN GIVE US WHATEVER WE WANT. ANYTHIN' IN THE WHOLE WORLD.
LIKE MY KID. HE'LL MAKE IT SO I CAN BE WITH KEMIA AGAIN. WHAT ABOUT YOU, ALEKSEI? WHAT'D HE PROMISE YOU?
THOOM
AS FOR WHAT HE HAS PROMISED?
THAT IS BETWEEN HIM AND ME.
SINCE MY WIFE DIED, THERE IS NOTHING I WANT.
RHINO. SANDMAN. REPORT TO THE CONTROL ROOM.
WE'RE RECEIVING A TRANSMISSION FROM OUR MAN IN THE FIELD.

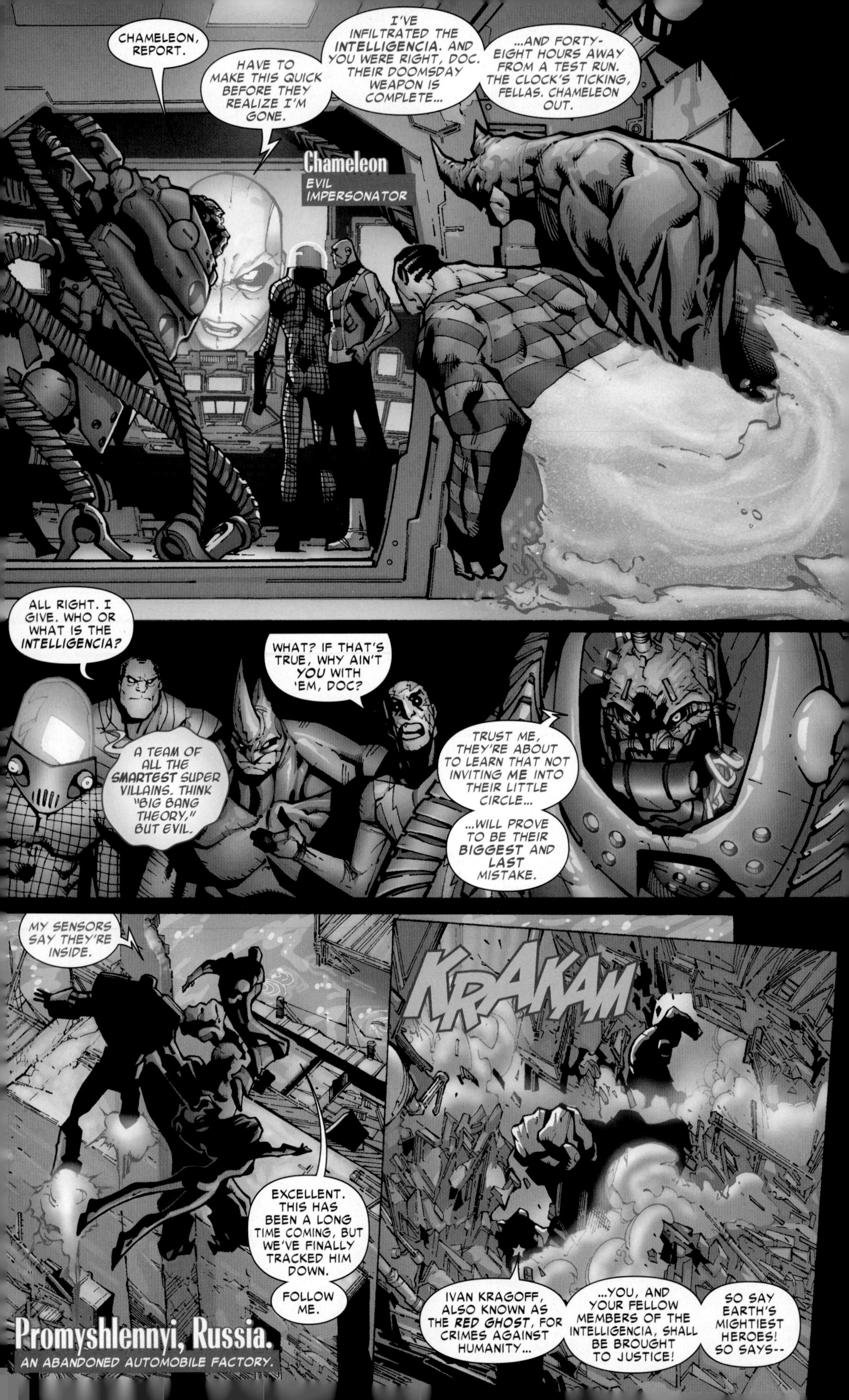
CHAMELEON, REPORT.
HAVE TO MAKE THIS QUICK BEFORE THEY REALIZE I'M GONE.
I'VE INFILTRATED THE INTELLIGENCIA. AND YOU WERE RIGHT, DOC. THEIR DOOMSDAY WEAPON IS COMPLETE...
...AND FORTY-EIGHT HOURS AWAY FROM A TEST RUN. THE CLOCK'S TICKING, FELLAS. CHAMELEON OUT.
Chameleon
EVIL IMPERSONATOR
ALL RIGHT. I GIVE. WHO OR WHAT IS THE INTELLIGENCIA?
A TEAM OF ALL THE SMARTEST SUPER VILLAINS. THINK "BIG BANG THEORY," BUT EVIL.
WHAT? IF THAT'S TRUE, WHY AIN'T YOU WITH 'EM, DOC?
TRUST ME, THEY'RE ABOUT TO LEARN THAT NOT INVITING ME INTO THEIR LITTLE CIRCLE...
...WILL PROVE TO BE THEIR BIGGEST AND LAST MISTAKE.
Promyshlennyi, Russia.
AN ABANDONED AUTOMOBILE FACTORY.
MY SENSORS SAY THEY'RE INSIDE.
EXCELLENT. THIS HAS BEEN A LONG TIME COMING, BUT WE'VE FINALLY TRACKED HIM DOWN.
FOLLOW ME.
KRAKAM
IVAN KRAGOFF, ALSO KNOWN AS THE RED GHOST, FOR CRIMES AGAINST HUMANITY...
...YOU, AND YOUR FELLOW MEMBERS OF THE INTELLIGENCIA, SHALL BE BROUGHT TO JUSTICE!
SO SAY EARTH'S MIGHTIEST HEROES! SO SAYS--

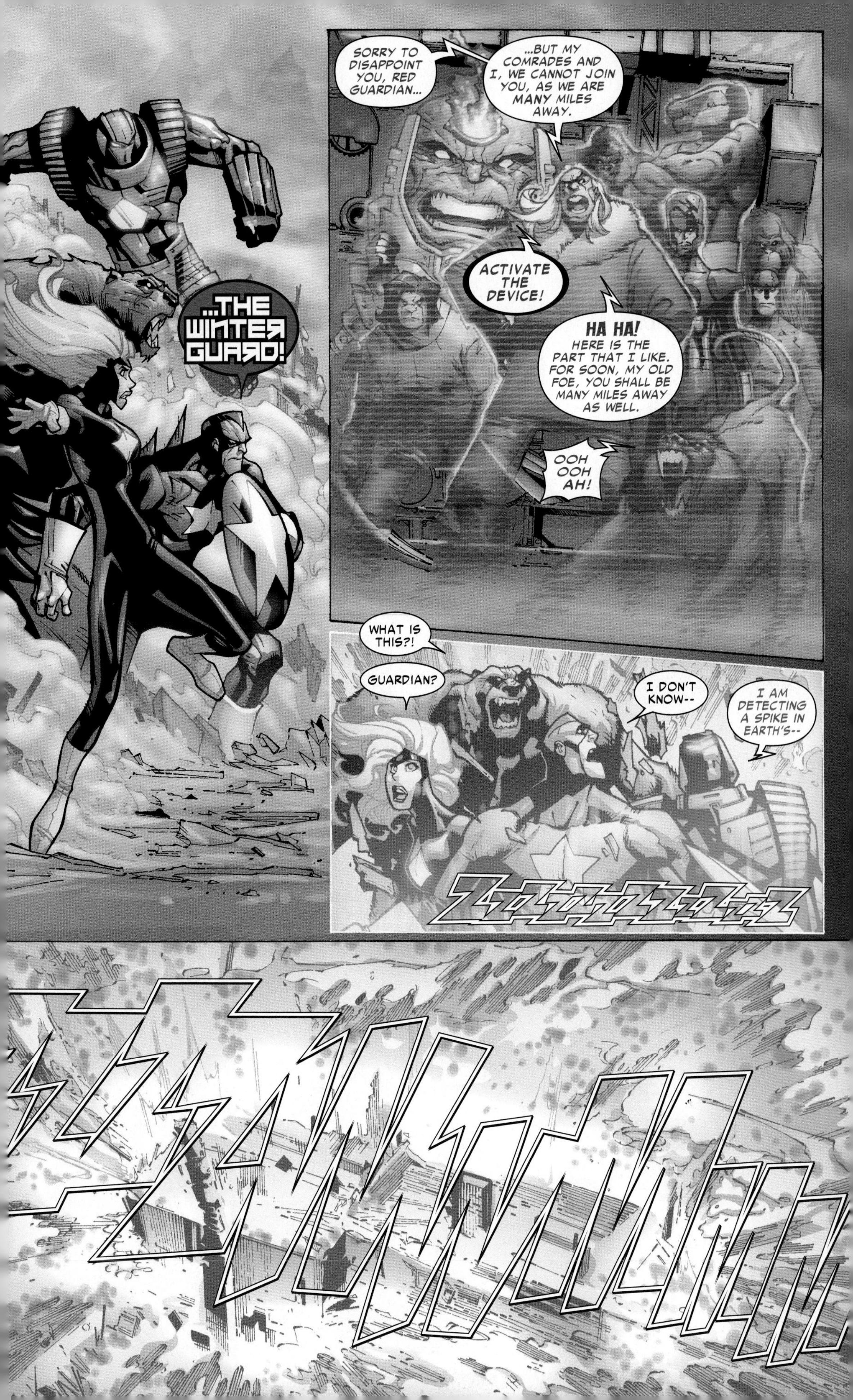
...THE WINTER GUARD!
SORRY TO DISAPPOINT YOU, RED GUARDIAN...
...BUT MY COMRADES AND I, WE CANNOT JOIN YOU, AS WE ARE MANY MILES AWAY.
ACTIVATE THE DEVICE!
HA HA! HERE IS THE PART THAT I LIKE. FOR SOON, MY OLD FOE, YOU SHALL BE MANY MILES AWAY AS WELL.
OOH OOH AH!
WHAT IS THIS?!
GUARDIAN?
I DON'T KNOW--
I AM DETECTING A SPIKE IN EARTH'S--

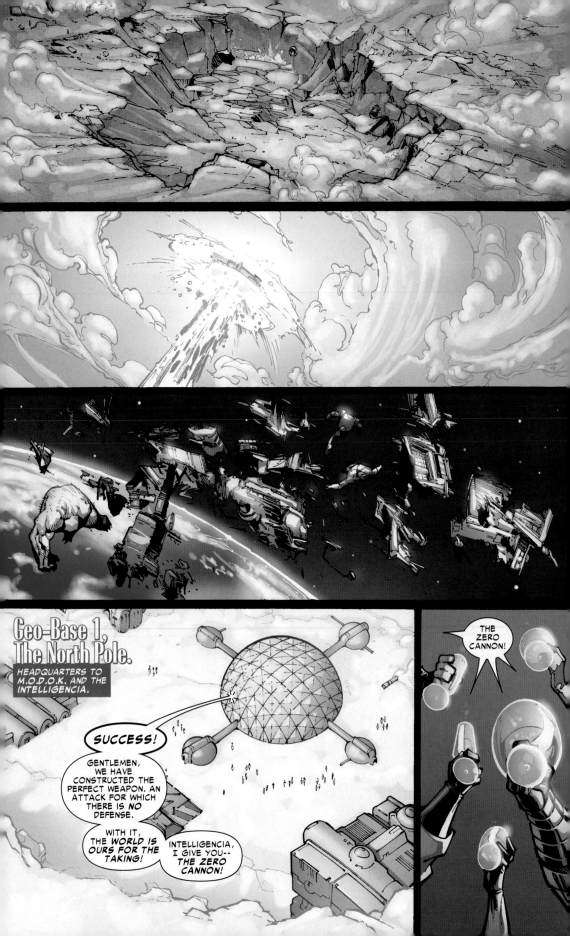

Geo-Base 1, The North Pole.

HEADQUARTERS TO M.O.D.O.K. AND THE INTELLIGENCIA.

SUCCESS!

GENTLEMEN, WE HAVE CONSTRUCTED THE PERFECT WEAPON. AN ATTACK FOR WHICH THERE IS *NO* DEFENSE.

WITH IT, THE *WORLD IS OURS* FOR THE TAKING!

INTELLIGENCIA, I GIVE YOU-- *THE ZERO CANNON!*

THE ZERO CANNON!

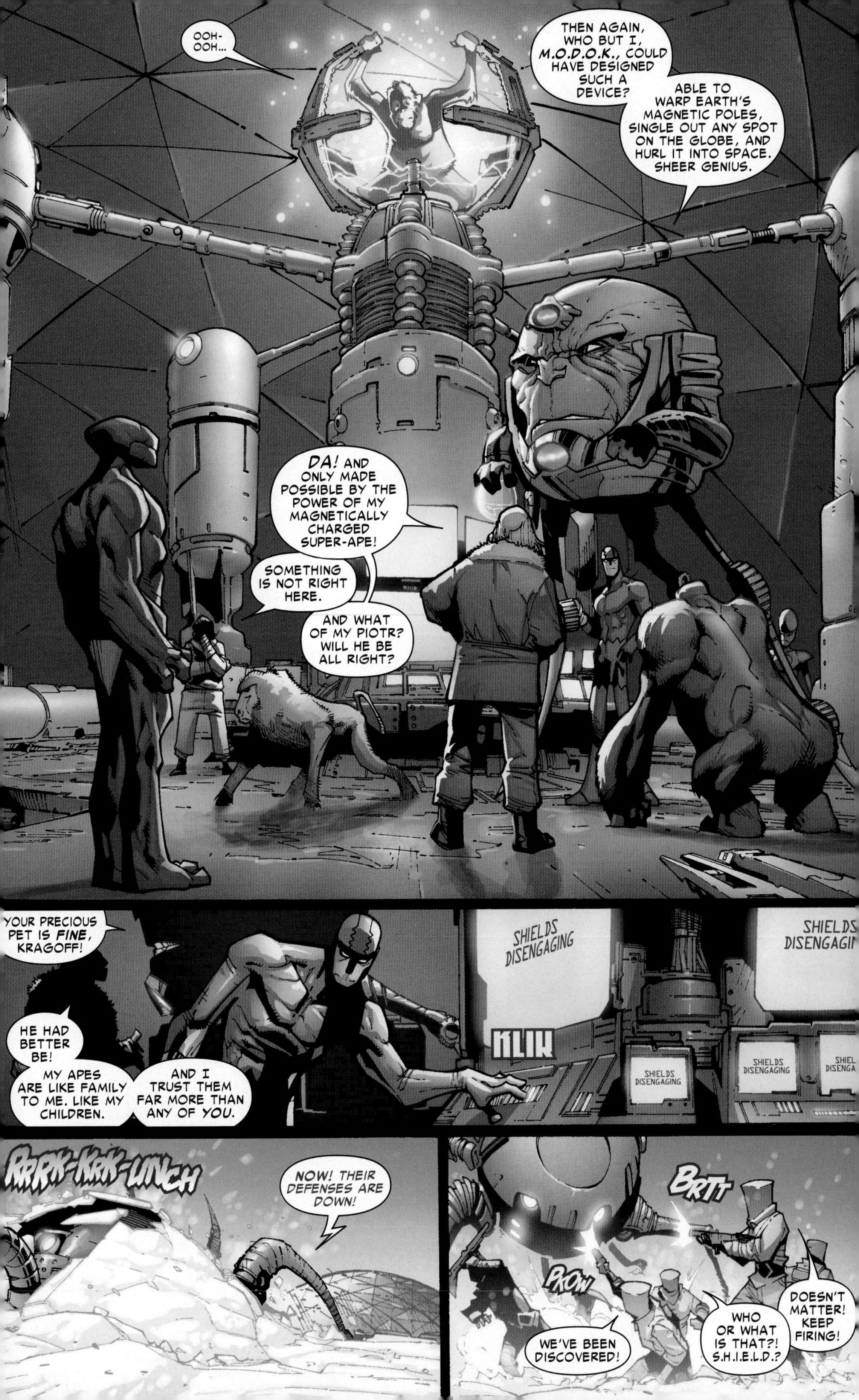
OOH-OOH...
THEN AGAIN, WHO BUT I, M.O.D.O.K., COULD HAVE DESIGNED SUCH A DEVICE?
ABLE TO WARP EARTH'S MAGNETIC POLES, SINGLE OUT ANY SPOT ON THE GLOBE, AND HURL IT INTO SPACE. SHEER GENIUS.
DA! AND ONLY MADE POSSIBLE BY THE POWER OF MY MAGNETICALLY CHARGED SUPER-APE!
SOMETHING IS NOT RIGHT HERE.
AND WHAT OF MY PIOTR? WILL HE BE ALL RIGHT?
YOUR PRECIOUS PET IS FINE, KRAGOFF!
SHIELDS DISENGAGING
SHIELDS DISENGAGI
HE HAD BETTER BE!
MY APES ARE LIKE FAMILY TO ME. LIKE MY CHILDREN.
AND I TRUST THEM FAR MORE THAN ANY OF YOU.
KLIK
SHIELDS DISENGAGING
SHIELDS DISENGAGING
SHIEL DISENGA
RRRK-KRRK-UNCH
NOW! THEIR DEFENSES ARE DOWN!
BRTT
PKOW
WE'VE BEEN DISCOVERED!
WHO OR WHAT IS THAT?! S.H.I.E.L.D.?
DOESN'T MATTER! KEEP FIRING!

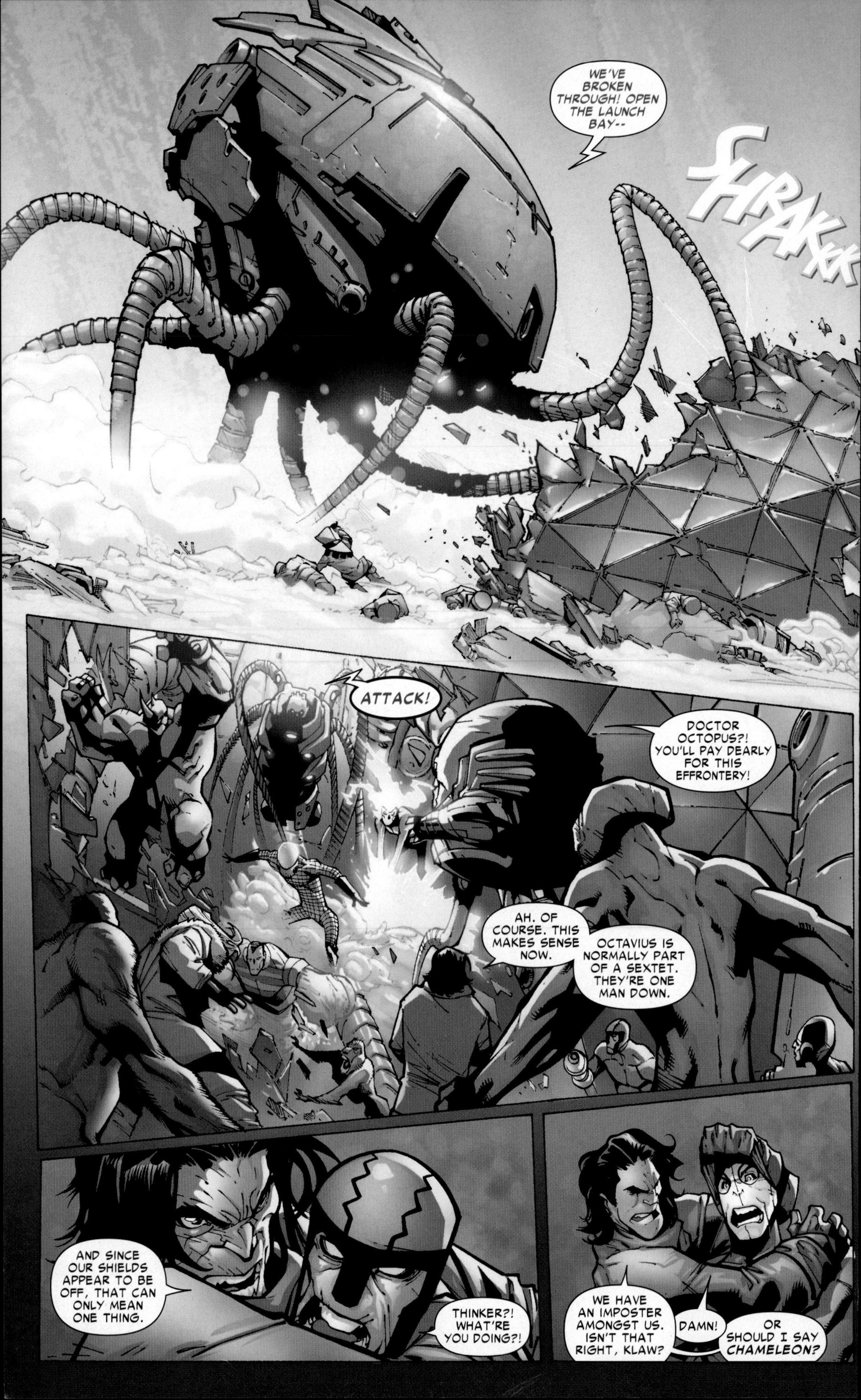
WE'VE BROKEN THROUGH! OPEN THE LAUNCH BAY--
SHRAKKK
ATTACK!
DOCTOR OCTOPUS?! YOU'LL PAY DEARLY FOR THIS EFFRONTERY!
AH. OF COURSE. THIS MAKES SENSE NOW.
OCTAVIUS IS NORMALLY PART OF A SEXTET. THEY'RE ONE MAN DOWN.
AND SINCE OUR SHIELDS APPEAR TO BE OFF, THAT CAN ONLY MEAN ONE THING.
THINKER?! WHAT'RE YOU DOING?!
WE HAVE AN IMPOSTER AMONGST US. ISN'T THAT RIGHT, KLAW?
DAMN!
OR SHOULD I SAY *CHAMELEON?*

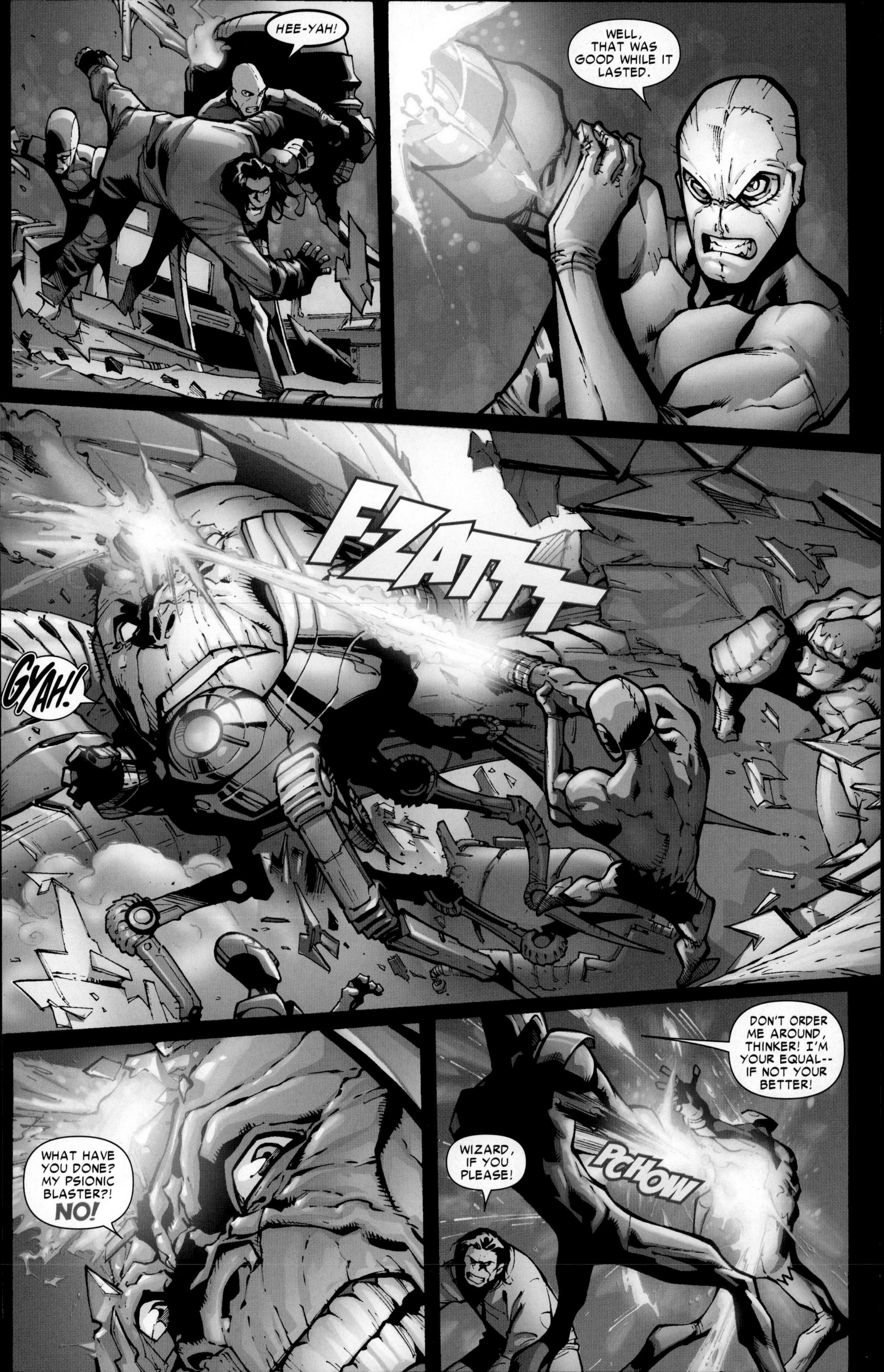
HEE-YAH!
WELL, THAT WAS GOOD WHILE IT LASTED.
F-ZATTTT
GYAH!
WHAT HAVE YOU DONE? MY PSIONIC BLASTER?! NO!
DON'T ORDER ME AROUND, THINKER! I'M YOUR EQUAL-- IF NOT YOUR BETTER!
WIZARD, IF YOU PLEASE!
PCHOW

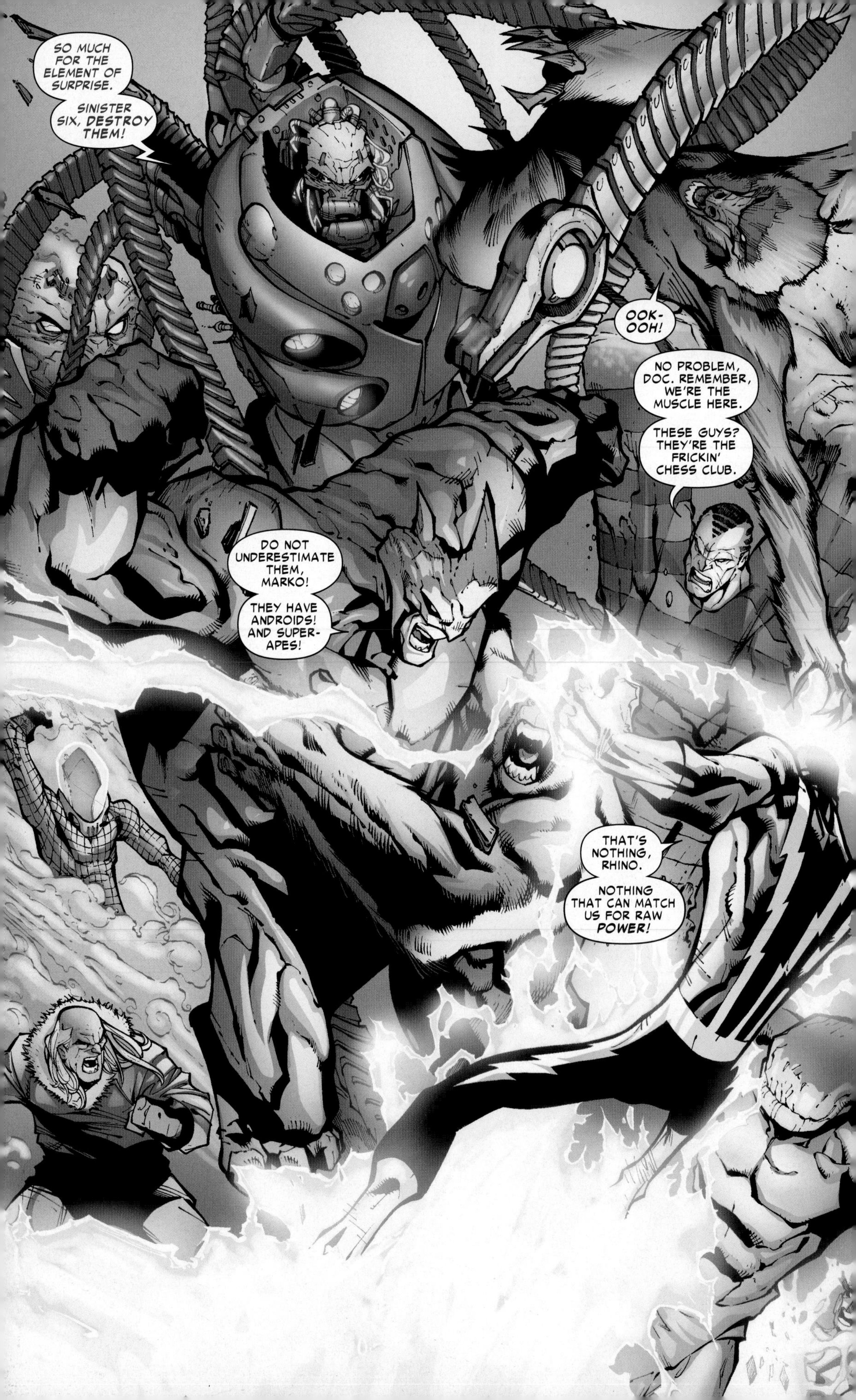
SO MUCH FOR THE ELEMENT OF SURPRISE.
SINISTER SIX, DESTROY THEM!
OOK-OOH!
NO PROBLEM, DOC. REMEMBER, WE'RE THE MUSCLE HERE.
THESE GUYS? THEY'RE THE FRICKIN' CHESS CLUB.
DO NOT UNDERESTIMATE THEM, MARKO!
THEY HAVE ANDROIDS! AND SUPER-APES!
THAT'S NOTHING, RHINO.
NOTHING THAT CAN MATCH US FOR RAW POWER!

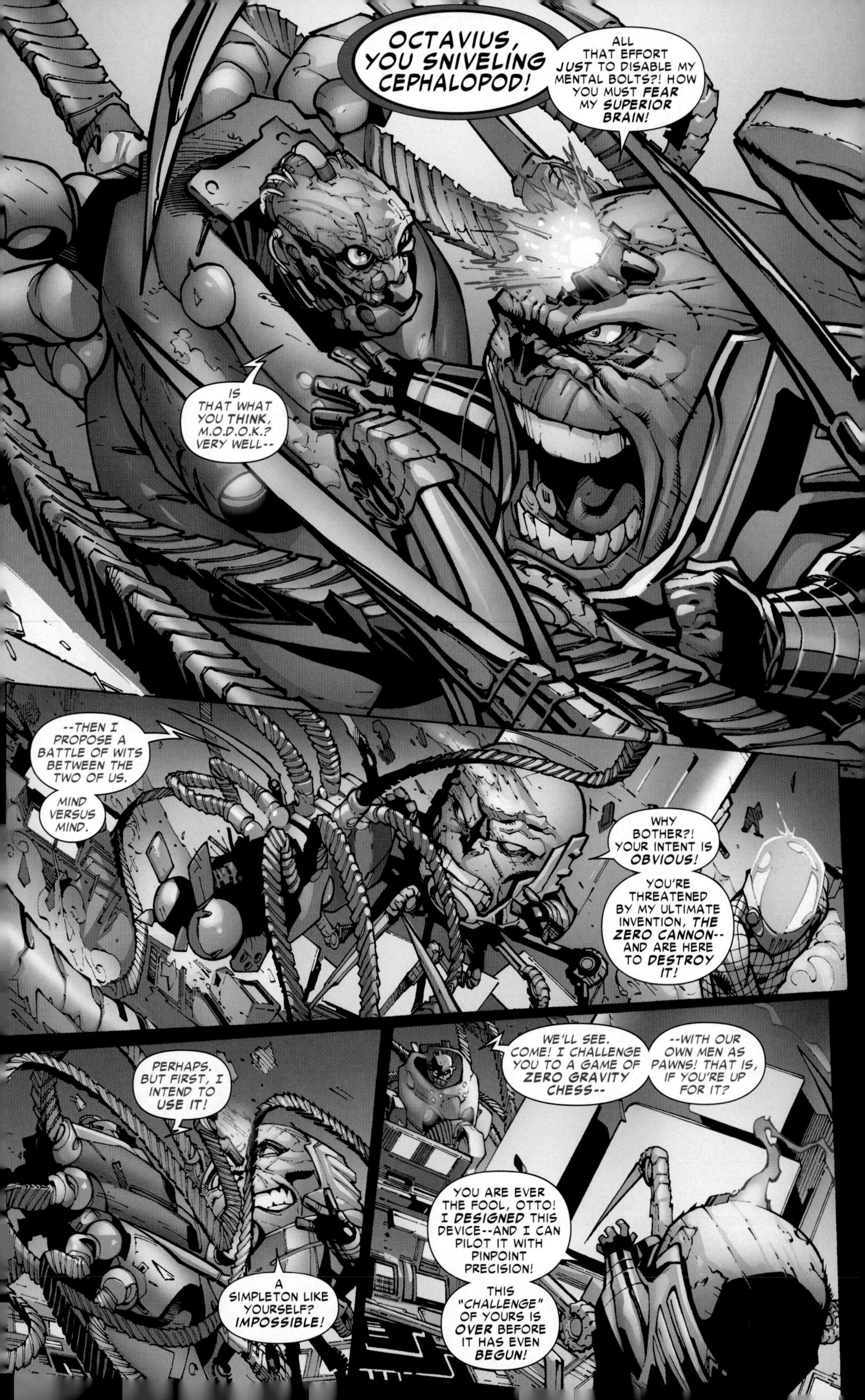
OCTAVIUS, YOU SNIVELING CEPHALOPOD!
ALL THAT EFFORT JUST TO DISABLE MY MENTAL BOLTS?! HOW YOU MUST FEAR MY SUPERIOR BRAIN!
IS THAT WHAT YOU THINK, M.O.D.O.K.? VERY WELL--
--THEN I PROPOSE A BATTLE OF WITS BETWEEN THE TWO OF US.
MIND VERSUS MIND.
WHY BOTHER?! YOUR INTENT IS OBVIOUS!
YOU'RE THREATENED BY MY ULTIMATE INVENTION, THE ZERO CANNON-- AND ARE HERE TO DESTROY IT!
PERHAPS. BUT FIRST, I INTEND TO USE IT!
A SIMPLETON LIKE YOURSELF? IMPOSSIBLE!
WE'LL SEE. COME! I CHALLENGE YOU TO A GAME OF ZERO GRAVITY CHESS--
--WITH OUR OWN MEN AS PAWNS! THAT IS, IF YOU'RE UP FOR IT?
YOU ARE EVER THE FOOL, OTTO! I DESIGNED THIS DEVICE--AND I CAN PILOT IT WITH PINPOINT PRECISION!
THIS "CHALLENGE" OF YOURS IS OVER BEFORE IT HAS EVEN BEGUN!

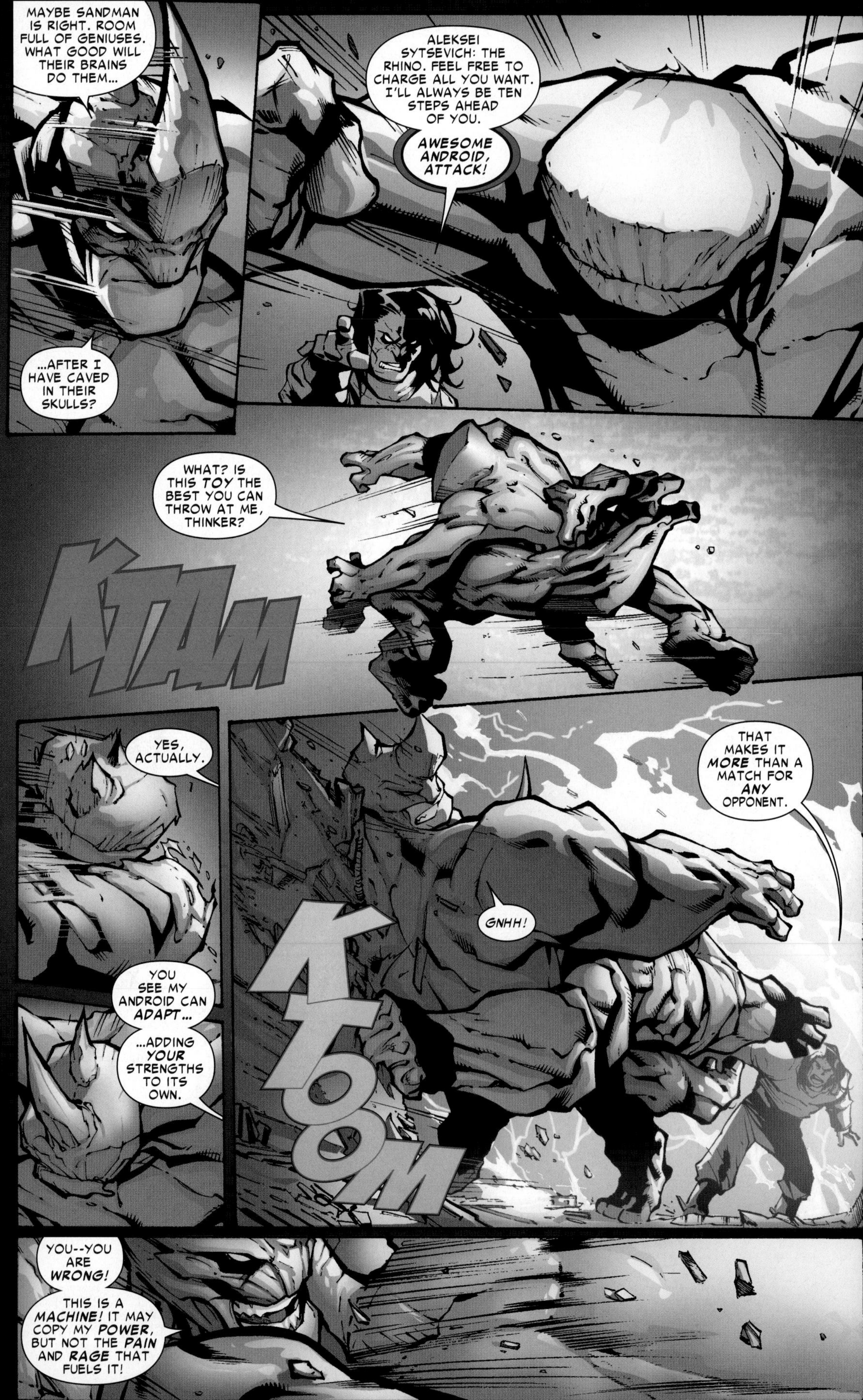
MAYBE SANDMAN IS RIGHT. ROOM FULL OF GENIUSES. WHAT GOOD WILL THEIR BRAINS DO THEM...
...AFTER I HAVE CAVED IN THEIR SKULLS?
ALEKSEI SYTSEVICH: THE RHINO. FEEL FREE TO CHARGE ALL YOU WANT. I'LL ALWAYS BE TEN STEPS AHEAD OF YOU.
AWESOME ANDROID, ATTACK!
WHAT? IS THIS TOY THE BEST YOU CAN THROW AT ME, THINKER?
KTAM
YES, ACTUALLY.
YOU SEE MY ANDROID CAN ADAPT...
...ADDING YOUR STRENGTHS TO ITS OWN.
THAT MAKES IT MORE THAN A MATCH FOR ANY OPPONENT.
GNHH!
KTOOM
YOU--YOU ARE WRONG!
THIS IS A MACHINE! IT MAY COPY MY POWER, BUT NOT THE PAIN AND RAGE THAT FUELS IT!

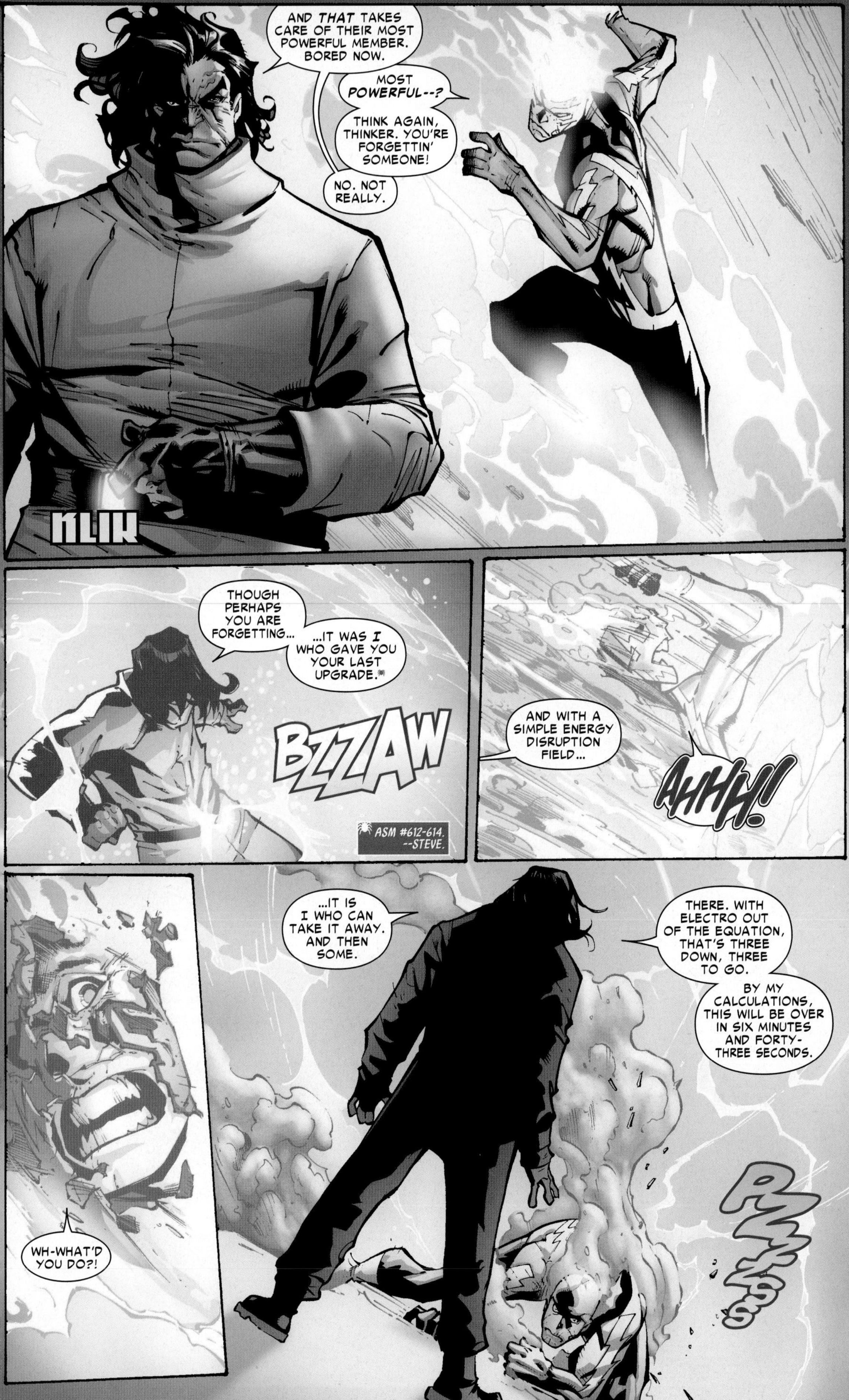
AND THAT TAKES CARE OF THEIR MOST POWERFUL MEMBER. BORED NOW.
MOST POWERFUL--?
THINK AGAIN, THINKER. YOU'RE FORGETTIN' SOMEONE!
NO. NOT REALLY.
KLIK
THOUGH PERHAPS YOU ARE FORGETTING...
...IT WAS I WHO GAVE YOU YOUR LAST UPGRADE.
BZZAW
ASM #612-614. --STEVE.
AND WITH A SIMPLE ENERGY DISRUPTION FIELD...
AHHH!
...IT IS I WHO CAN TAKE IT AWAY. AND THEN SOME.
WH-WHAT'D YOU DO?!
THERE. WITH ELECTRO OUT OF THE EQUATION, THAT'S THREE DOWN, THREE TO GO.
BY MY CALCULATIONS, THIS WILL BE OVER IN SIX MINUTES AND FORTY-THREE SECONDS.

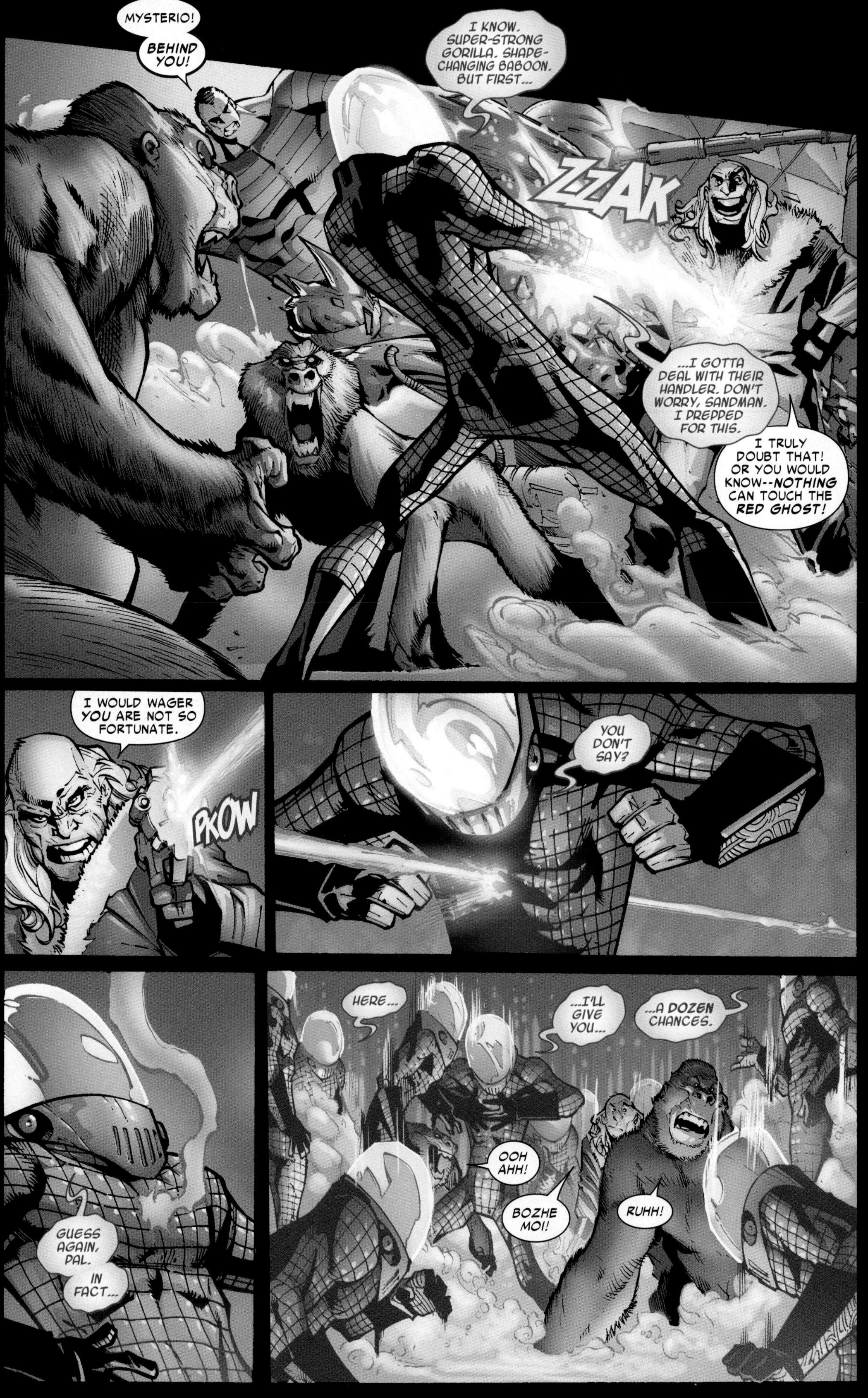
MYSTERIO!
BEHIND YOU!
I KNOW. SUPER-STRONG GORILLA. SHAPE-CHANGING BABOON. BUT FIRST...
ZZZAK
...I GOTTA DEAL WITH THEIR HANDLER. DON'T WORRY, SANDMAN. I PREPPED FOR THIS.
I TRULY DOUBT THAT! OR YOU WOULD KNOW--NOTHING CAN TOUCH THE RED GHOST!
I WOULD WAGER YOU ARE NOT SO FORTUNATE.
PKOW
YOU DON'T SAY?
GUESS AGAIN, PAL.
IN FACT...
HERE...
...I'LL GIVE YOU...
...A DOZEN CHANCES.
OOH AHH!
BOZHE MOI!
RUHH!

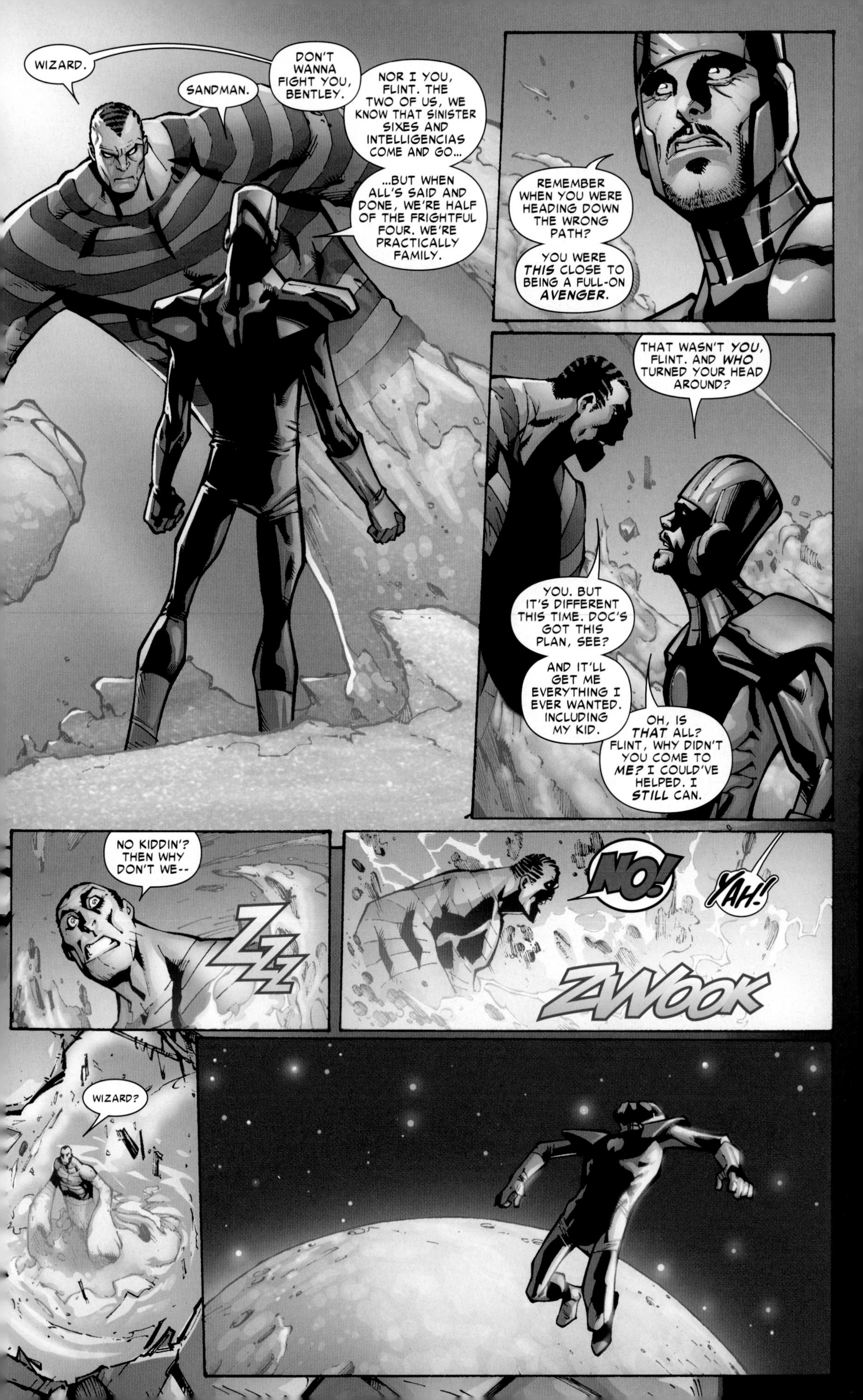
WIZARD.
SANDMAN.
DON'T WANNA FIGHT YOU, BENTLEY.
NOR I YOU, FLINT. THE TWO OF US, WE KNOW THAT SINISTER SIXES AND INTELLIGENCIAS COME AND GO...
...BUT WHEN ALL'S SAID AND DONE, WE'RE HALF OF THE FRIGHTFUL FOUR. WE'RE PRACTICALLY FAMILY.
REMEMBER WHEN YOU WERE HEADING DOWN THE WRONG PATH?
YOU WERE THIS CLOSE TO BEING A FULL-ON AVENGER.
THAT WASN'T YOU, FLINT. AND WHO TURNED YOUR HEAD AROUND?
YOU. BUT IT'S DIFFERENT THIS TIME. DOC'S GOT THIS PLAN, SEE?
AND IT'LL GET ME EVERYTHING I EVER WANTED. INCLUDING MY KID.
OH, IS THAT ALL? FLINT, WHY DIDN'T YOU COME TO ME? I COULD'VE HELPED. I STILL CAN.
NO KIDDIN'? THEN WHY DON'T WE--
ZZZ
NO!
YAH!
ZWOOK
WIZARD?

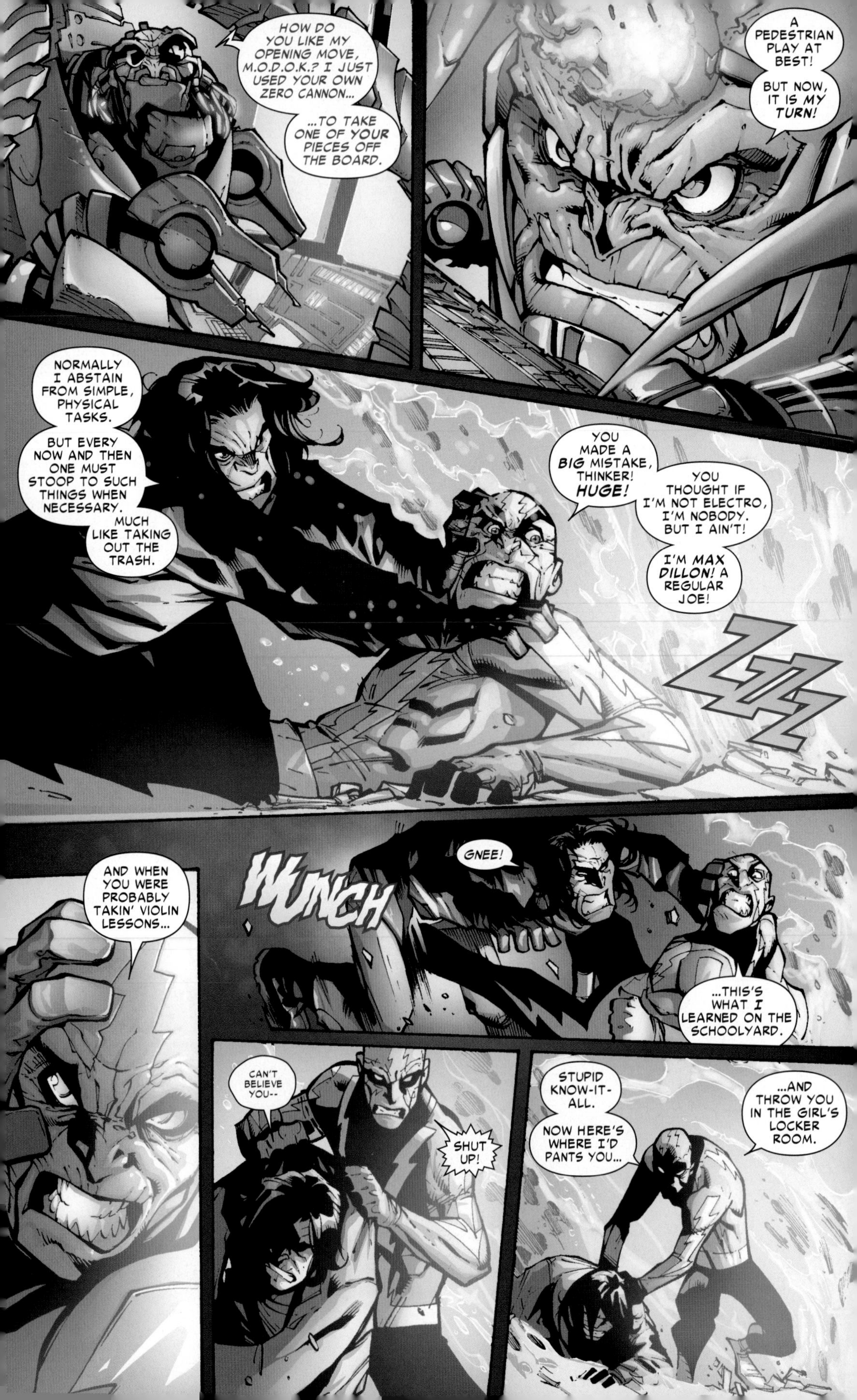
HOW DO YOU LIKE MY OPENING MOVE, M.O.D.O.K.? I JUST USED YOUR OWN ZERO CANNON...
...TO TAKE ONE OF YOUR PIECES OFF THE BOARD.
A PEDESTRIAN PLAY AT BEST!
BUT NOW, IT IS MY TURN!
NORMALLY I ABSTAIN FROM SIMPLE, PHYSICAL TASKS.
BUT EVERY NOW AND THEN ONE MUST STOOP TO SUCH THINGS WHEN NECESSARY.
MUCH LIKE TAKING OUT THE TRASH.
YOU MADE A BIG MISTAKE, THINKER! HUGE!
YOU THOUGHT IF I'M NOT ELECTRO, I'M NOBODY. BUT I AIN'T!
I'M MAX DILLON! A REGULAR JOE!
ZZZZ
AND WHEN YOU WERE PROBABLY TAKIN' VIOLIN LESSONS...
WUNCH
GNEE!
...THIS'S WHAT I LEARNED ON THE SCHOOLYARD.
CAN'T BELIEVE YOU--
SHUT UP!
STUPID KNOW-IT-ALL.
NOW HERE'S WHERE I'D PANTS YOU...
...AND THROW YOU IN THE GIRL'S LOCKER ROOM.

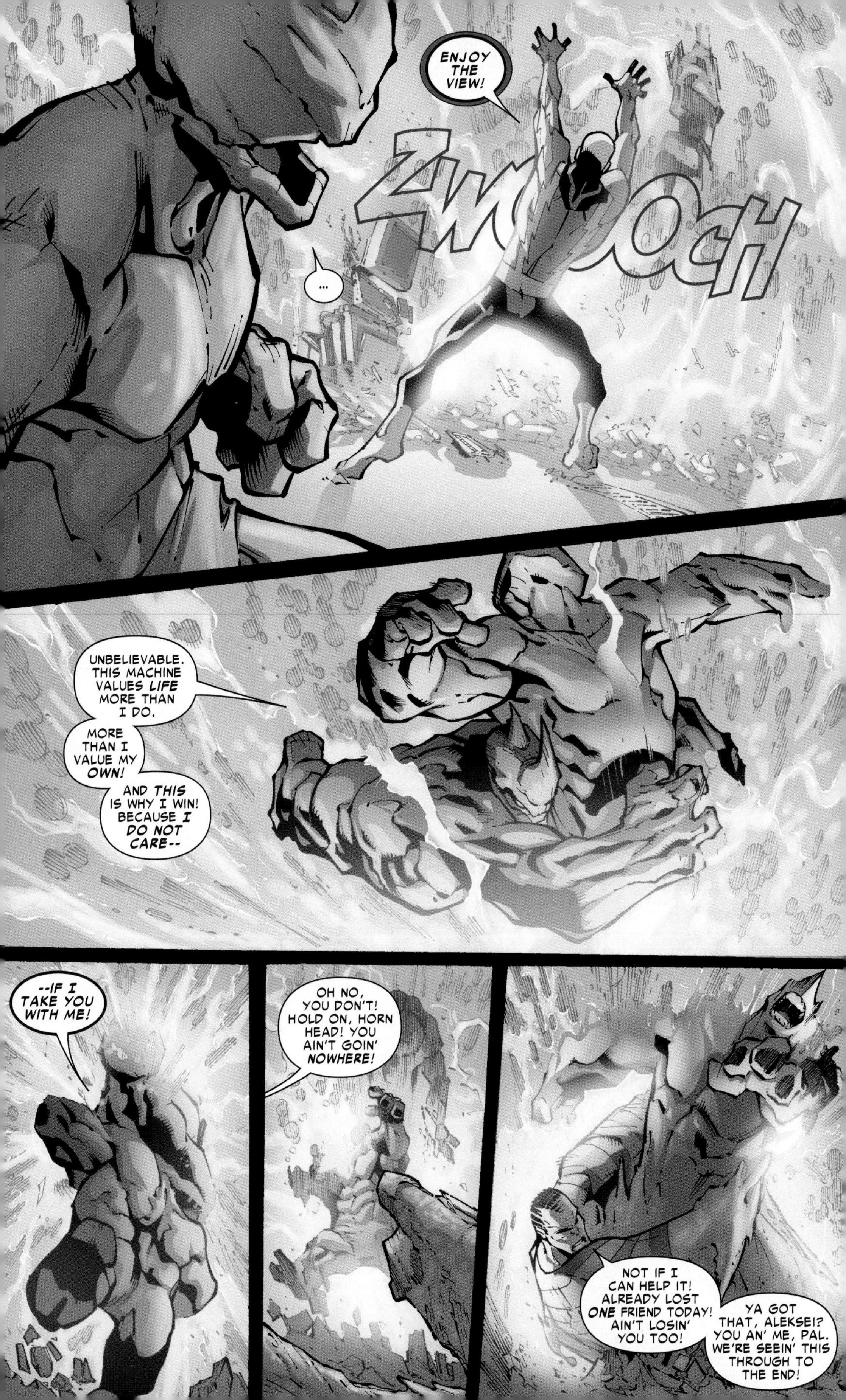
ENJOY THE VIEW!
ZWOOOCH
...
UNBELIEVABLE. THIS MACHINE VALUES *LIFE* MORE THAN I DO.
MORE THAN I VALUE MY *OWN*!
AND *THIS* IS WHY I WIN! BECAUSE *I DO NOT CARE*--
--*IF I TAKE YOU WITH ME!*
OH NO, YOU DON'T! HOLD ON, HORN HEAD! YOU AIN'T GOIN' *NOWHERE*!
NOT IF I CAN HELP IT! ALREADY LOST **ONE** FRIEND TODAY! AIN'T LOSIN' YOU TOO!
YA GOT THAT, ALEKSEI? YOU AN' ME, PAL. WE'RE SEEIN' THIS THROUGH TO THE END!

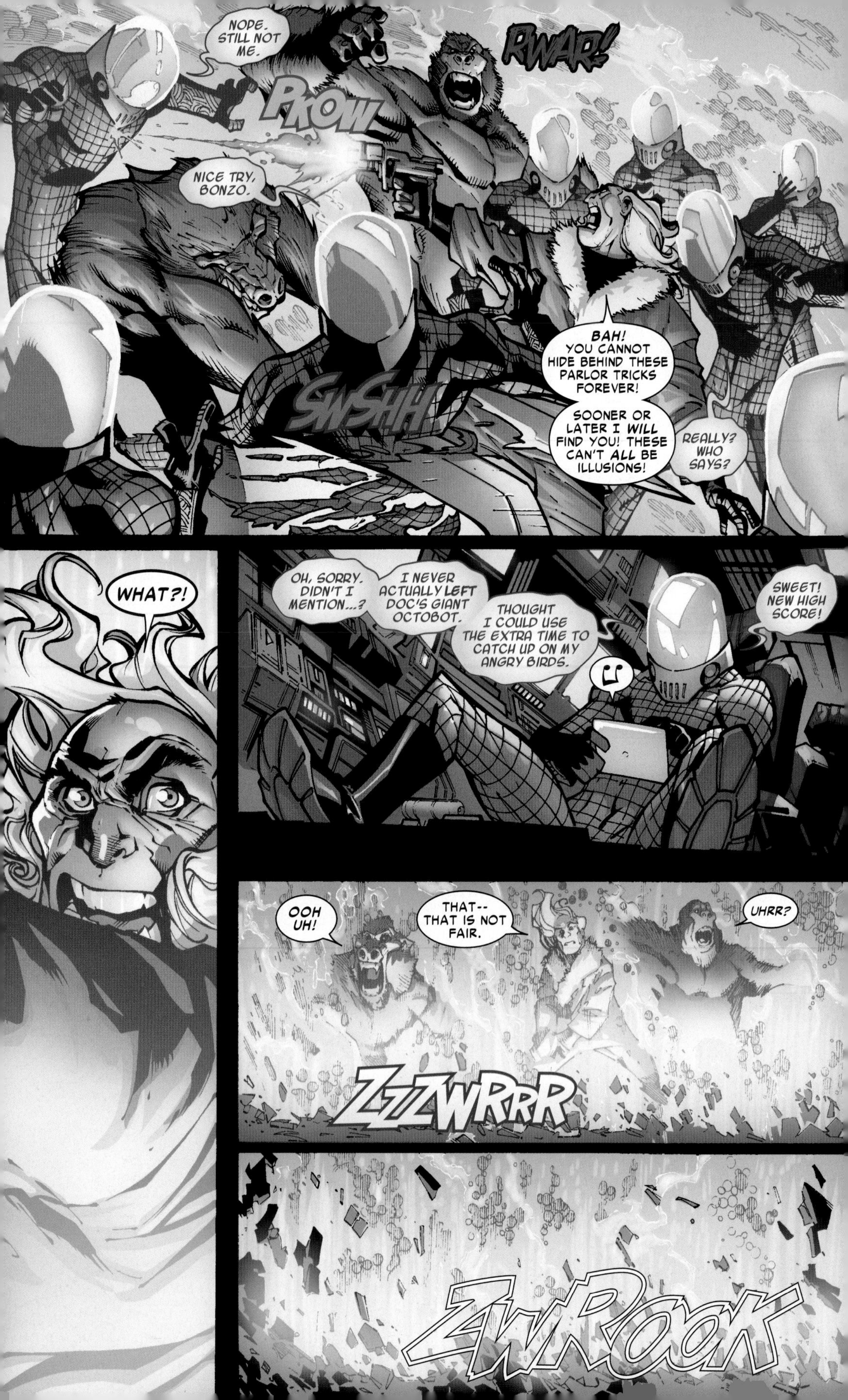
NOPE. STILL NOT ME.
RWAR!
PKOW
NICE TRY, BONZO.
BAH! YOU CANNOT HIDE BEHIND THESE PARLOR TRICKS FOREVER!
SOONER OR LATER I WILL FIND YOU! THESE CAN'T ALL BE ILLUSIONS!
SWSHH
REALLY? WHO SAYS?
WHAT?!
OH, SORRY. DIDN'T I MENTION...?
I NEVER ACTUALLY LEFT DOC'S GIANT OCTOBOT.
THOUGHT I COULD USE THE EXTRA TIME TO CATCH UP ON MY ANGRY BIRDS.
SWEET! NEW HIGH SCORE!
OOH UH!
THAT-- THAT IS NOT FAIR.
UHRR?
ZZZWRRR
ZWROOK

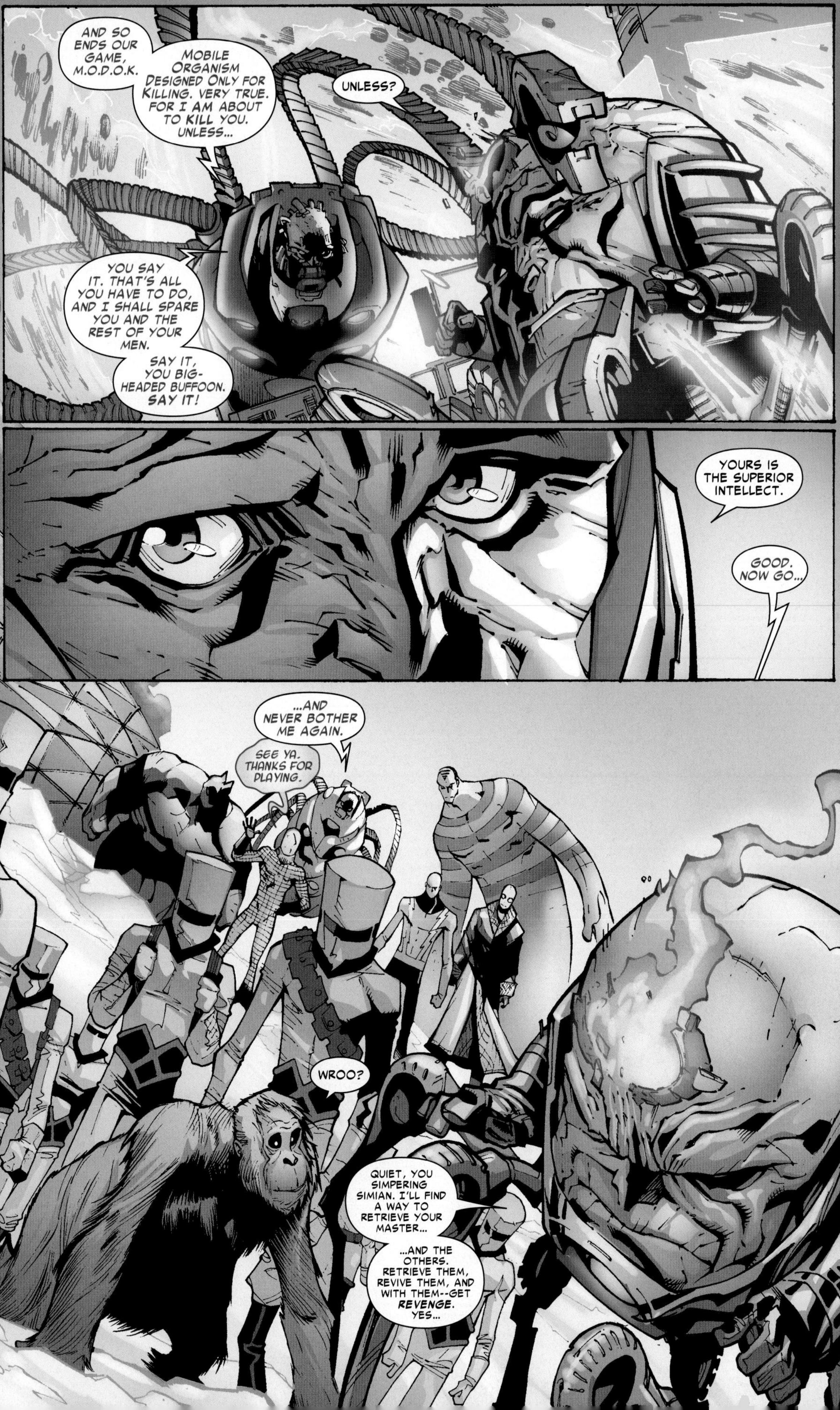
AND SO ENDS OUR GAME, M.O.D.O.K.
MOBILE ORGANISM DESIGNED ONLY FOR KILLING. VERY TRUE. FOR I AM ABOUT TO **KILL** YOU. UNLESS...
UNLESS?
YOU SAY IT. THAT'S ALL YOU HAVE TO DO, AND I SHALL SPARE YOU AND THE REST OF YOUR MEN.
SAY IT, YOU BIG-HEADED BUFFOON. **SAY IT!**
YOURS IS THE SUPERIOR INTELLECT.
GOOD. NOW GO...
...AND NEVER BOTHER ME AGAIN.
SEE YA. THANKS FOR PLAYING.
WROO?
QUIET, YOU SIMPERING SIMIAN. I'LL FIND A WAY TO RETRIEVE YOUR MASTER...
...AND THE OTHERS. RETRIEVE THEM, REVIVE THEM, AND WITH THEM--GET **REVENGE**. YES...

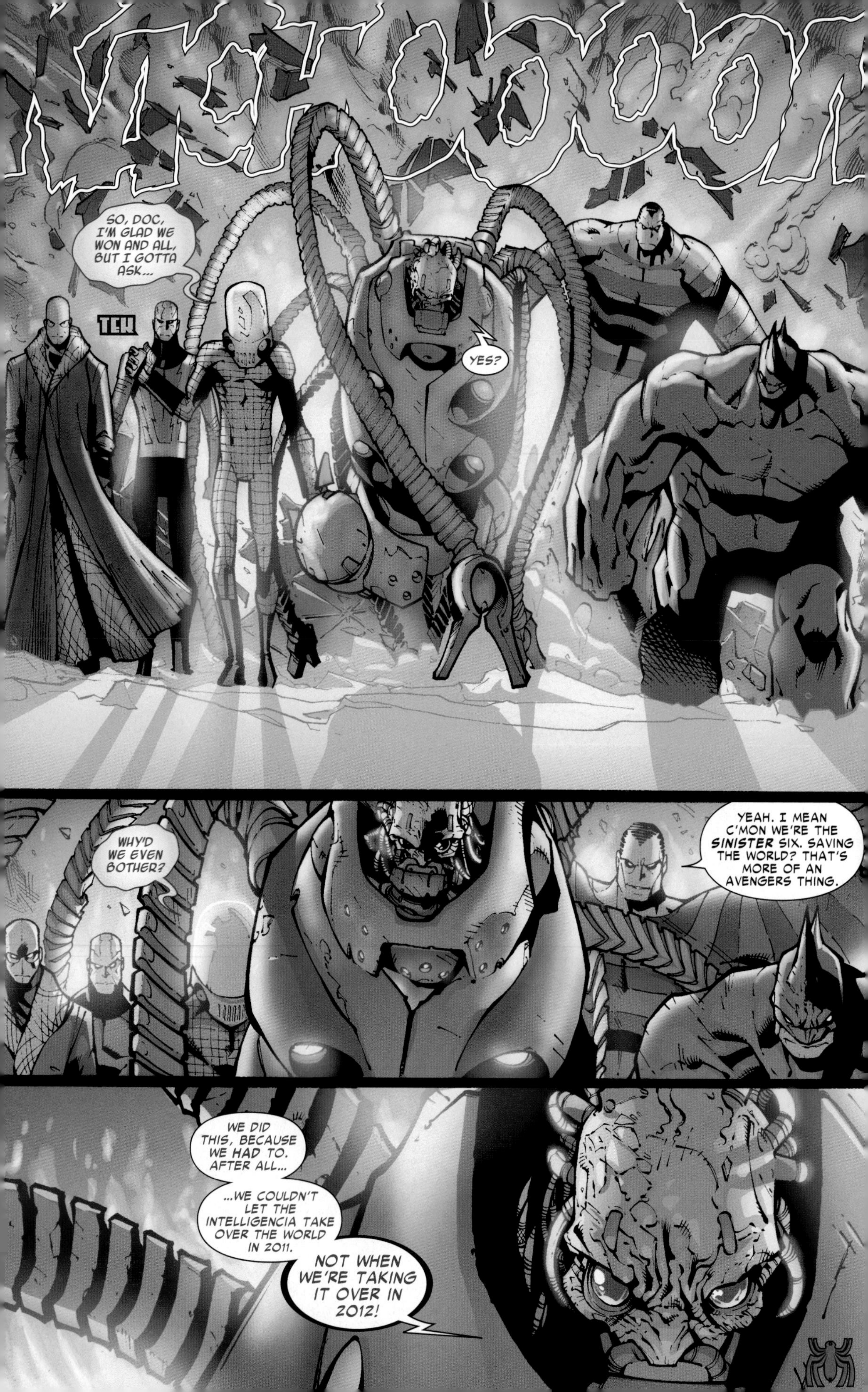
NYAKOOOOOOM
SO, DOC, I'M GLAD WE WON AND ALL, BUT I GOTTA ASK...
TEH
YES?
WHY'D WE EVEN BOTHER?
YEAH. I MEAN C'MON WE'RE THE SINISTER SIX. SAVING THE WORLD? THAT'S MORE OF AN AVENGERS THING.
WE DID THIS, BECAUSE WE HAD TO. AFTER ALL...
...WE COULDN'T LET THE INTELLIGENCIA TAKE OVER THE WORLD IN 2011.
NOT WHEN WE'RE TAKING IT OVER IN 2012!

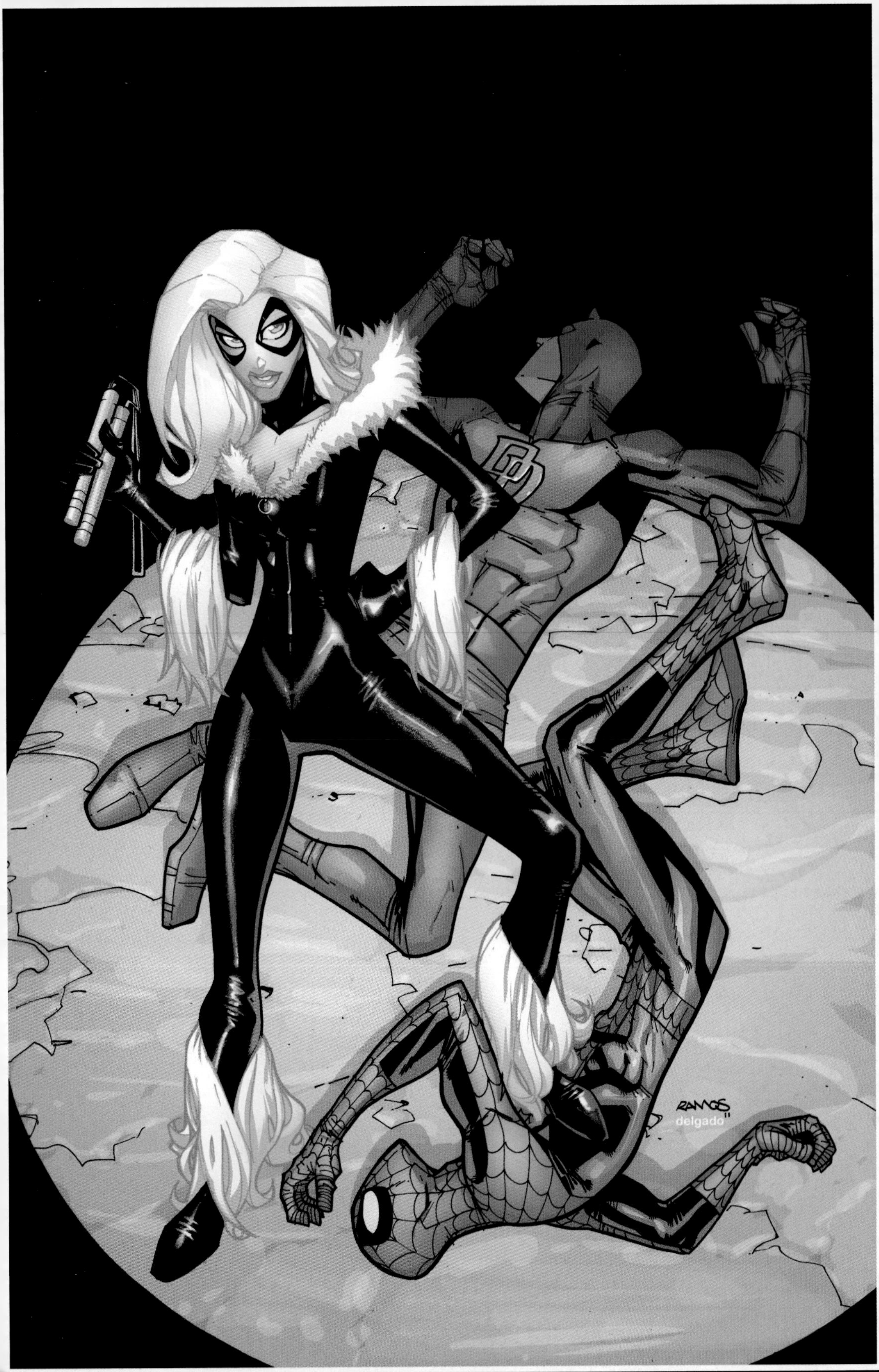
RAMOS
delgado

AMAZING SPIDER-MAN #677

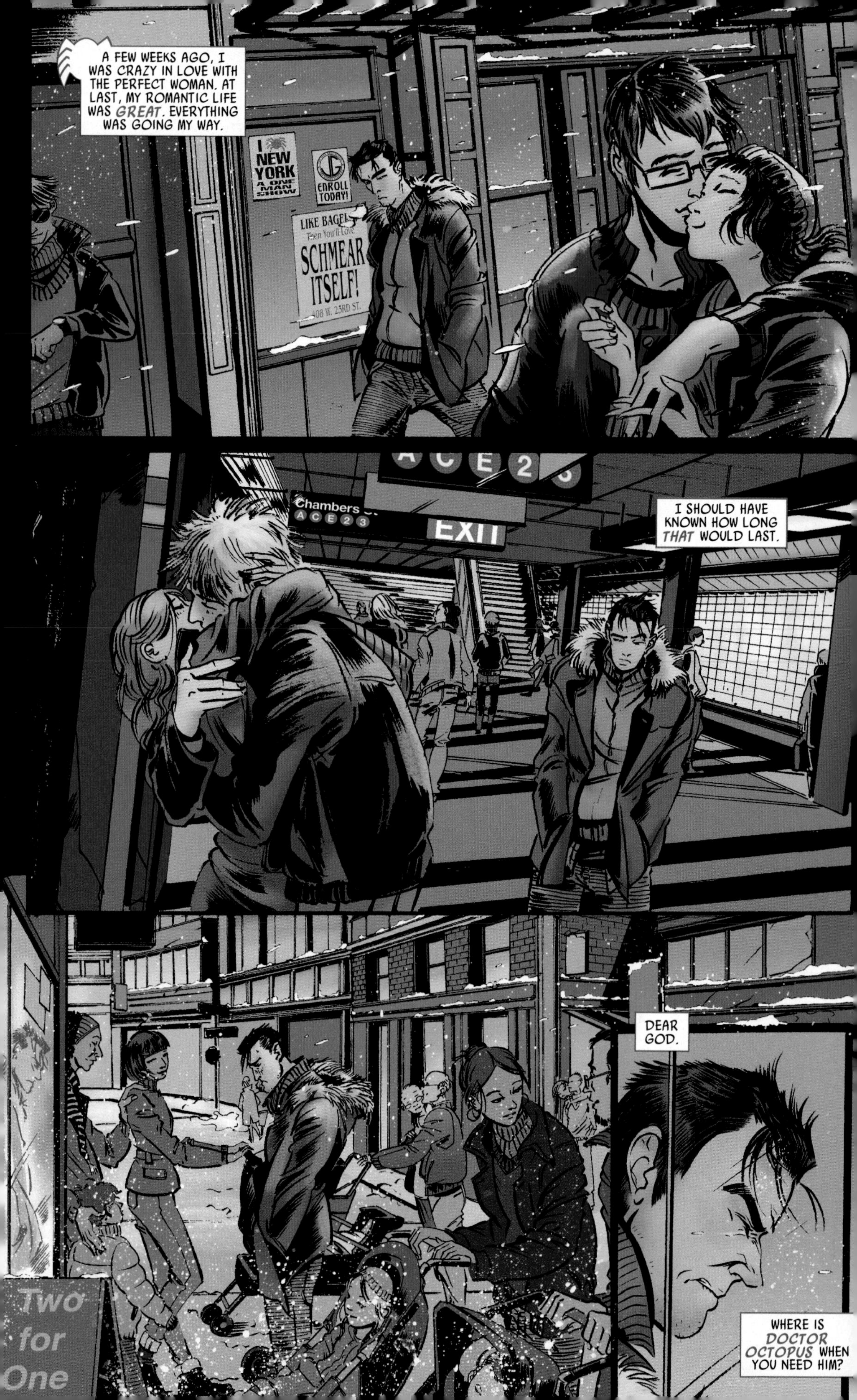

A FEW WEEKS AGO, I WAS CRAZY IN LOVE WITH THE PERFECT WOMAN. AT LAST, MY ROMANTIC LIFE WAS *GREAT*. EVERYTHING WAS GOING MY WAY.
I NEW YORK A ONE MAN SHOW
ENROLL TODAY!
SCHMEAR ITSELF!
EXIT
I SHOULD HAVE KNOWN HOW LONG *THAT* WOULD LAST.
DEAR GOD.
Two for One
WHERE IS *DOCTOR OCTOPUS* WHEN YOU NEED HIM?

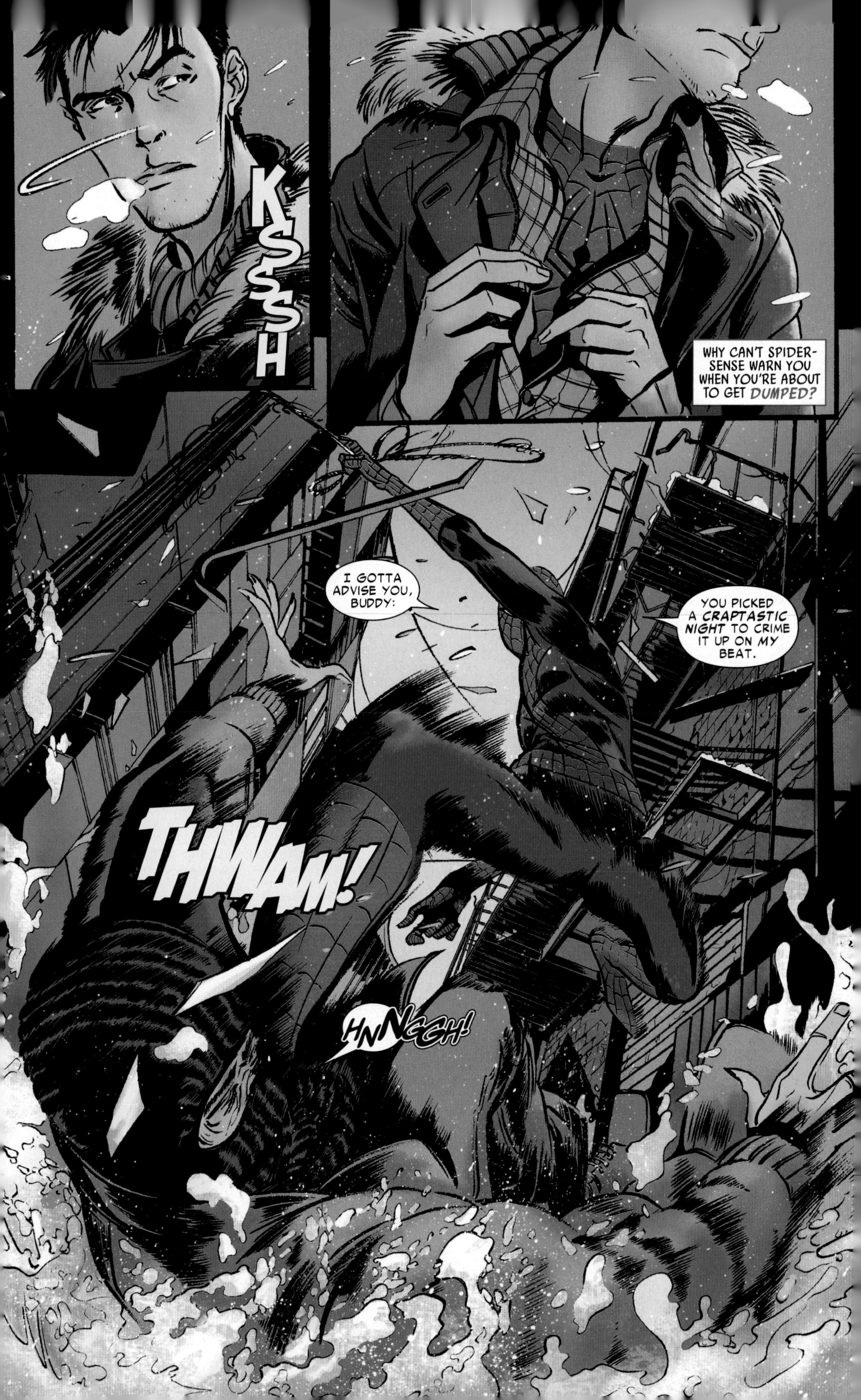
KSSSH
WHY CAN'T SPIDER-SENSE WARN YOU WHEN YOU'RE ABOUT TO GET DUMPED?
I GOTTA ADVISE YOU, BUDDY:
YOU PICKED A CRAPTASTIC NIGHT TO CRIME IT UP ON MY BEAT.
THWAM!
HNNGGH!

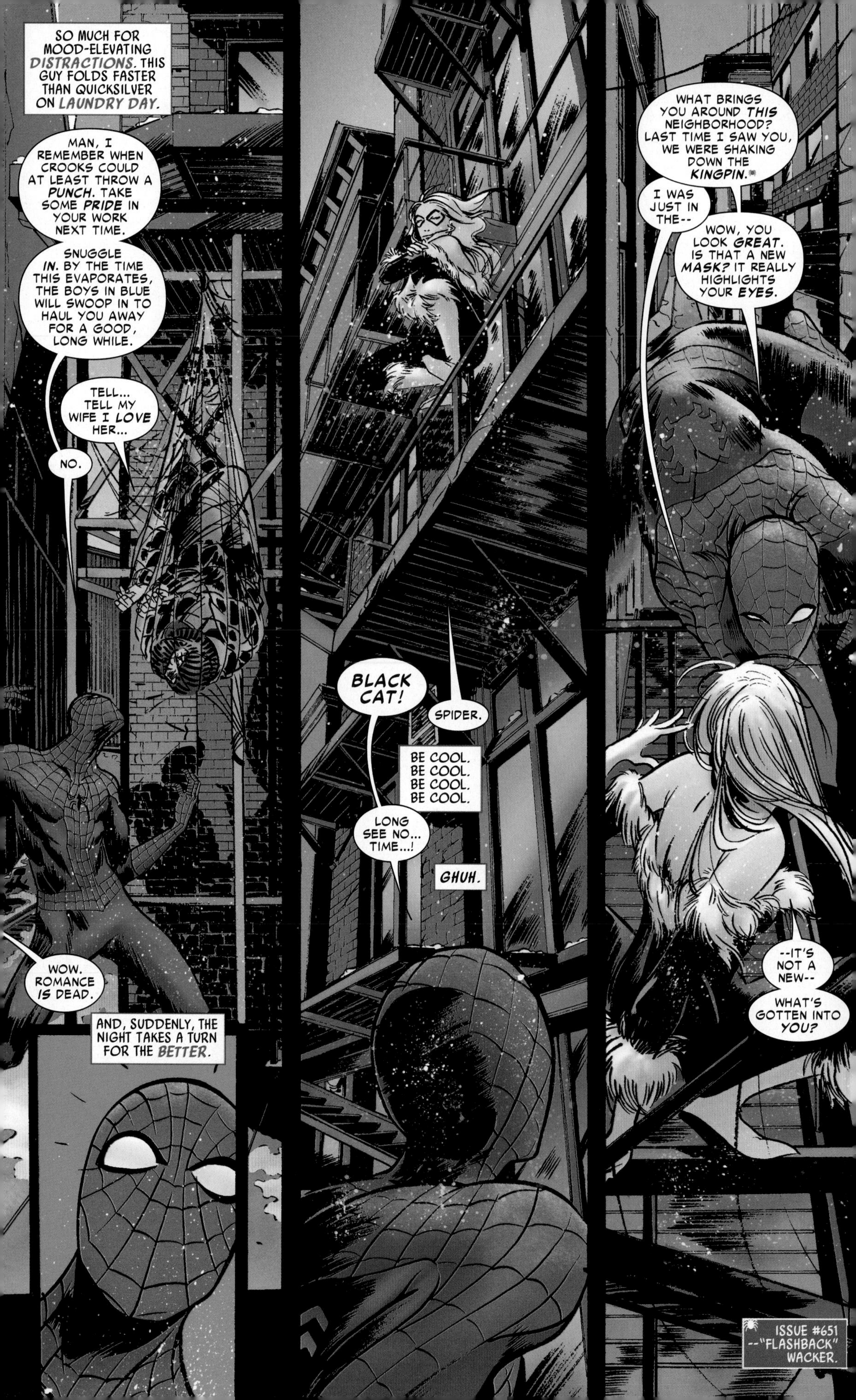

SO MUCH FOR MOOD-ELEVATING DISTRACTIONS. THIS GUY FOLDS FASTER THAN QUICKSILVER ON LAUNDRY DAY.
MAN, I REMEMBER WHEN CROOKS COULD AT LEAST THROW A PUNCH. TAKE SOME PRIDE IN YOUR WORK NEXT TIME.
SNUGGLE IN. BY THE TIME THIS EVAPORATES, THE BOYS IN BLUE WILL SWOOP IN TO HAUL YOU AWAY FOR A GOOD, LONG WHILE.
TELL... TELL MY WIFE I LOVE HER...
NO.
WOW. ROMANCE IS DEAD.
AND, SUDDENLY, THE NIGHT TAKES A TURN FOR THE BETTER.
BLACK CAT!
SPIDER.
BE COOL. BE COOL. BE COOL. BE COOL.
LONG SEE NO... TIME...!
GHUH.
WHAT BRINGS YOU AROUND THIS NEIGHBORHOOD? LAST TIME I SAW YOU, WE WERE SHAKING DOWN THE KINGPIN.
I WAS JUST IN THE--
WOW, YOU LOOK GREAT. IS THAT A NEW MASK? IT REALLY HIGHLIGHTS YOUR EYES.
--IT'S NOT A NEW--
WHAT'S GOTTEN INTO YOU?
ISSUE #651 --"FLASHBACK" WACKER.

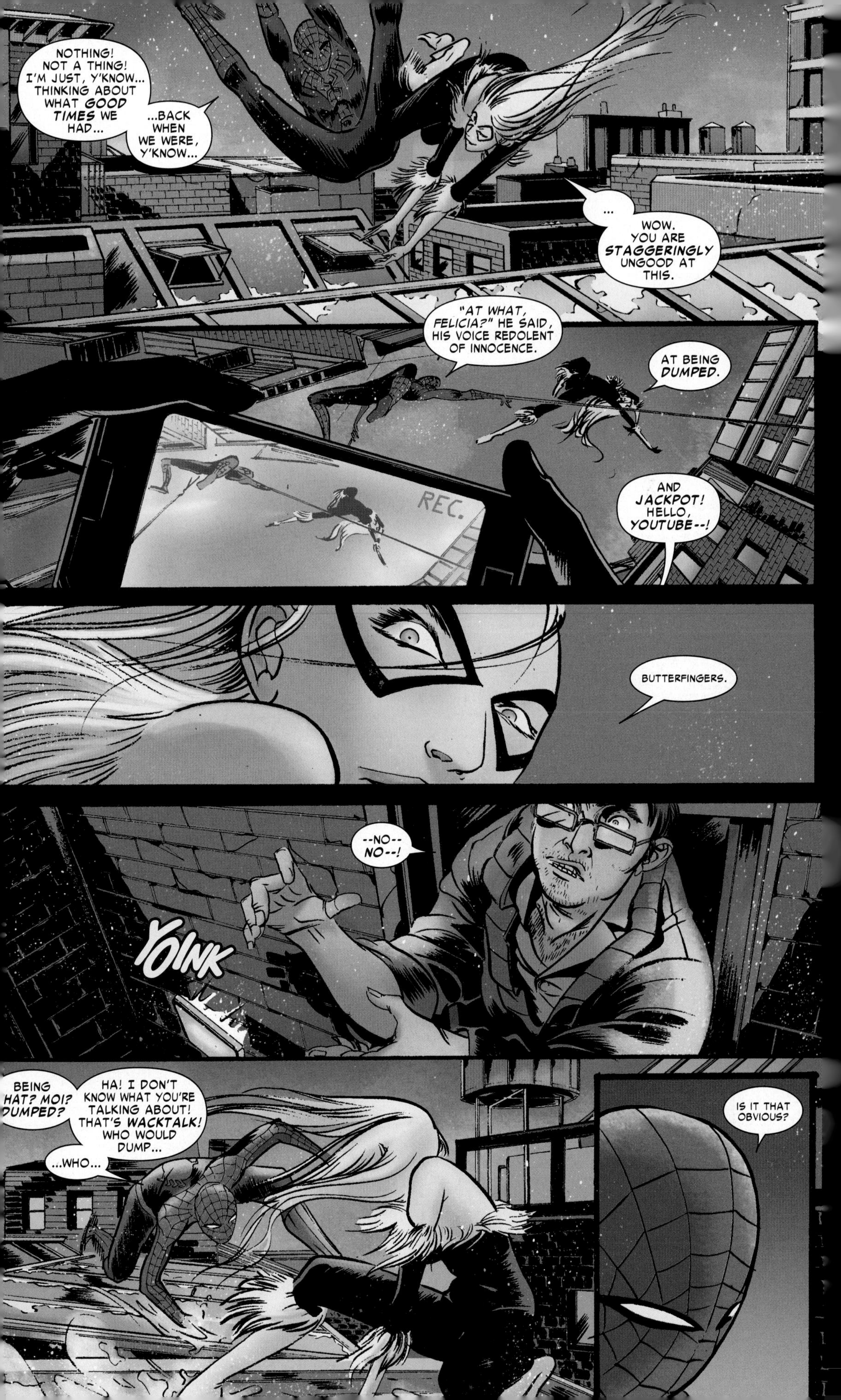

NOTHING! NOT A THING! I'M JUST, Y'KNOW... THINKING ABOUT WHAT GOOD TIMES WE HAD...
...BACK WHEN WE WERE, Y'KNOW...
... WOW. YOU ARE STAGGERINGLY UNGOOD AT THIS.
"AT WHAT, FELICIA?" HE SAID, HIS VOICE REDOLENT OF INNOCENCE.
AT BEING DUMPED.
REC.
AND JACKPOT! HELLO, YOUTUBE--!
BUTTERFINGERS.
--NO-- NO--!
YOINK
BEING HAT? MOI? DUMPED?
HA! I DON'T KNOW WHAT YOU'RE TALKING ABOUT! THAT'S WACKTALK! WHO WOULD DUMP...
...WHO...
IS IT THAT OBVIOUS?

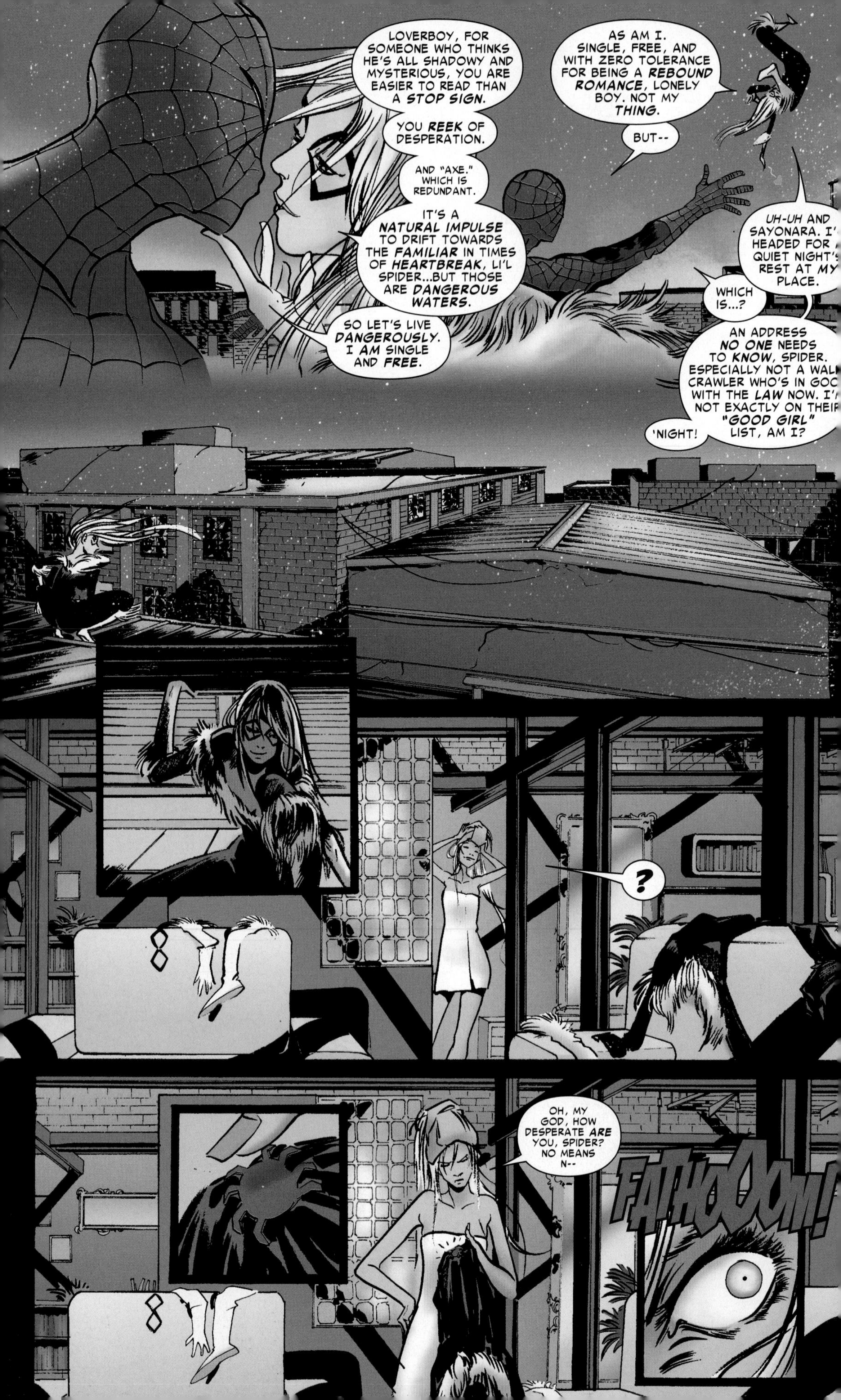
LOVERBOY, FOR SOMEONE WHO THINKS HE'S ALL SHADOWY AND MYSTERIOUS, YOU ARE EASIER TO READ THAN A STOP SIGN.
YOU REEK OF DESPERATION.
AND "AXE." WHICH IS REDUNDANT.
IT'S A NATURAL IMPULSE TO DRIFT TOWARDS THE FAMILIAR IN TIMES OF HEARTBREAK, LI'L SPIDER...BUT THOSE ARE DANGEROUS WATERS.
SO LET'S LIVE DANGEROUSLY. I AM SINGLE AND FREE.
AS AM I. SINGLE, FREE, AND WITH ZERO TOLERANCE FOR BEING A REBOUND ROMANCE, LONELY BOY. NOT MY THING.
BUT--
WHICH IS...?
'NIGHT!
?
OH, MY GOD, HOW DESPERATE ARE YOU, SPIDER? NO MEANS N--
FATHOOOM!

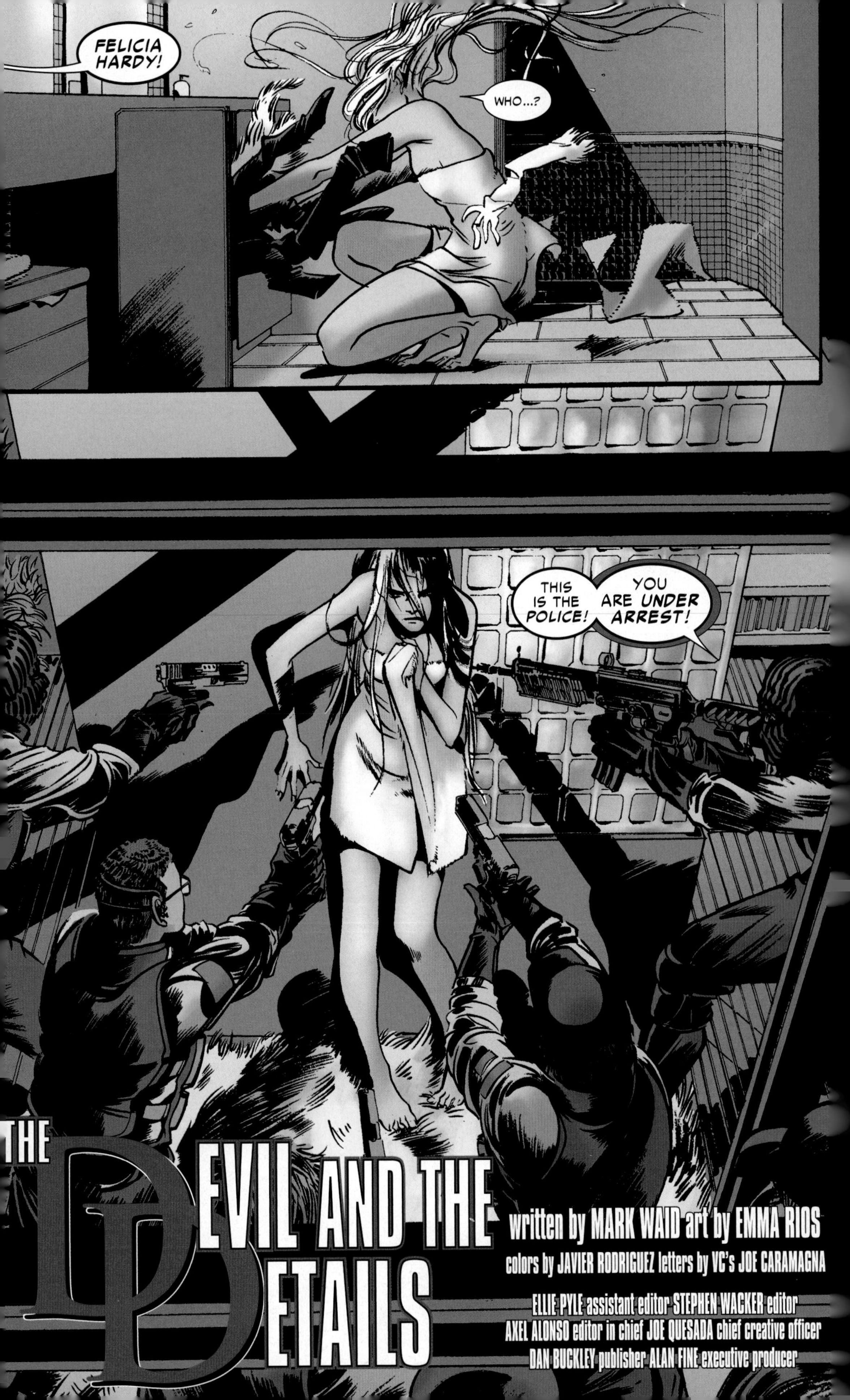
FELICIA HARDY!
WHO...?
THIS IS THE POLICE!
YOU ARE UNDER ARREST!
THE DEVIL AND THE DETAILS
written by MARK WAID art by EMMA RIOS
colors by JAVIER RODRIGUEZ letters by VC's JOE CARAMAGNA
ELLIE PYLE assistant editor STEPHEN WACKER editor
AXEL ALONSO editor in chief JOE QUESADA chief creative officer
DAN BUCKLEY publisher ALAN FINE executive producer

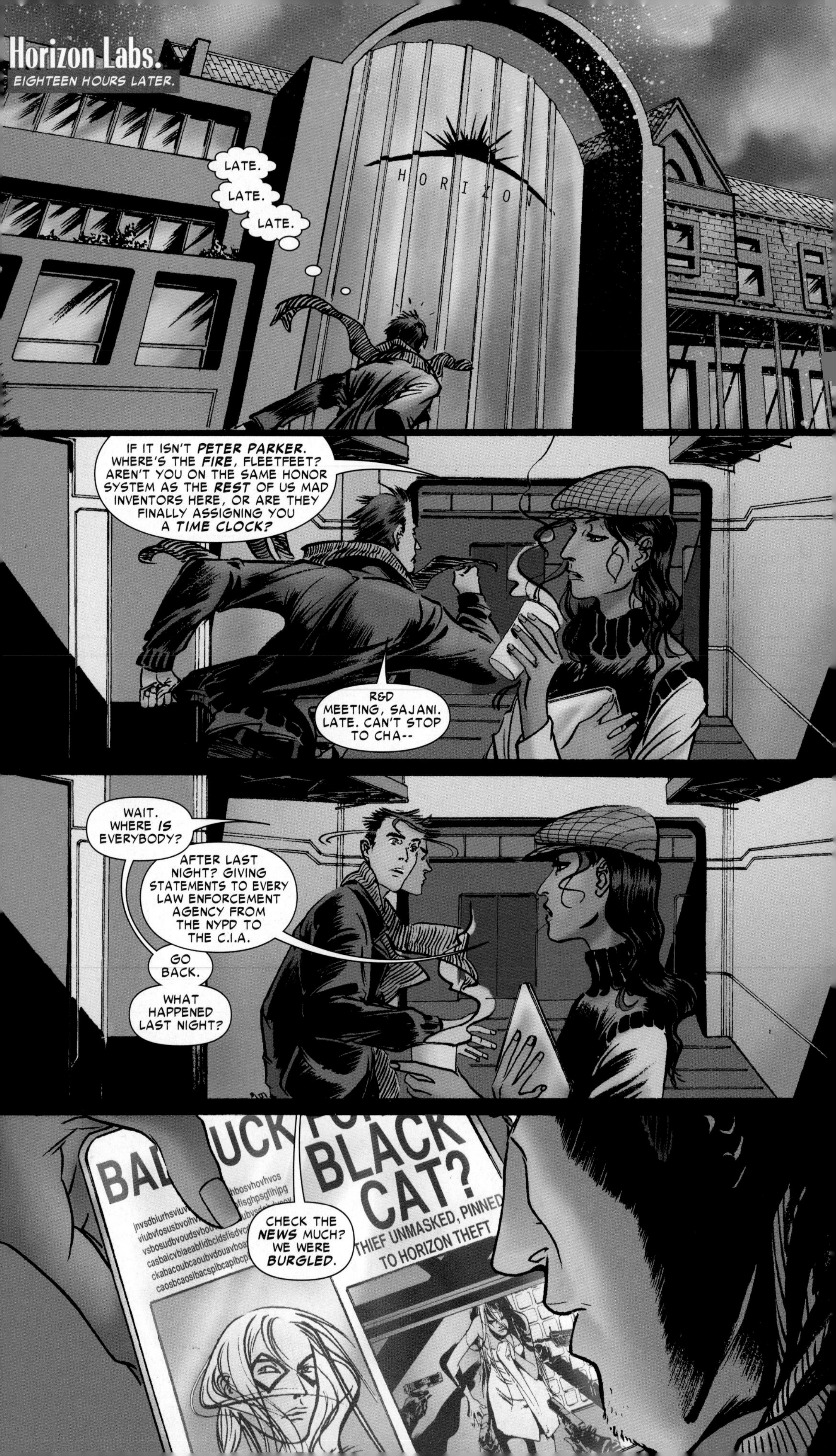

Horizon Labs.
EIGHTEEN HOURS LATER.
LATE.
LATE.
LATE.
HORIZON
IF IT ISN'T PETER PARKER. WHERE'S THE FIRE, FLEETFEET? AREN'T YOU ON THE SAME HONOR SYSTEM AS THE REST OF US MAD INVENTORS HERE, OR ARE THEY FINALLY ASSIGNING YOU A TIME CLOCK?
R&D MEETING, SAJANI. LATE. CAN'T STOP TO CHA--
WAIT. WHERE IS EVERYBODY?
AFTER LAST NIGHT? GIVING STATEMENTS TO EVERY LAW ENFORCEMENT AGENCY FROM THE NYPD TO THE C.I.A.
GO BACK.
WHAT HAPPENED LAST NIGHT?
BLACK CAT?
THIEF UNMASKED, PINNED TO HORIZON THEFT
CHECK THE NEWS MUCH? WE WERE BURGLED.

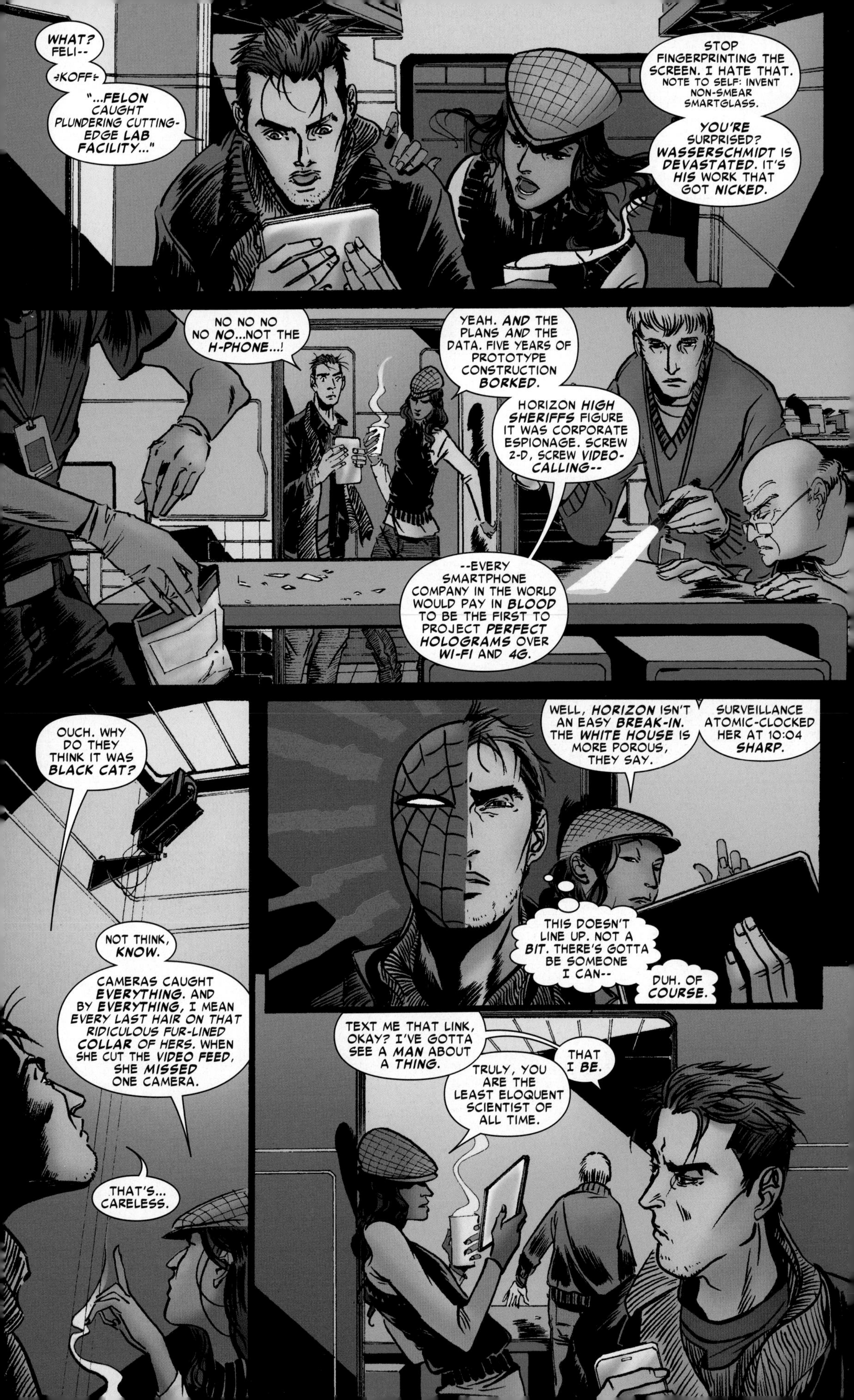
WHAT? FELI--
-KOFF-
"...FELON CAUGHT PLUNDERING CUTTING-EDGE LAB FACILITY..."
STOP FINGERPRINTING THE SCREEN. I HATE THAT. NOTE TO SELF: INVENT NON-SMEAR SMARTGLASS.
YOU'RE SURPRISED? WASSERSCHMIDT IS DEVASTATED. IT'S HIS WORK THAT GOT NICKED.
NO NO NO NO NO...NOT THE H-PHONE...!
YEAH. AND THE PLANS AND THE DATA. FIVE YEARS OF PROTOTYPE CONSTRUCTION BORKED.
HORIZON HIGH SHERIFFS FIGURE IT WAS CORPORATE ESPIONAGE. SCREW 2-D, SCREW VIDEO-CALLING--
--EVERY SMARTPHONE COMPANY IN THE WORLD WOULD PAY IN BLOOD TO BE THE FIRST TO PROJECT PERFECT HOLOGRAMS OVER WI-FI AND 4G.
OUCH. WHY DO THEY THINK IT WAS BLACK CAT?
NOT THINK, KNOW.
CAMERAS CAUGHT EVERYTHING. AND BY EVERYTHING, I MEAN EVERY LAST HAIR ON THAT RIDICULOUS FUR-LINED COLLAR OF HERS. WHEN SHE CUT THE VIDEO FEED, SHE MISSED ONE CAMERA.
THAT'S... CARELESS.
WELL, HORIZON ISN'T AN EASY BREAK-IN. THE WHITE HOUSE IS MORE POROUS, THEY SAY.
SURVEILLANCE ATOMIC-CLOCKED HER AT 10:04 SHARP.
THIS DOESN'T LINE UP. NOT A BIT. THERE'S GOTTA BE SOMEONE I CAN--
DUH. OF COURSE.
TEXT ME THAT LINK, OKAY? I'VE GOTTA SEE A MAN ABOUT A THING.
THAT I BE.
TRULY, YOU ARE THE LEAST ELOQUENT SCIENTIST OF ALL TIME.

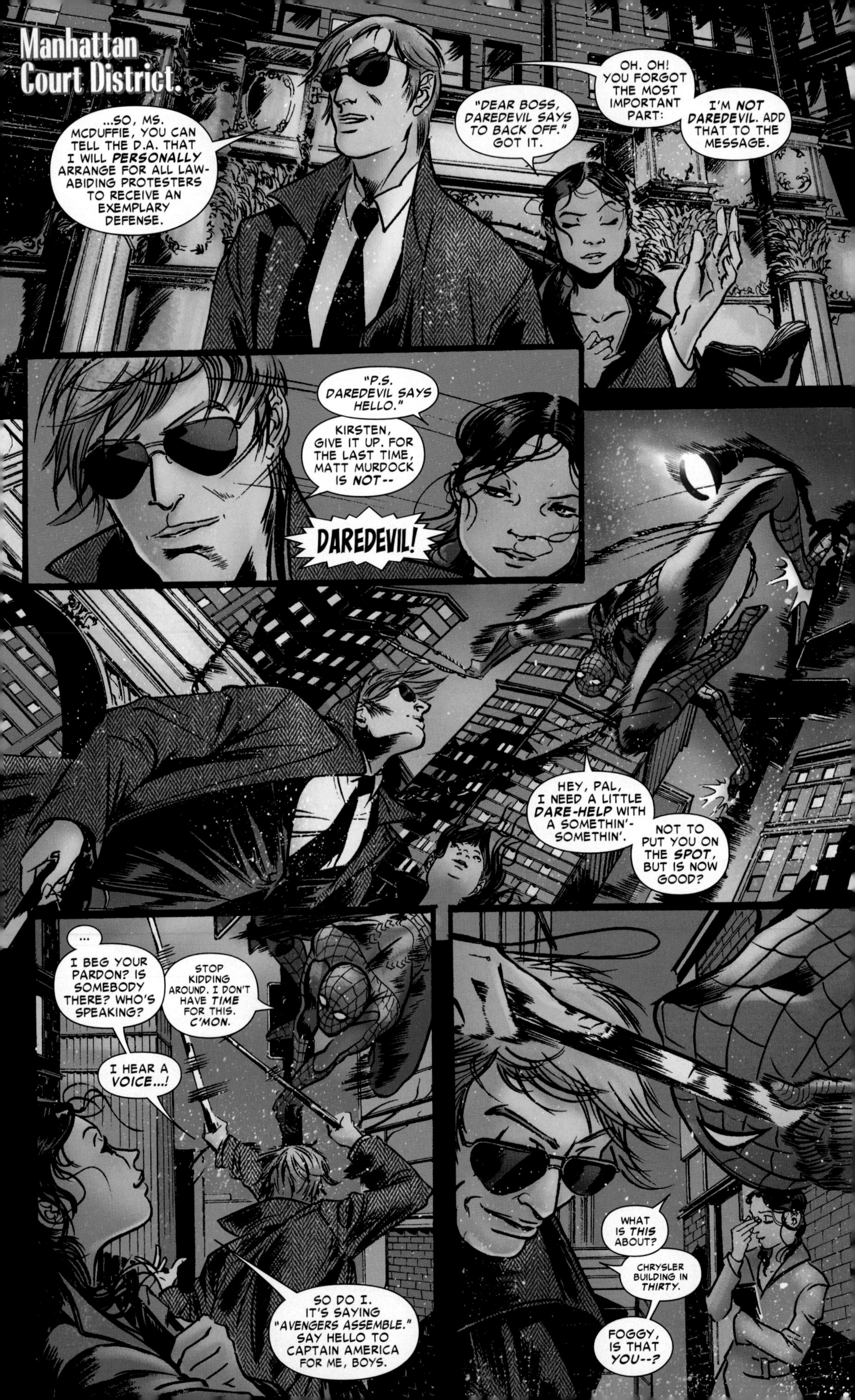
Manhattan Court District.
...SO, MS. MCDUFFIE, YOU CAN TELL THE D.A. THAT I WILL PERSONALLY ARRANGE FOR ALL LAW-ABIDING PROTESTERS TO RECEIVE AN EXEMPLARY DEFENSE.
"DEAR BOSS, DAREDEVIL SAYS TO BACK OFF." GOT IT.
OH. OH! YOU FORGOT THE MOST IMPORTANT PART:
I'M NOT DAREDEVIL. ADD THAT TO THE MESSAGE.
"P.S. DAREDEVIL SAYS HELLO."
KIRSTEN, GIVE IT UP. FOR THE LAST TIME, MATT MURDOCK IS NOT--
DAREDEVIL!
HEY, PAL, I NEED A LITTLE DARE-HELP WITH A SOMETHIN'-SOMETHIN'.
NOT TO PUT YOU ON THE SPOT, BUT IS NOW GOOD?
...
I BEG YOUR PARDON? IS SOMEBODY THERE? WHO'S SPEAKING?
STOP KIDDING AROUND. I DON'T HAVE TIME FOR THIS. C'MON.
I HEAR A VOICE...!
SO DO I. IT'S SAYING "AVENGERS ASSEMBLE." SAY HELLO TO CAPTAIN AMERICA FOR ME, BOYS.
WHAT IS THIS ABOUT?
CHRYSLER BUILDING IN THIRTY.
FOGGY, IS THAT YOU--?

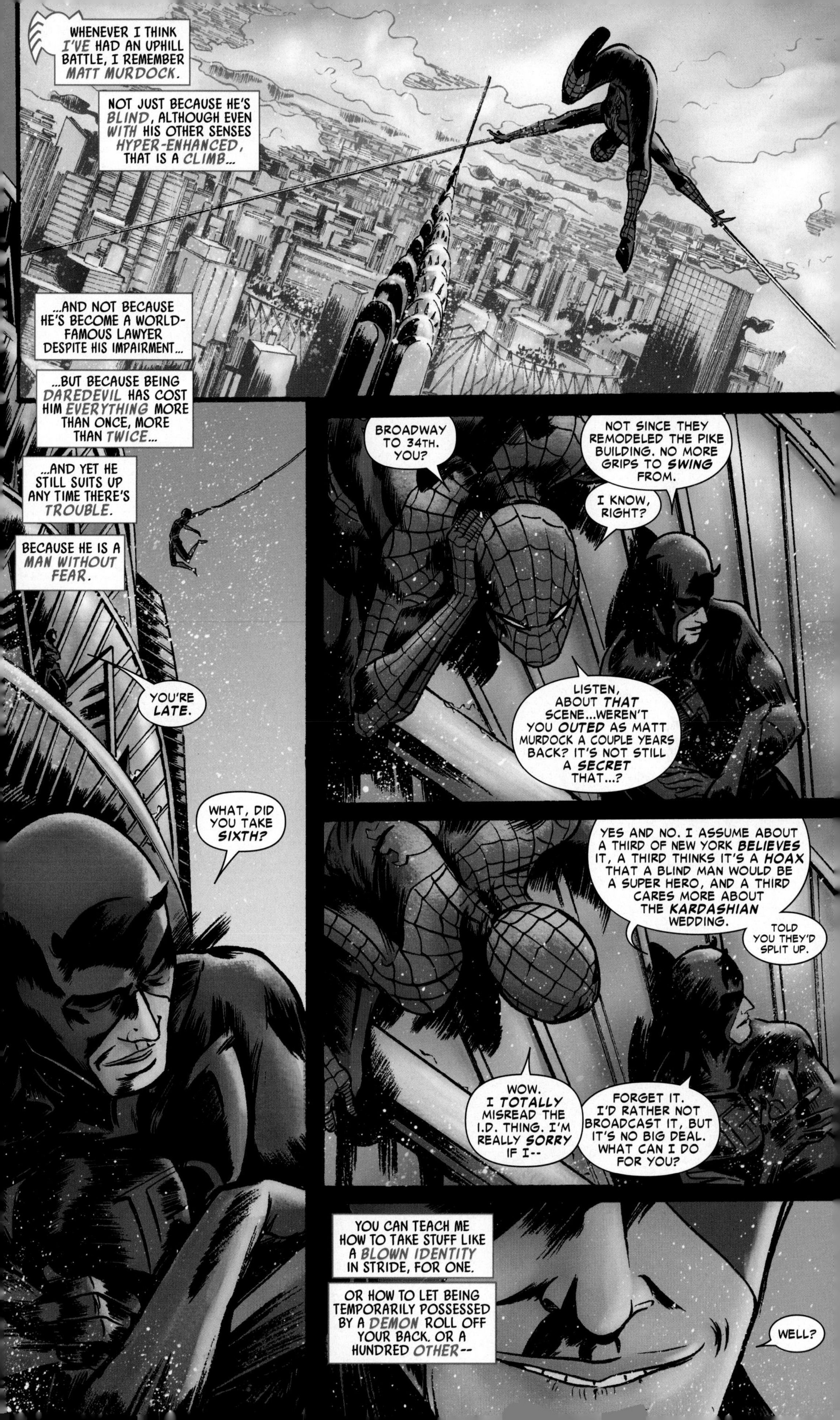
WHENEVER I THINK I'VE HAD AN UPHILL BATTLE, I REMEMBER MATT MURDOCK.
NOT JUST BECAUSE HE'S BLIND, ALTHOUGH EVEN WITH HIS OTHER SENSES HYPER-ENHANCED, THAT IS A CLIMB...
...AND NOT BECAUSE HE'S BECOME A WORLD-FAMOUS LAWYER DESPITE HIS IMPAIRMENT...
...BUT BECAUSE BEING DAREDEVIL HAS COST HIM EVERYTHING MORE THAN ONCE, MORE THAN TWICE...
...AND YET HE STILL SUITS UP ANY TIME THERE'S TROUBLE.
BECAUSE HE IS A MAN WITHOUT FEAR.
YOU'RE LATE.
WHAT, DID YOU TAKE SIXTH?
BROADWAY TO 34TH. YOU?
NOT SINCE THEY REMODELED THE PIKE BUILDING. NO MORE GRIPS TO SWING FROM.
I KNOW, RIGHT?
LISTEN, ABOUT THAT SCENE...WEREN'T YOU OUTED AS MATT MURDOCK A COUPLE YEARS BACK? IT'S NOT STILL A SECRET THAT...?
YES AND NO. I ASSUME ABOUT A THIRD OF NEW YORK BELIEVES IT, A THIRD THINKS IT'S A HOAX THAT A BLIND MAN WOULD BE A SUPER HERO, AND A THIRD CARES MORE ABOUT THE KARDASHIAN WEDDING.
TOLD YOU THEY'D SPLIT UP.
WOW. I TOTALLY MISREAD THE I.D. THING. I'M REALLY SORRY IF I--
FORGET IT. I'D RATHER NOT BROADCAST IT, BUT IT'S NO BIG DEAL. WHAT CAN I DO FOR YOU?
YOU CAN TEACH ME HOW TO TAKE STUFF LIKE A BLOWN IDENTITY IN STRIDE, FOR ONE.
OR HOW TO LET BEING TEMPORARILY POSSESSED BY A DEMON ROLL OFF YOUR BACK. OR A HUNDRED OTHER--
WELL?

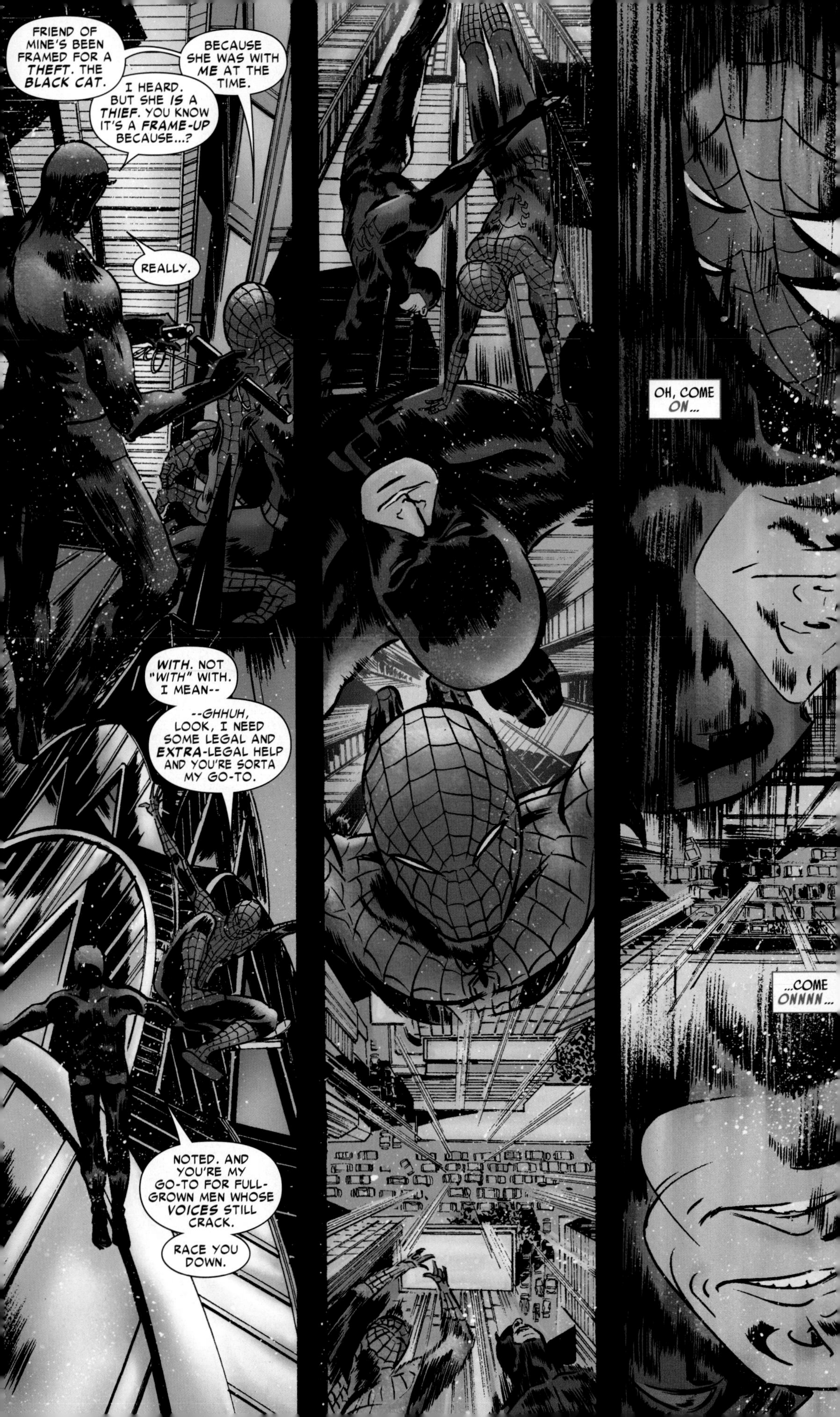

FRIEND OF MINE'S BEEN FRAMED FOR A *THEFT*. THE *BLACK CAT*.
I HEARD. BUT SHE *IS* A *THIEF*. YOU KNOW IT'S A *FRAME-UP* BECAUSE...?
BECAUSE SHE WAS WITH *ME* AT THE TIME.
REALLY.
WITH. NOT "*WITH*" WITH. I MEAN--
--GHHUH, LOOK, I NEED SOME LEGAL AND **EXTRA**-LEGAL HELP AND YOU'RE SORTA MY GO-TO.
NOTED. AND YOU'RE MY GO-TO FOR FULL-GROWN MEN WHOSE **VOICES** STILL CRACK.
RACE YOU DOWN.
OH, COME *ON*...
...COME *ONNNN*...

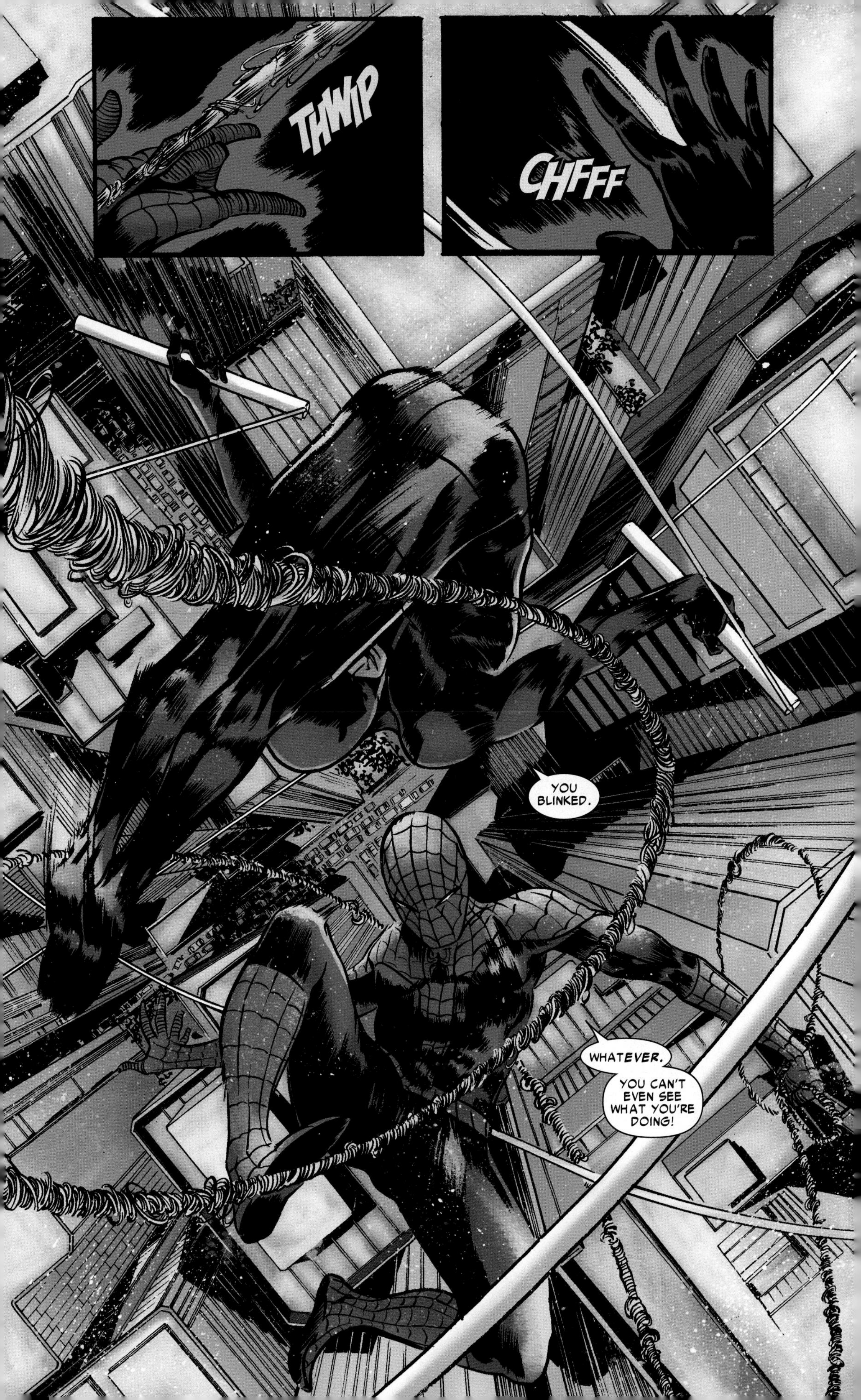
THWIP
CHFFF
YOU BLINKED.
WHATEVER.
YOU CAN'T EVEN SEE WHAT YOU'RE DOING!

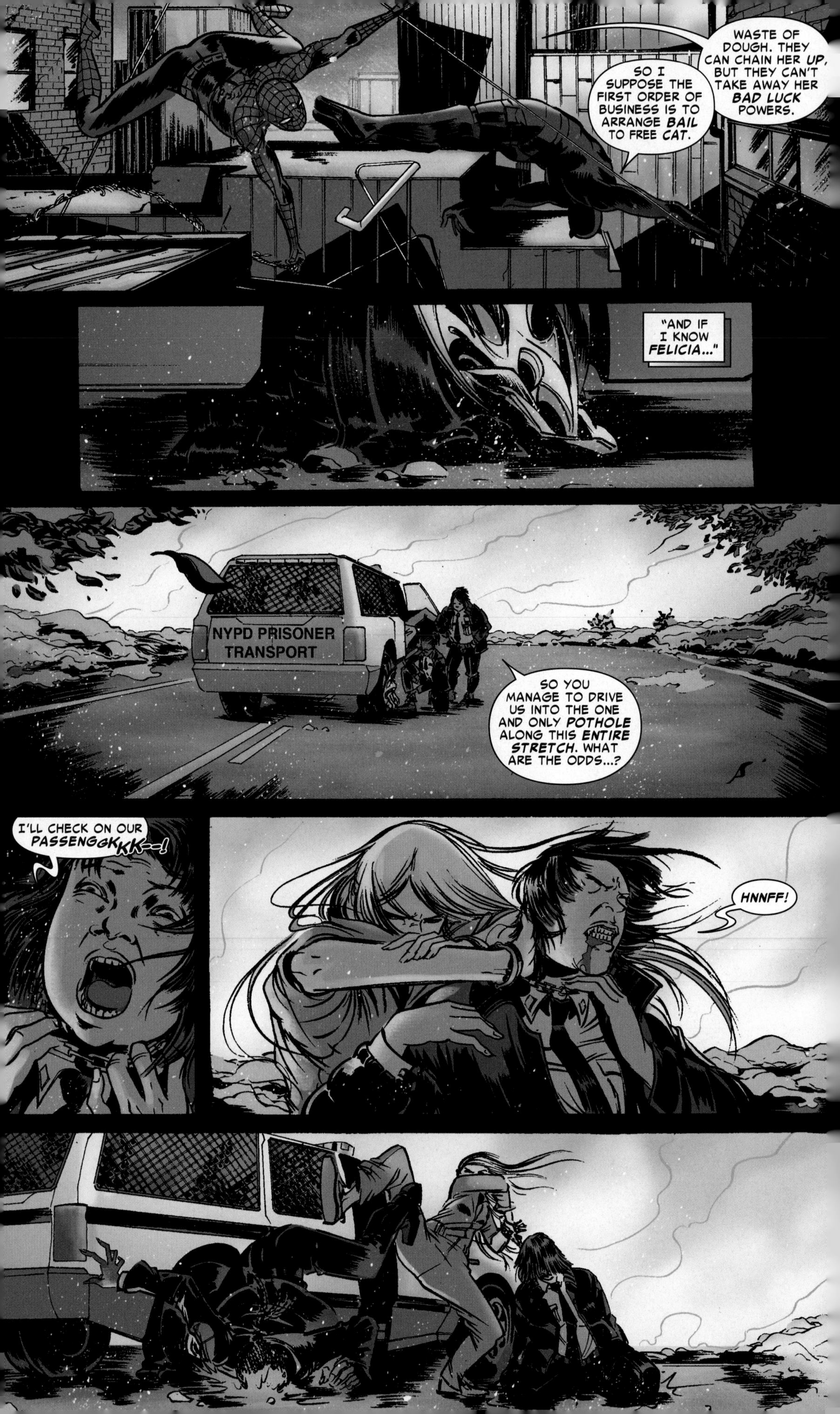
SO I SUPPOSE THE FIRST ORDER OF BUSINESS IS TO ARRANGE BAIL TO FREE CAT.
WASTE OF DOUGH. THEY CAN CHAIN HER UP, BUT THEY CAN'T TAKE AWAY HER BAD LUCK POWERS.
"AND IF I KNOW FELICIA..."
NYPD PRISONER TRANSPORT
SO YOU MANAGE TO DRIVE US INTO THE ONE AND ONLY POTHOLE ALONG THIS ENTIRE STRETCH. WHAT ARE THE ODDS...?
I'LL CHECK ON OUR PASSENGGKKK--!
HNNFF!

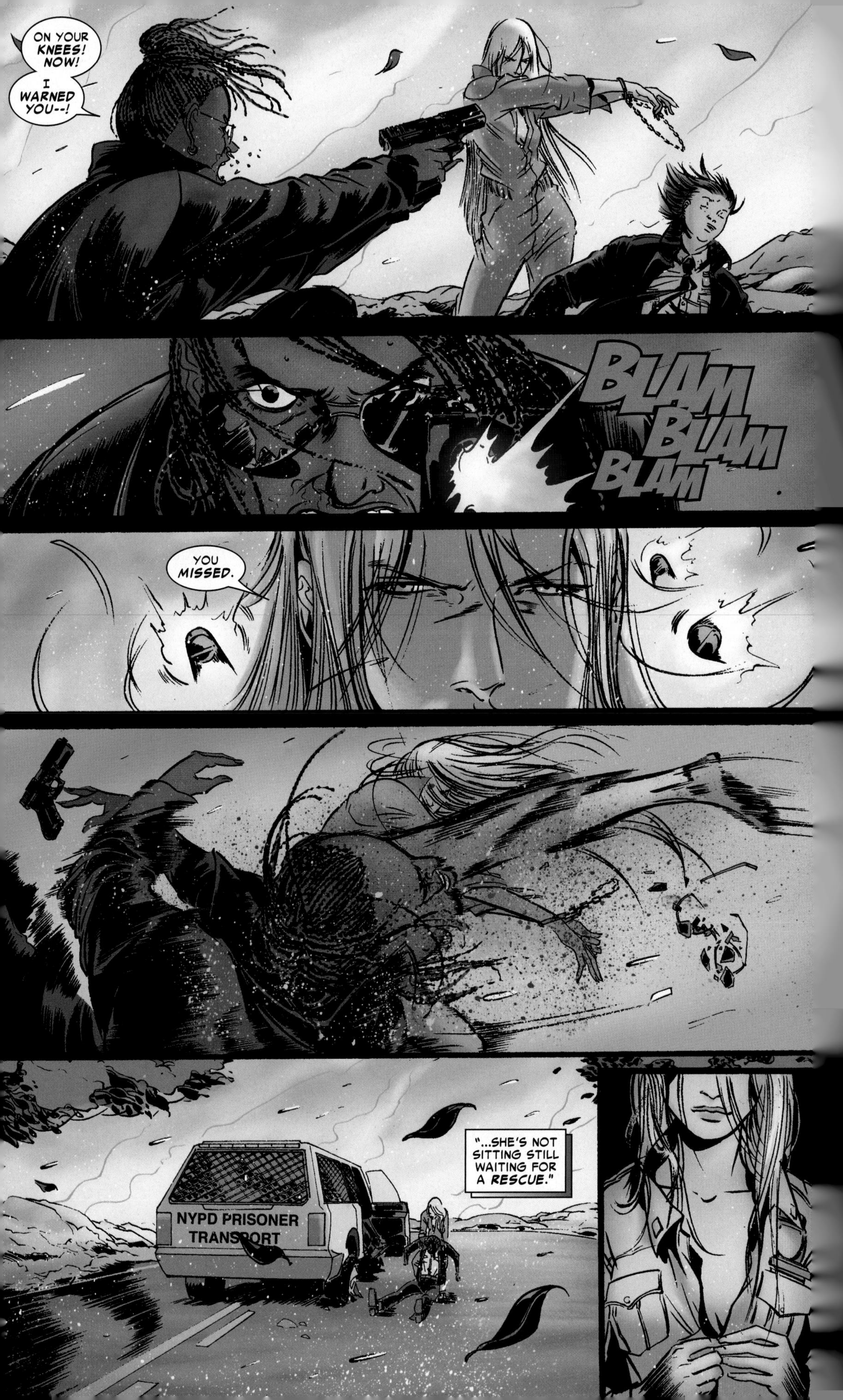
ON YOUR KNEES! NOW!
I WARNED YOU--!
BLAM BLAM BLAM
YOU MISSED.
NYPD PRISONER TRANSPORT
"...SHE'S NOT SITTING STILL WAITING FOR A RESCUE."

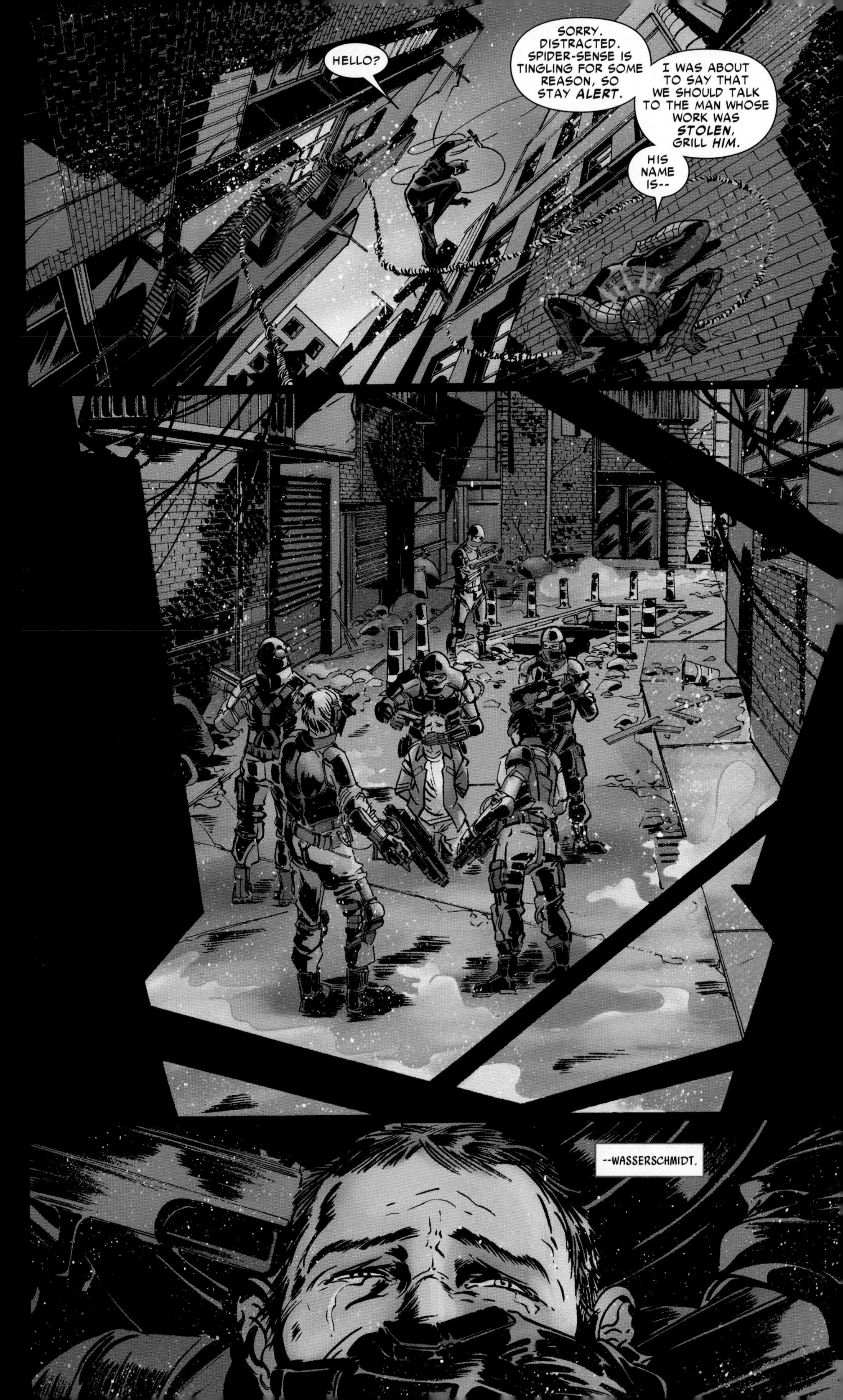
HELLO?
SORRY. DISTRACTED. SPIDER-SENSE IS TINGLING FOR SOME REASON, SO STAY ALERT.
I WAS ABOUT TO SAY THAT WE SHOULD TALK TO THE MAN WHOSE WORK WAS STOLEN, GRILL HIM.
HIS NAME IS--
--WASSERSCHMIDT.

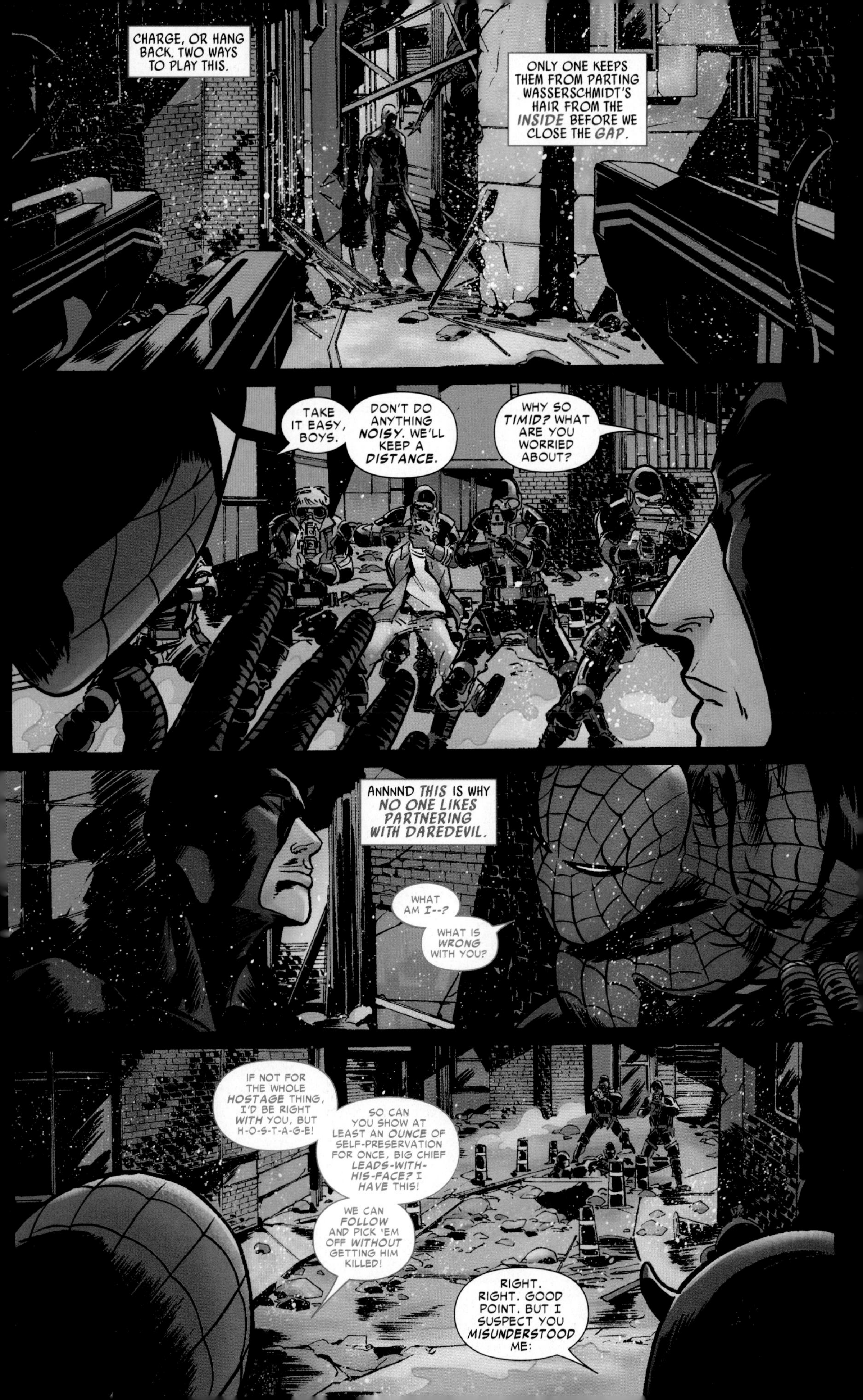
CHARGE, OR HANG BACK. TWO WAYS TO PLAY THIS.
ONLY ONE KEEPS THEM FROM PARTING WASSERSCHMIDT'S HAIR FROM THE INSIDE BEFORE WE CLOSE THE GAP.
TAKE IT EASY, BOYS.
DON'T DO ANYTHING NOISY. WE'LL KEEP A DISTANCE.
WHY SO TIMID? WHAT ARE YOU WORRIED ABOUT?
ANNNND THIS IS WHY NO ONE LIKES PARTNERING WITH DAREDEVIL.
WHAT AM I--?
WHAT IS WRONG WITH YOU?
IF NOT FOR THE WHOLE HOSTAGE THING, I'D BE RIGHT WITH YOU, BUT H-O-S-T-A-G-E!
SO CAN YOU SHOW AT LEAST AN OUNCE OF SELF-PRESERVATION FOR ONCE, BIG CHIEF LEADS-WITH-HIS-FACE? I HAVE THIS!
WE CAN FOLLOW AND PICK 'EM OFF WITHOUT GETTING HIM KILLED!
RIGHT. RIGHT. GOOD POINT. BUT I SUSPECT YOU MISUNDERSTOOD ME:

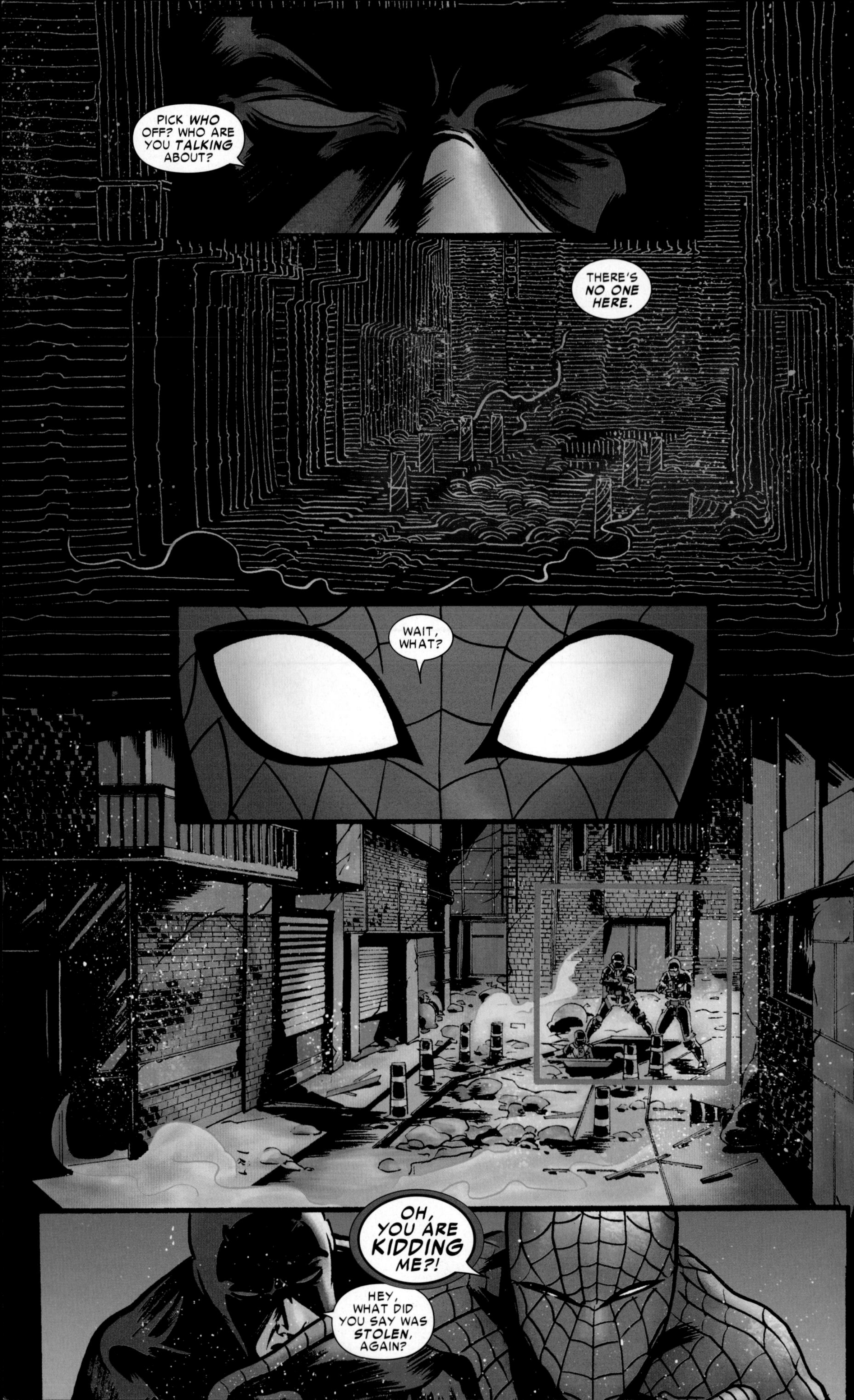
PICK WHO OFF? WHO ARE YOU TALKING ABOUT?
THERE'S NO ONE HERE.
WAIT, WHAT?
OH, YOU ARE KIDDING ME?!
HEY, WHAT DID YOU SAY WAS STOLEN, AGAIN?

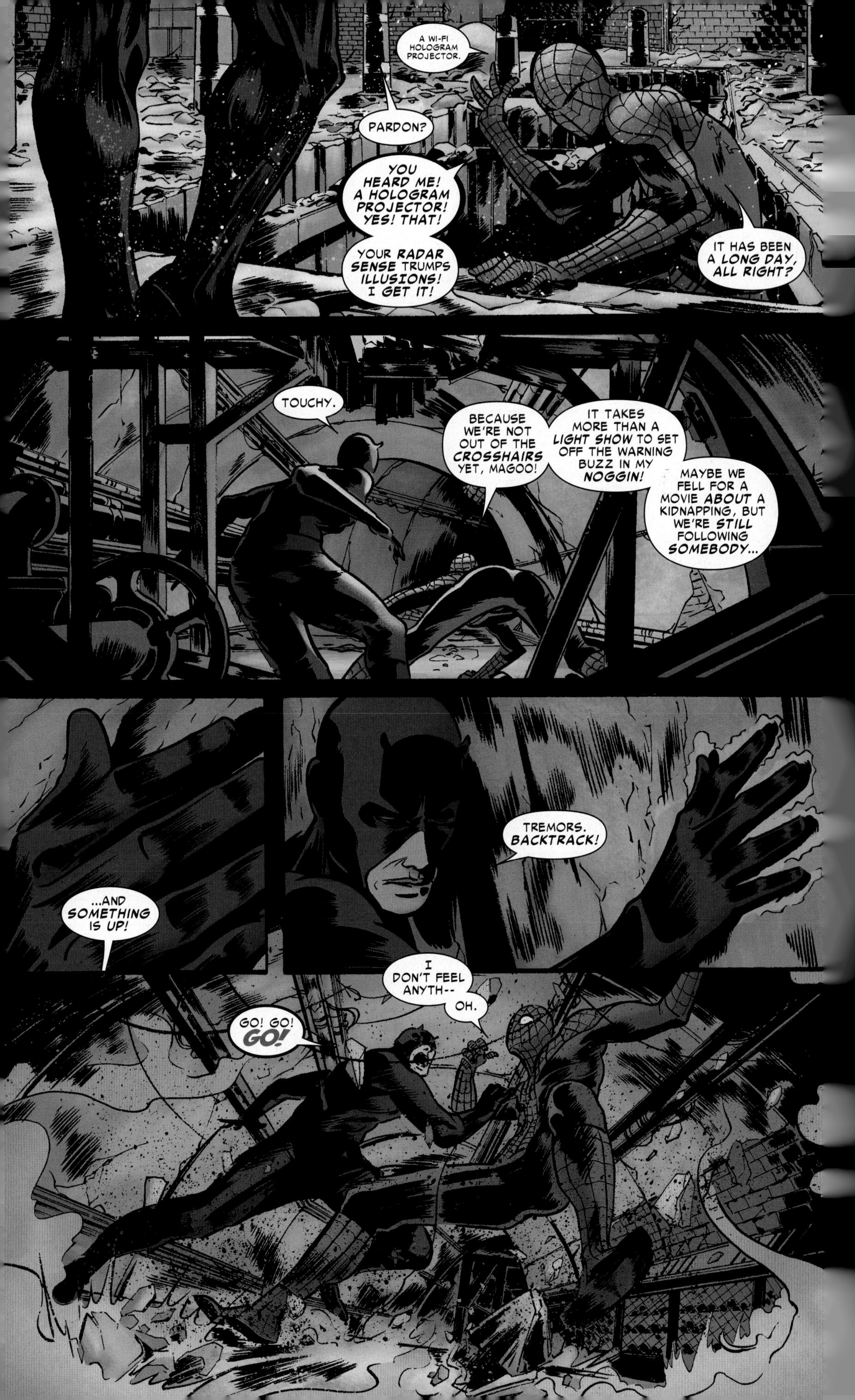
A WI-FI HOLOGRAM PROJECTOR.
PARDON?
YOU HEARD ME! A HOLOGRAM PROJECTOR! YES! THAT!
YOUR RADAR SENSE TRUMPS ILLUSIONS! I GET IT!
IT HAS BEEN A LONG DAY, ALL RIGHT?
TOUCHY.
BECAUSE WE'RE NOT OUT OF THE CROSSHAIRS YET, MAGOO!
IT TAKES MORE THAN A LIGHT SHOW TO SET OFF THE WARNING BUZZ IN MY NOGGIN!
MAYBE WE FELL FOR A MOVIE ABOUT A KIDNAPPING, BUT WE'RE STILL FOLLOWING SOMEBODY...
...AND SOMETHING IS UP!
TREMORS. BACKTRACK!
I DON'T FEEL ANYTH--
OH.
GO! GO! GO!

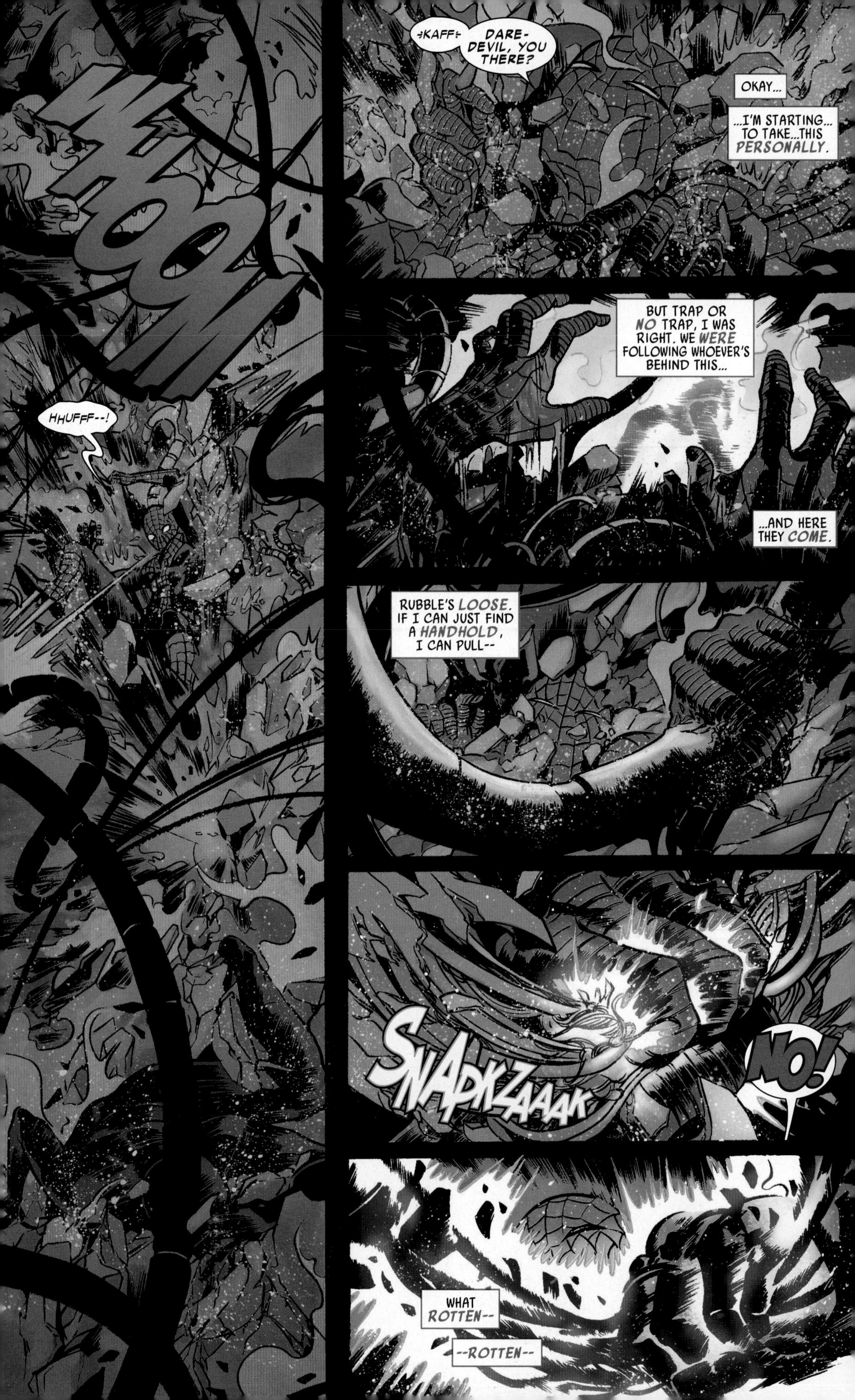
WHOOM
HHUFFF--!
⸗KAFF⸗ DARE-DEVIL, YOU THERE?
OKAY...
...I'M STARTING... TO TAKE...THIS PERSONALLY.
BUT TRAP OR NO TRAP, I WAS RIGHT. WE WERE FOLLOWING WHOEVER'S BEHIND THIS...
...AND HERE THEY COME.
RUBBLE'S LOOSE. IF I CAN JUST FIND A HANDHOLD, I CAN PULL--
SNAPKZAAAK
NO!
WHAT ROTTEN--
--ROTTEN--

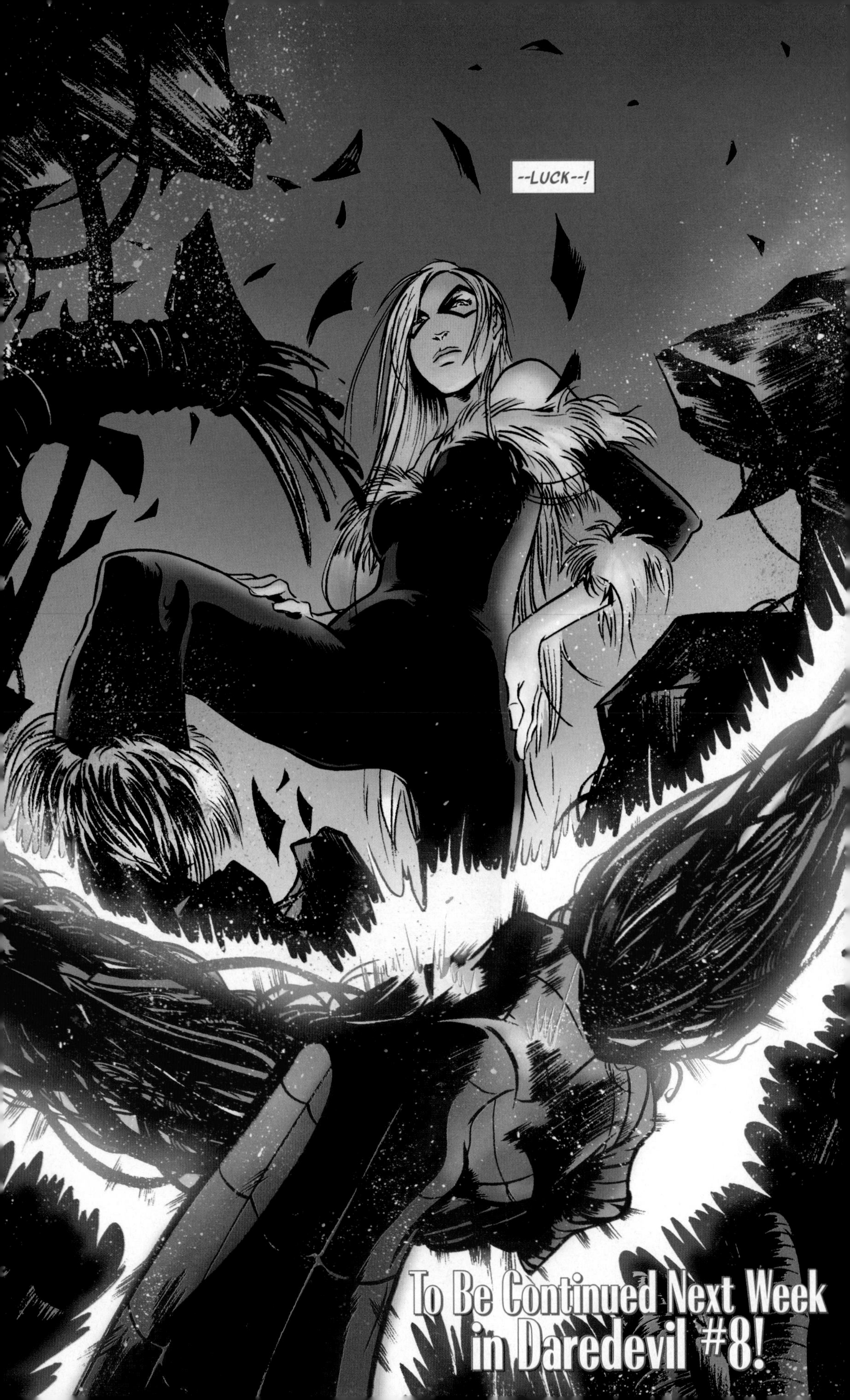
--LUCK--!
To Be Continued Next Week in Daredevil #8!

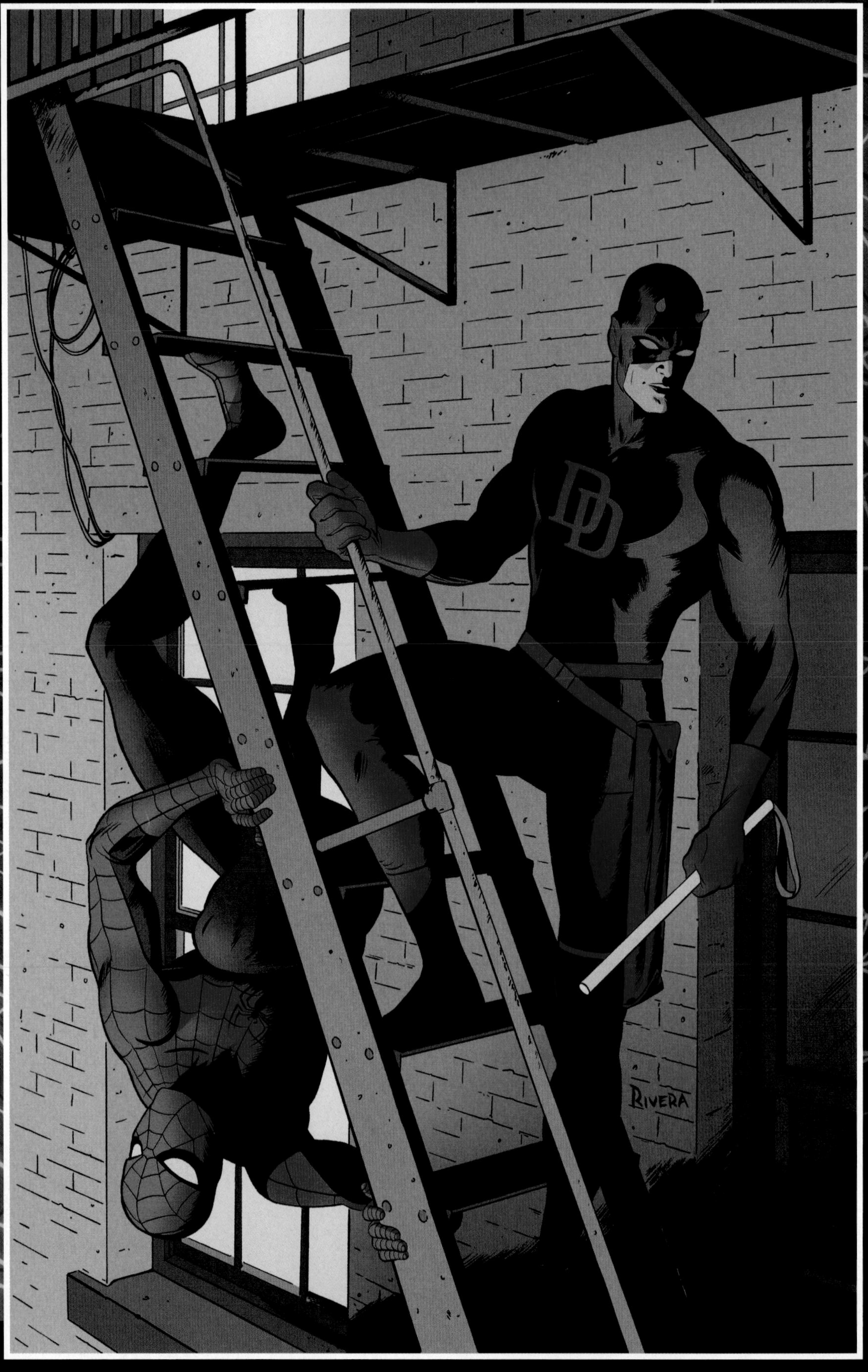
RIVERA

DAREDEVIL #8
COVER BY PAOLO RIVERA

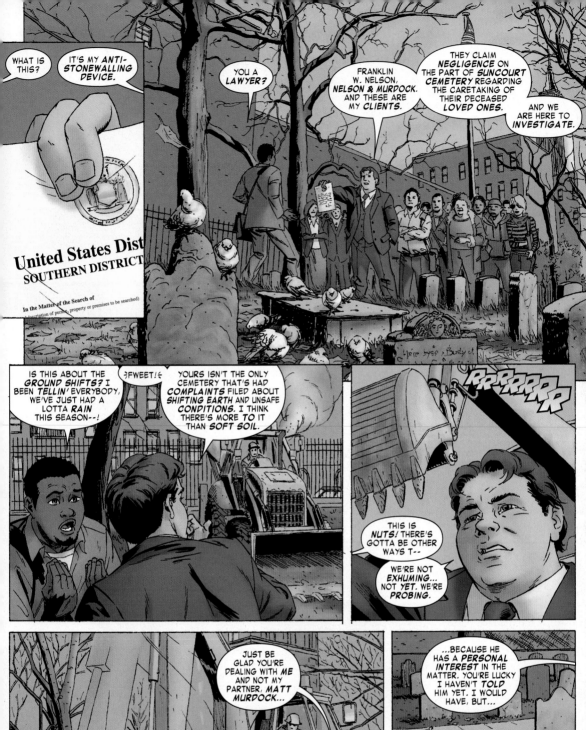

WHAT IS THIS?

IT'S MY *ANTI-STONEWALLING DEVICE*.

YOU A *LAWYER*?

FRANKLIN W. NELSON, *NELSON & MURDOCK*. AND THESE ARE MY *CLIENTS*.

THEY CLAIM *NEGLIGENCE* ON THE PART OF *SUNCOURT CEMETERY* REGARDING THE CARETAKING OF THEIR DECEASED *LOVED ONES*.

AND WE ARE HERE TO *INVESTIGATE*.

United States Dist
SOUTHERN DISTRICT

In the Matter of the Search of
Description of person, property or premises to be searched)

IS THIS ABOUT THE *GROUND SHIFTS?* I BEEN *TELLIN'* EVERYBODY, WE'VE JUST HAD A LOTTA *RAIN* THIS SEASON--!

≥FWEET!≤

YOURS ISN'T THE ONLY CEMETERY THAT'S HAD *COMPLAINTS* FILED ABOUT *SHIFTING EARTH* AND UNSAFE *CONDITIONS*. I THINK THERE'S MORE *TO IT* THAN *SOFT SOIL*.

RRRRRRRR

THIS IS *NUTS!* THERE'S GOTTA BE OTHER WAYS T--

WE'RE NOT *EXHUMING*... NOT *YET*. WE'RE *PROBING*.

JUST BE GLAD YOU'RE DEALING WITH *ME* AND NOT MY PARTNER, *MATT MURDOCK*...

...BECAUSE HE HAS A *PERSONAL INTEREST* IN THE MATTER. YOU'RE LUCKY I HAVEN'T *TOLD* HIM YET. I WOULD HAVE, BUT...

HE FOUGHT A GOOD FIGHT

JACK MURDOCK

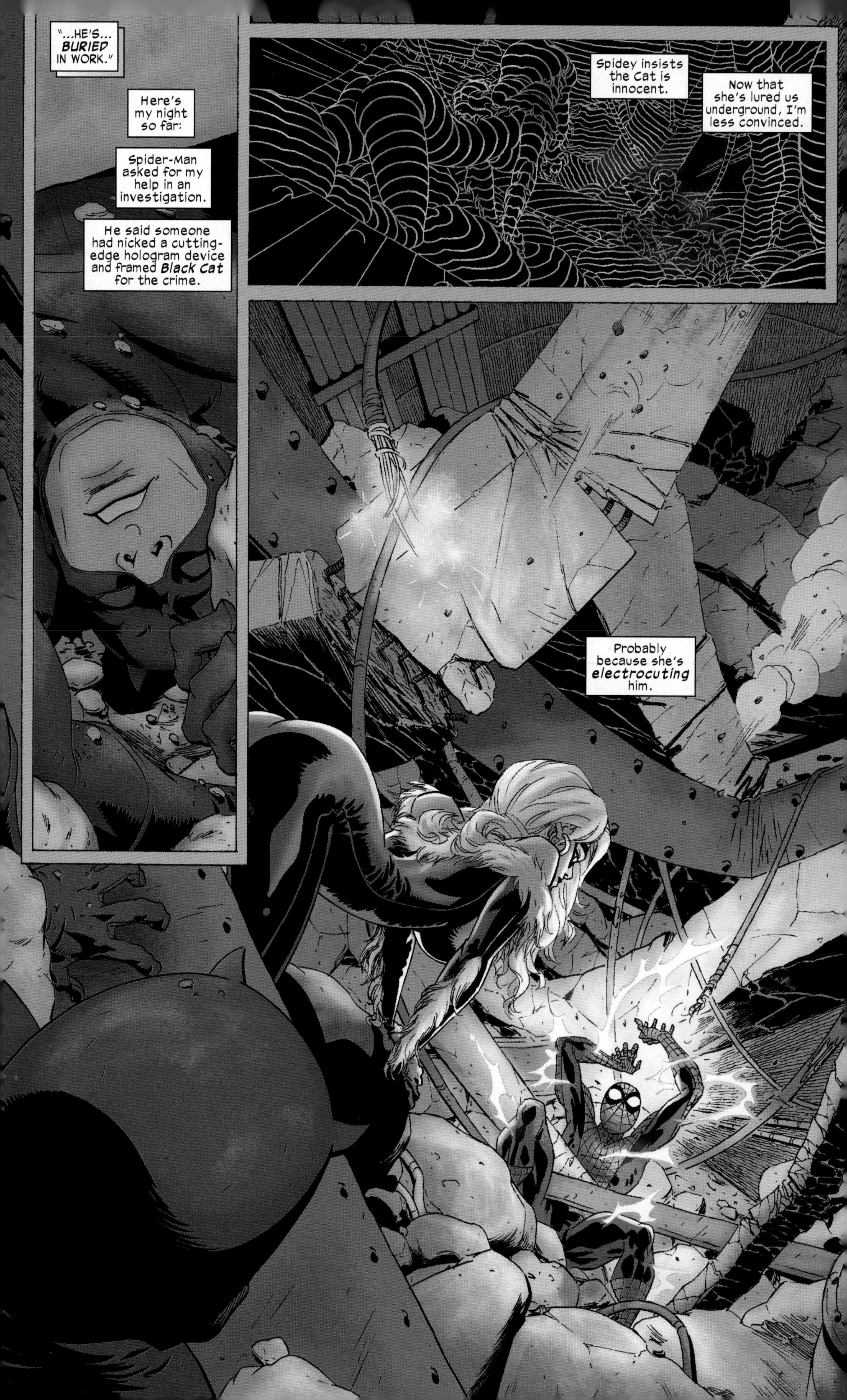
"...HE'S... BURIED IN WORK."
Here's my night so far:
Spider-Man asked for my help in an investigation.
He said someone had nicked a cutting-edge hologram device and framed Black Cat for the crime.
Spidey insists the Cat is innocent.
Now that she's lured us underground, I'm less convinced.
Probably because she's electrocuting him.

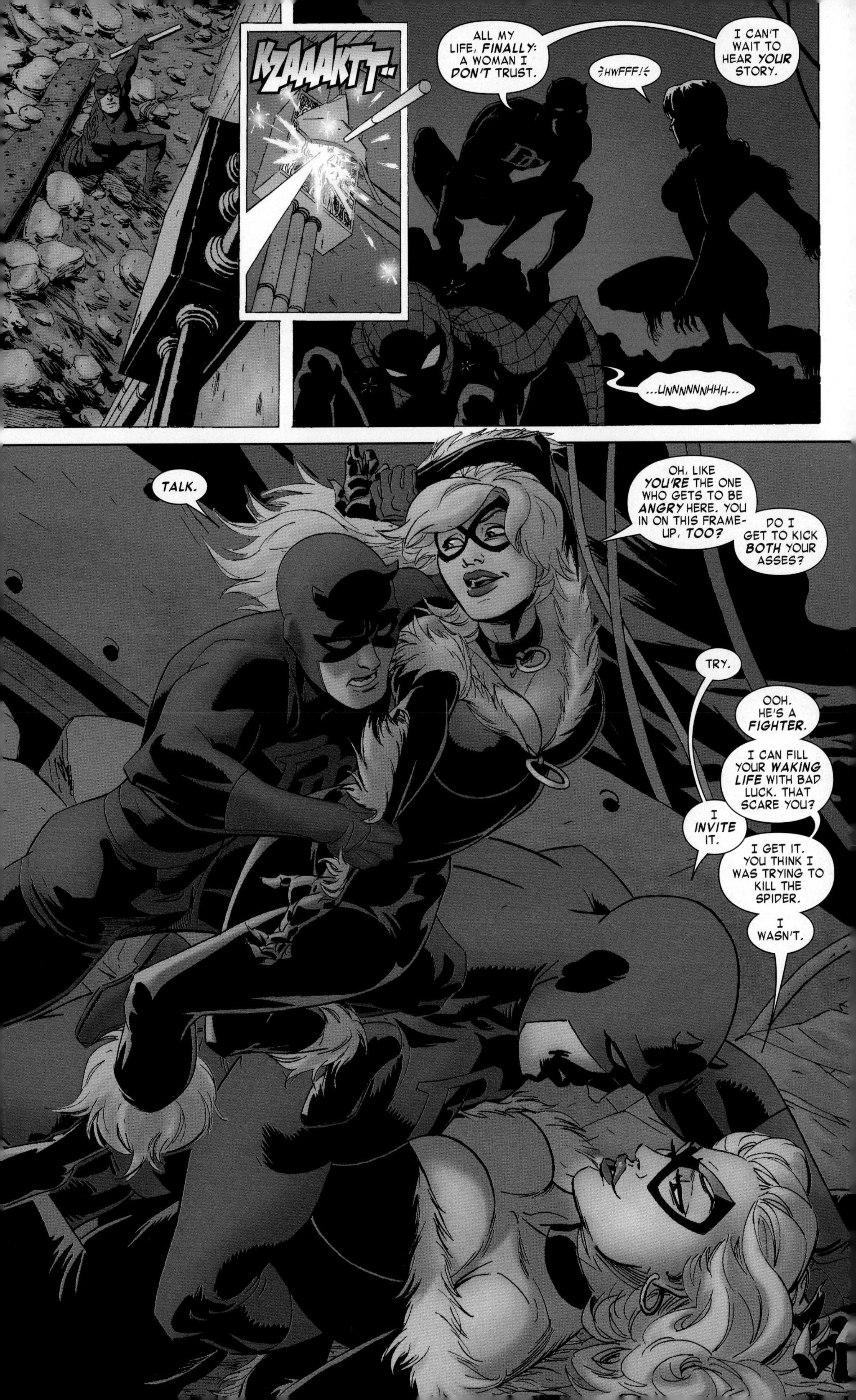
KZAAAKTTT-
ALL MY LIFE, FINALLY: A WOMAN I DON'T TRUST.
I CAN'T WAIT TO HEAR YOUR STORY.
HWFFF!
...UNNNNNNHHH...
TALK.
OH, LIKE YOU'RE THE ONE WHO GETS TO BE ANGRY HERE. YOU IN ON THIS FRAME-UP, TOO?
DO I GET TO KICK BOTH YOUR ASSES?
TRY.
OOH. HE'S A FIGHTER.
I CAN FILL YOUR WAKING LIFE WITH BAD LUCK. THAT SCARE YOU?
I INVITE IT.
I GET IT. YOU THINK I WAS TRYING TO KILL THE SPIDER.
I WASN'T.

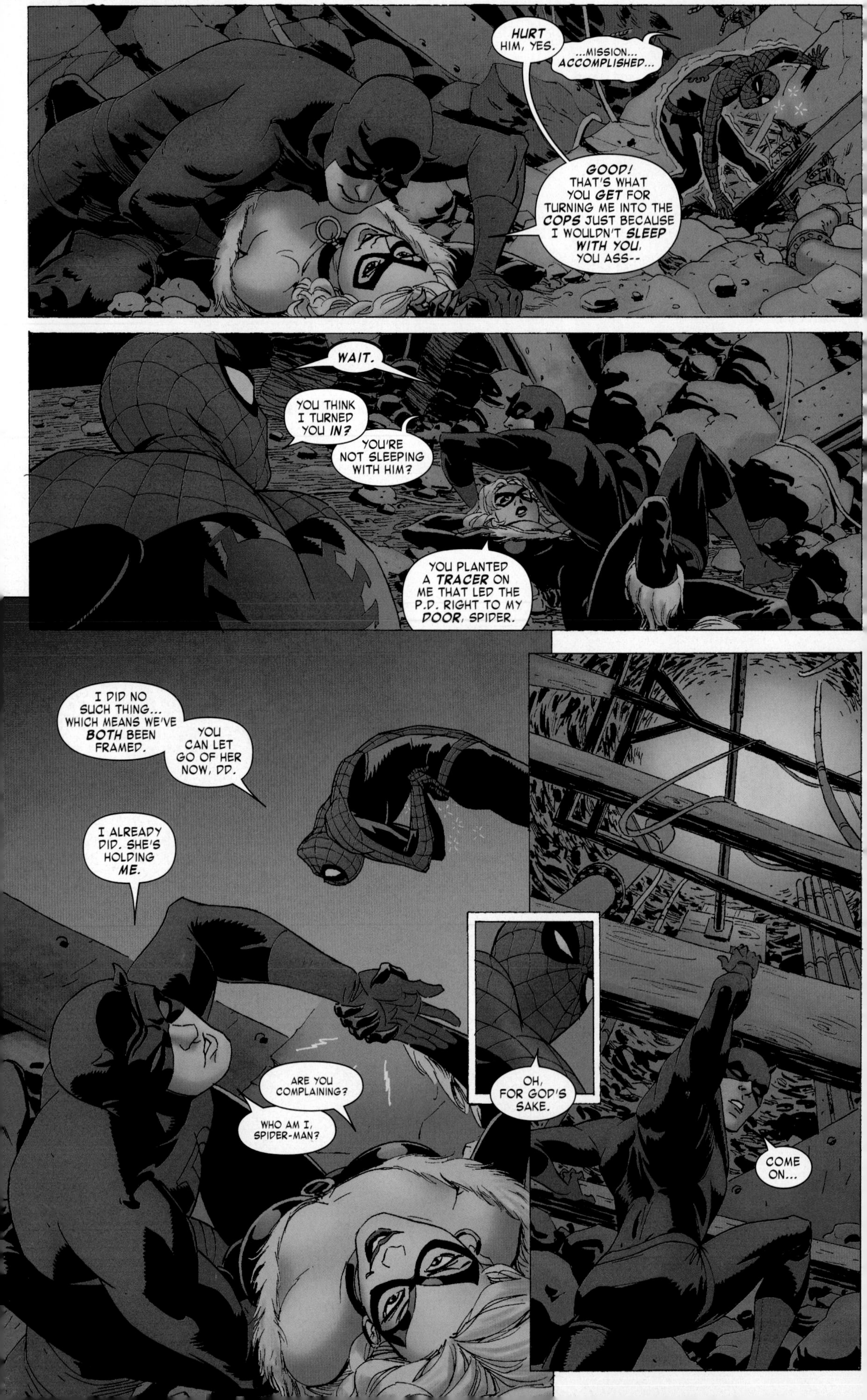
HURT HIM, YES.
...MISSION... ACCOMPLISHED...
GOOD! THAT'S WHAT YOU GET FOR TURNING ME INTO THE COPS JUST BECAUSE I WOULDN'T SLEEP WITH YOU, YOU ASS--
WAIT.
YOU THINK I TURNED YOU IN?
YOU'RE NOT SLEEPING WITH HIM?
YOU PLANTED A TRACER ON ME THAT LED THE P.D. RIGHT TO MY DOOR, SPIDER.
I DID NO SUCH THING... WHICH MEANS WE'VE BOTH BEEN FRAMED.
YOU CAN LET GO OF HER NOW, DD.
I ALREADY DID. SHE'S HOLDING ME.
ARE YOU COMPLAINING?
WHO AM I, SPIDER-MAN?
OH, FOR GOD'S SAKE.
COME ON...

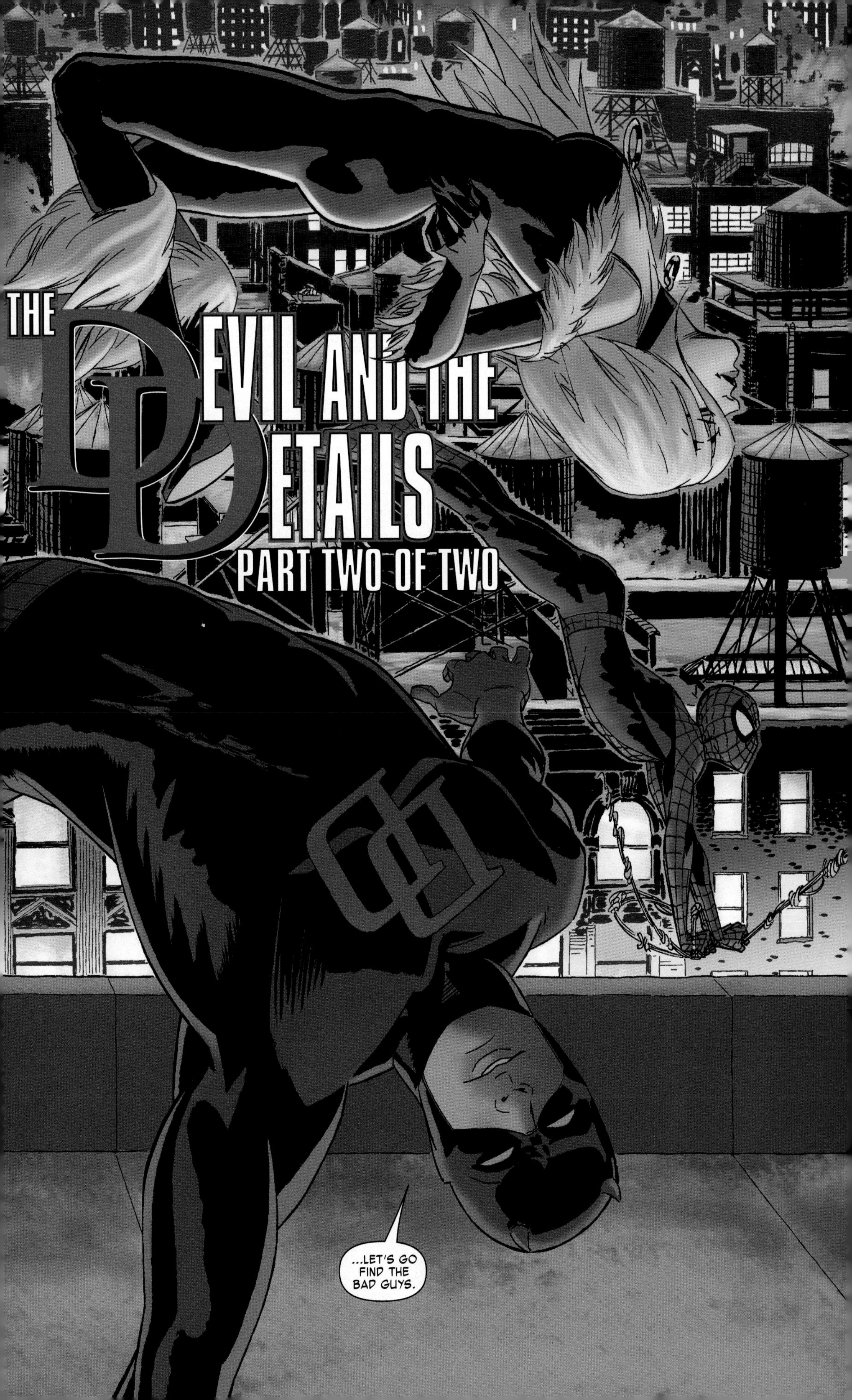
THE DEVIL AND THE DETAILS
PART TWO OF TWO
...LET'S GO FIND THE BAD GUYS.

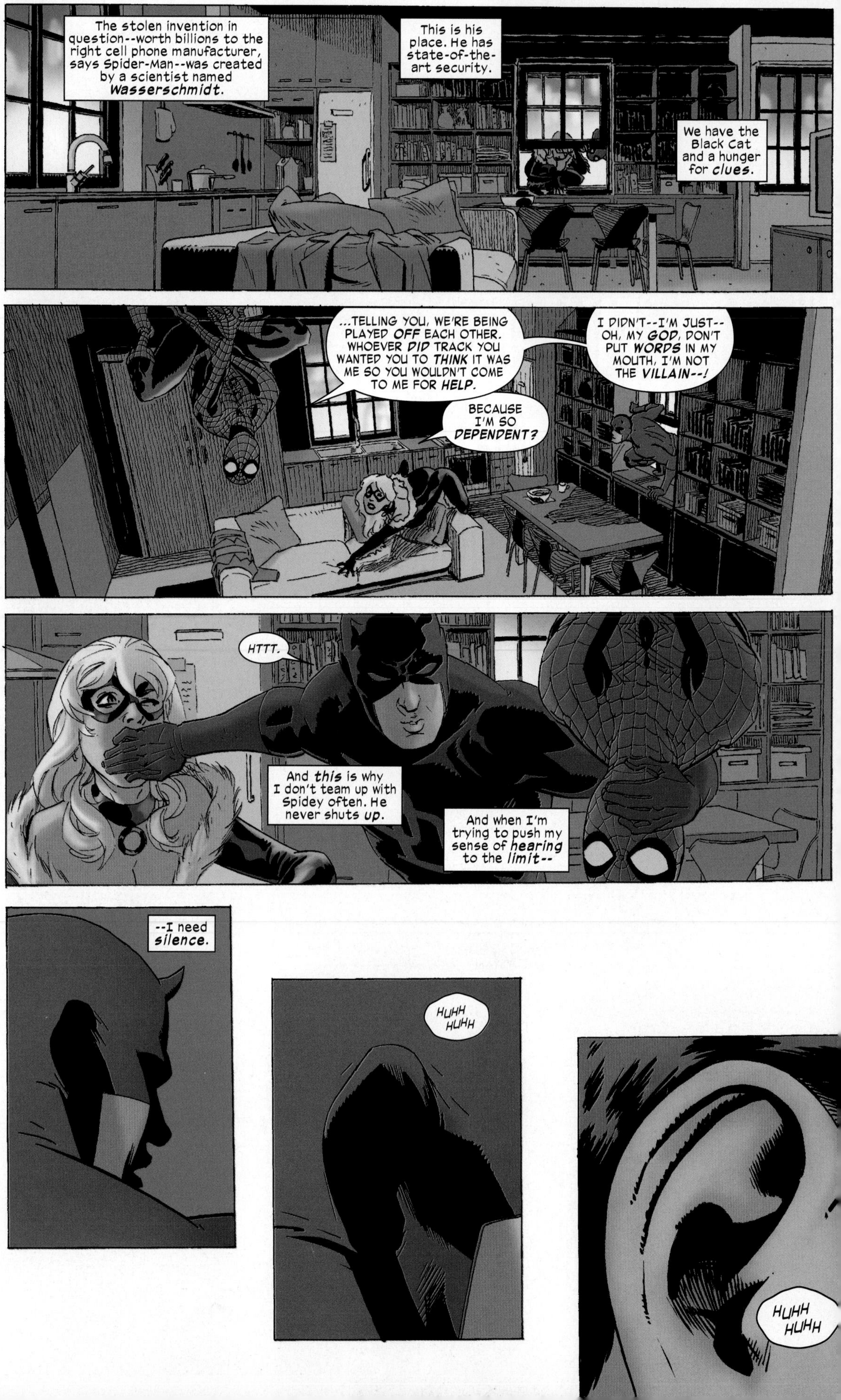
The stolen invention in question--worth billions to the right cell phone manufacturer, says Spider-Man--was created by a scientist named Wasserschmidt.
This is his place. He has state-of-the-art security.
We have the Black Cat and a hunger for clues.
...TELLING YOU, WE'RE BEING PLAYED OFF EACH OTHER. WHOEVER DID TRACK YOU WANTED YOU TO THINK IT WAS ME SO YOU WOULDN'T COME TO ME FOR HELP.
BECAUSE I'M SO DEPENDENT?
I DIDN'T--I'M JUST--OH, MY GOD, DON'T PUT WORDS IN MY MOUTH, I'M NOT THE VILLAIN--!
HTTT.
And this is why I don't team up with Spidey often. He never shuts up.
And when I'm trying to push my sense of hearing to the limit--
--I need silence.
HUHH HUHH
HUHH HUHH

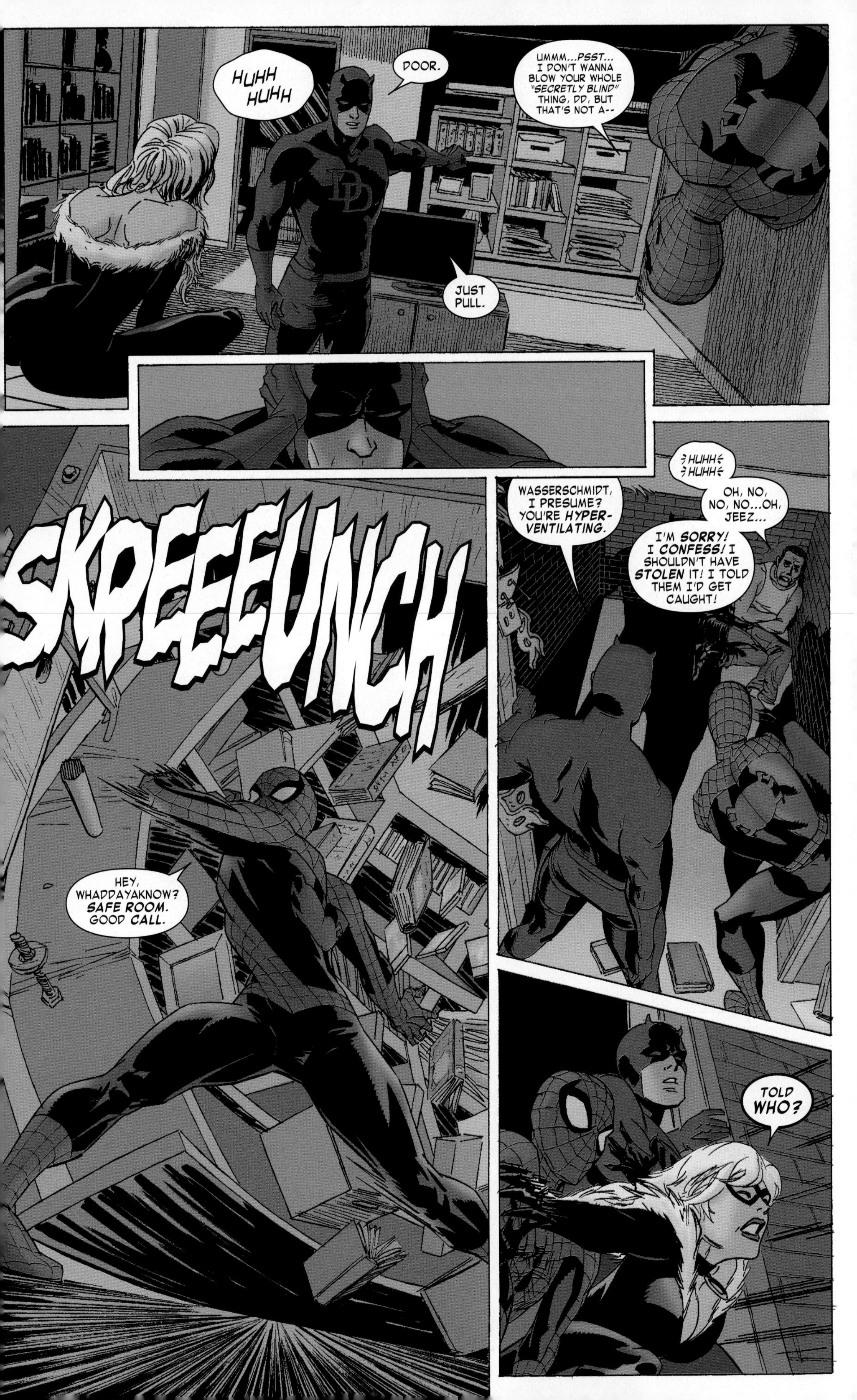
HUHH
HUHH
DOOR.
UMMM...PSST... I DON'T WANNA BLOW YOUR WHOLE "SECRETLY BLIND" THING, DD, BUT THAT'S NOT A--
JUST PULL.
SKREEEUNCH
HEY, WHADDAYAKNOW? SAFE ROOM. GOOD CALL.
HUHH
HUHH
WASSERSCHMIDT, I PRESUME? YOU'RE HYPER-VENTILATING.
OH, NO, NO, NO...OH, JEEZ...
I'M SORRY! I CONFESS! I SHOULDN'T HAVE STOLEN IT! I TOLD THEM I'D GET CAUGHT!
TOLD WHO?

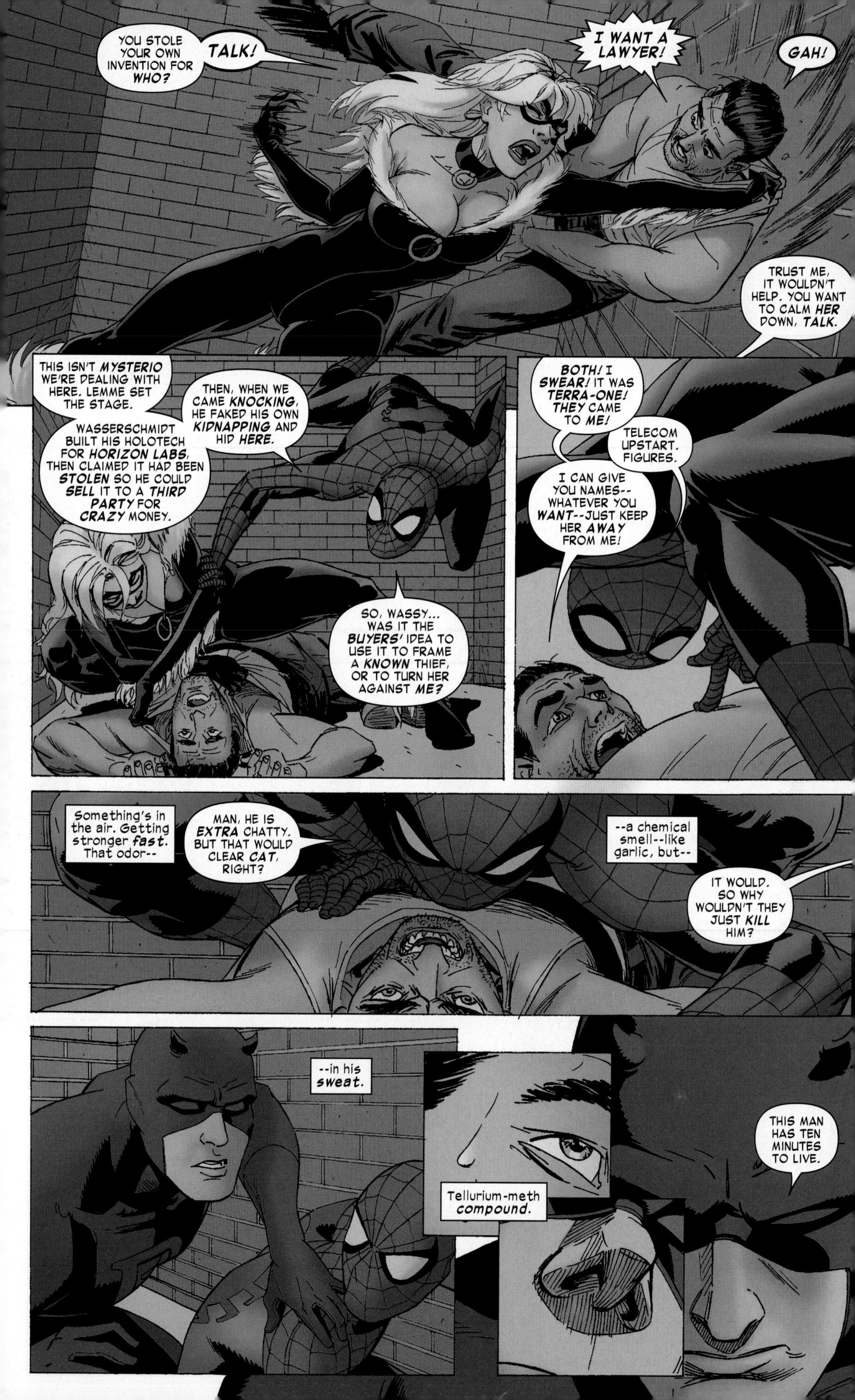

YOU STOLE YOUR OWN INVENTION FOR WHO?
TALK!
I WANT A LAWYER!
GAH!
TRUST ME, IT WOULDN'T HELP. YOU WANT TO CALM HER DOWN, TALK.
THIS ISN'T MYSTERIO WE'RE DEALING WITH HERE. LEMME SET THE STAGE.
WASSERSCHMIDT BUILT HIS HOLOTECH FOR HORIZON LABS, THEN CLAIMED IT HAD BEEN STOLEN SO HE COULD SELL IT TO A THIRD PARTY FOR CRAZY MONEY.
THEN, WHEN WE CAME KNOCKING, HE FAKED HIS OWN KIDNAPPING AND HID HERE.
SO, WASSY... WAS IT THE BUYERS' IDEA TO USE IT TO FRAME A KNOWN THIEF, OR TO TURN HER AGAINST ME?
BOTH! I SWEAR! IT WAS TERRA-ONE! THEY CAME TO ME!
TELECOM UPSTART. FIGURES.
I CAN GIVE YOU NAMES-- WHATEVER YOU WANT--JUST KEEP HER AWAY FROM ME!
Something's in the air. Getting stronger fast. That odor--
MAN, HE IS EXTRA CHATTY. BUT THAT WOULD CLEAR CAT, RIGHT?
--a chemical smell--like garlic, but--
IT WOULD. SO WHY WOULDN'T THEY JUST KILL HIM?
--in his sweat.
Tellurium-meth compound.
THIS MAN HAS TEN MINUTES TO LIVE.

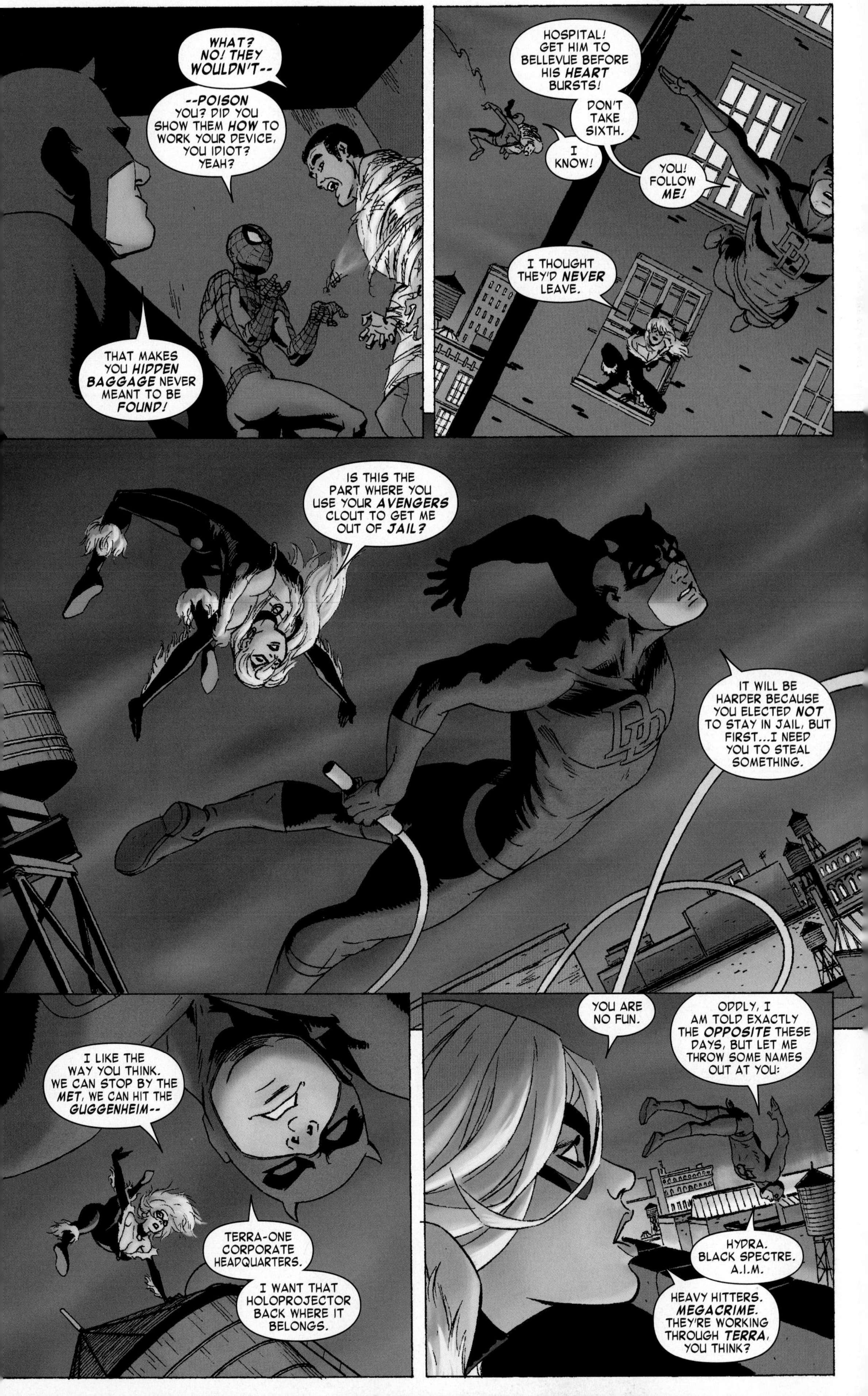
WHAT? NO! THEY WOULDN'T--
--POISON YOU? DID YOU SHOW THEM HOW TO WORK YOUR DEVICE, YOU IDIOT? YEAH?
THAT MAKES YOU HIDDEN BAGGAGE NEVER MEANT TO BE FOUND!
HOSPITAL! GET HIM TO BELLEVUE BEFORE HIS HEART BURSTS!
DON'T TAKE SIXTH.
I KNOW!
YOU! FOLLOW ME!
I THOUGHT THEY'D NEVER LEAVE.
IS THIS THE PART WHERE YOU USE YOUR AVENGERS CLOUT TO GET ME OUT OF JAIL?
IT WILL BE HARDER BECAUSE YOU ELECTED NOT TO STAY IN JAIL, BUT FIRST...I NEED YOU TO STEAL SOMETHING.
I LIKE THE WAY YOU THINK. WE CAN STOP BY THE MET, WE CAN HIT THE GUGGENHEIM--
TERRA-ONE CORPORATE HEADQUARTERS.
I WANT THAT HOLOPROJECTOR BACK WHERE IT BELONGS.
YOU ARE NO FUN.
ODDLY, I AM TOLD EXACTLY THE OPPOSITE THESE DAYS, BUT LET ME THROW SOME NAMES OUT AT YOU:
HYDRA. BLACK SPECTRE. A.I.M.
HEAVY HITTERS. MEGACRIME. THEY'RE WORKING THROUGH TERRA, YOU THINK?

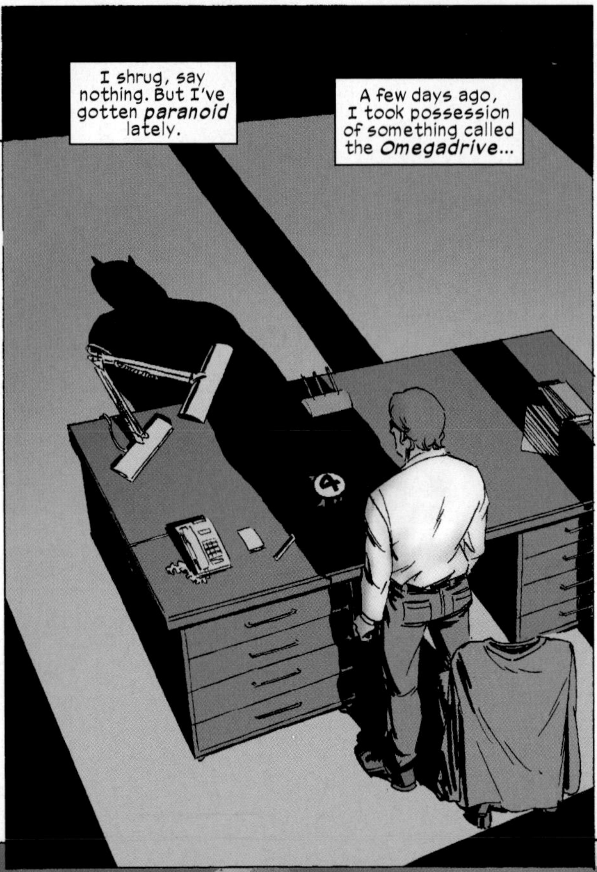
I shrug, say nothing. But I've gotten *paranoid* lately.
A few days ago, I took possession of something called the *Omegadrive*...

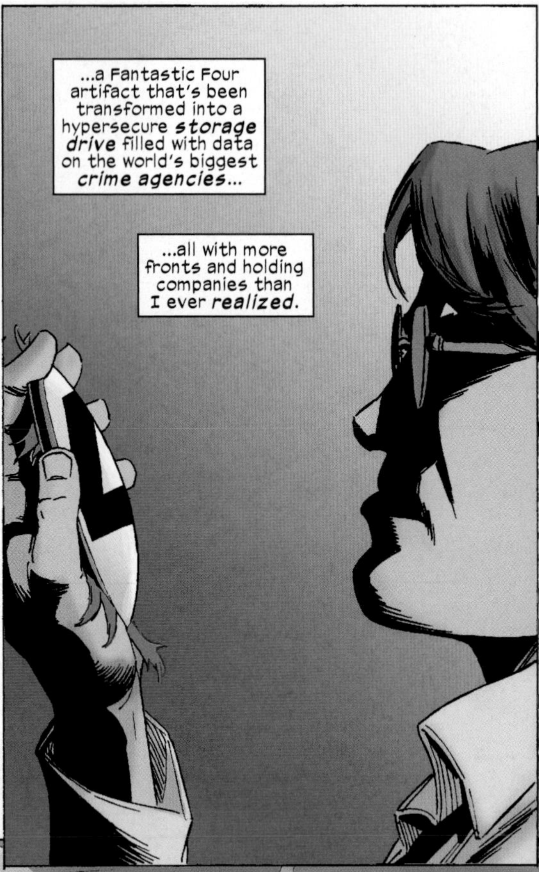
...a Fantastic Four artifact that's been transformed into a hypersecure *storage drive* filled with data on the world's biggest *crime agencies*...
...all with more fronts and holding companies than I ever *realized*.

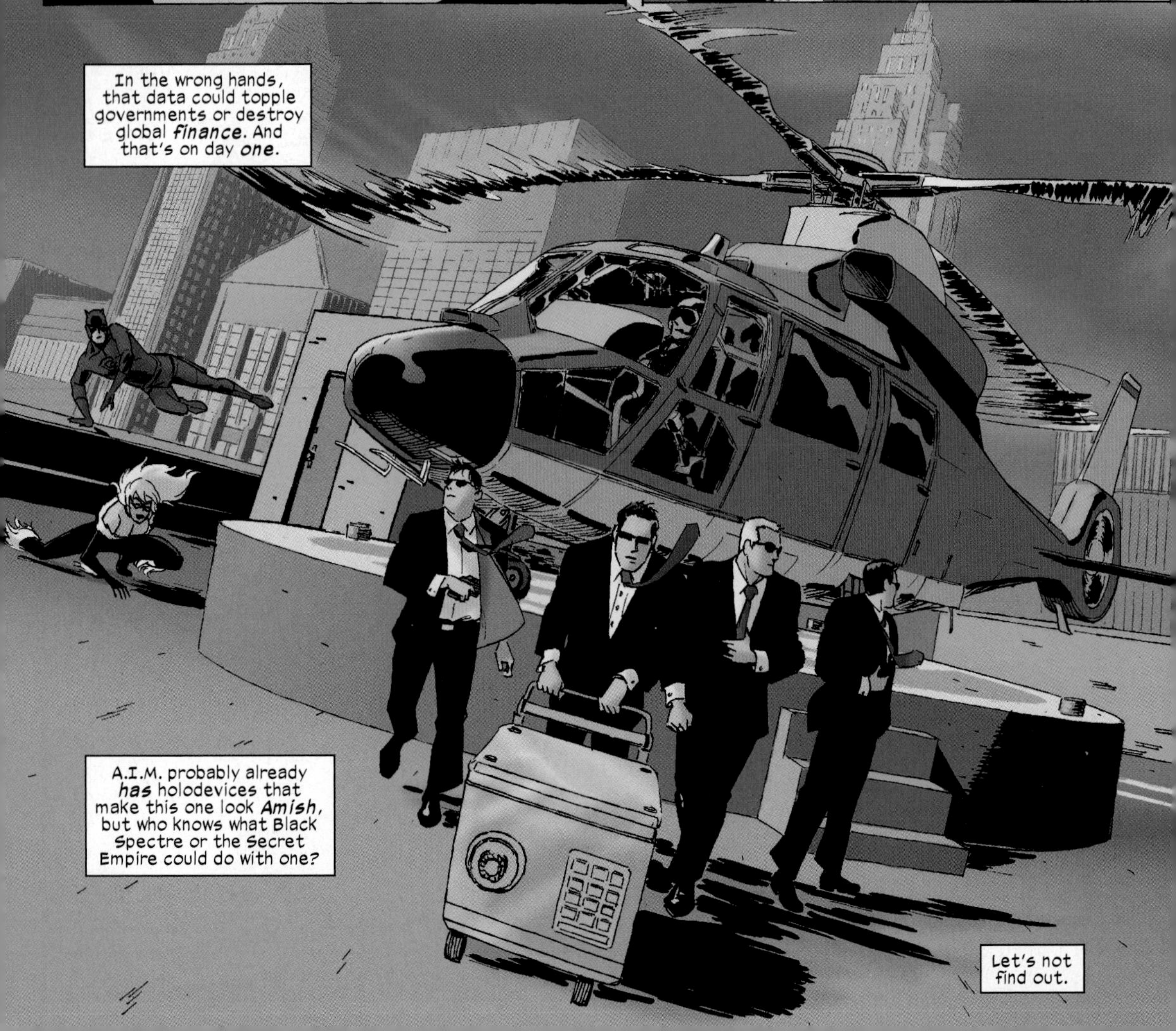
In the wrong hands, that data could topple governments or destroy global *finance*. And that's on day *one*.
A.I.M. probably already *has* holodevices that make this one look *Amish*, but who knows what Black Spectre or the Secret Empire could do with one?
Let's not find out.

INCOMING!

OPEN FIRE!

HEY, I THINK WE FOUND YOUR *HOLOGIZMO.*

ON THAT *CART,* THAT IS, NOT *SHOOTING* AT US. YOU HAVE A *PLAN?*

PLANNING IS OVERRATED.

IT'S ALWAYS MORE EXCITING TO BE SURPRISED.

YOU NEVER KNOW WHAT NEW TOOLS YOU MIGHT DISCOVER.

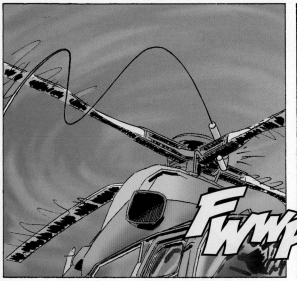

FWWP-P-P

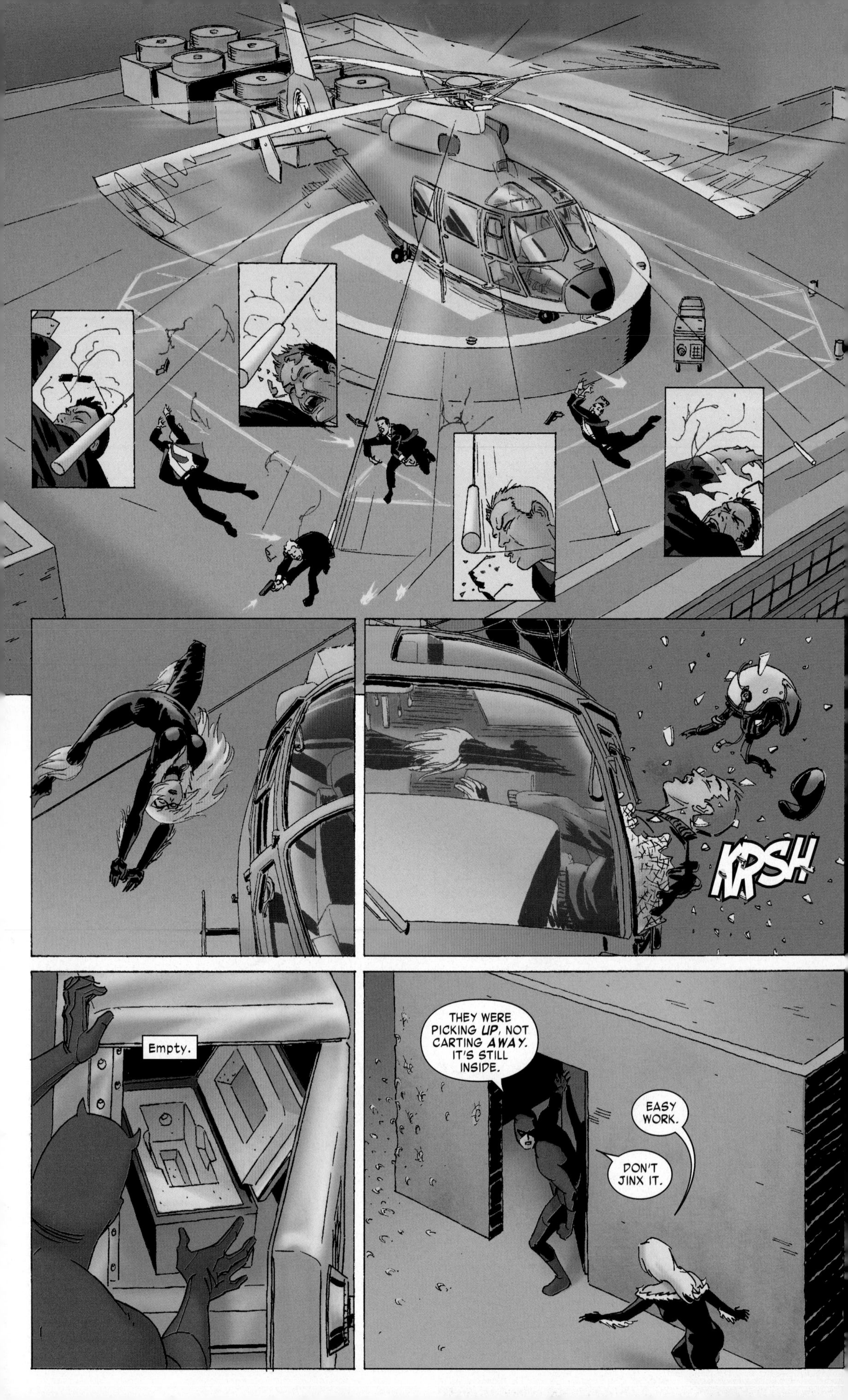
KRSH
Empty.
THEY WERE PICKING UP, NOT CARTING AWAY. IT'S STILL INSIDE.
EASY WORK.
DON'T JINX IT.

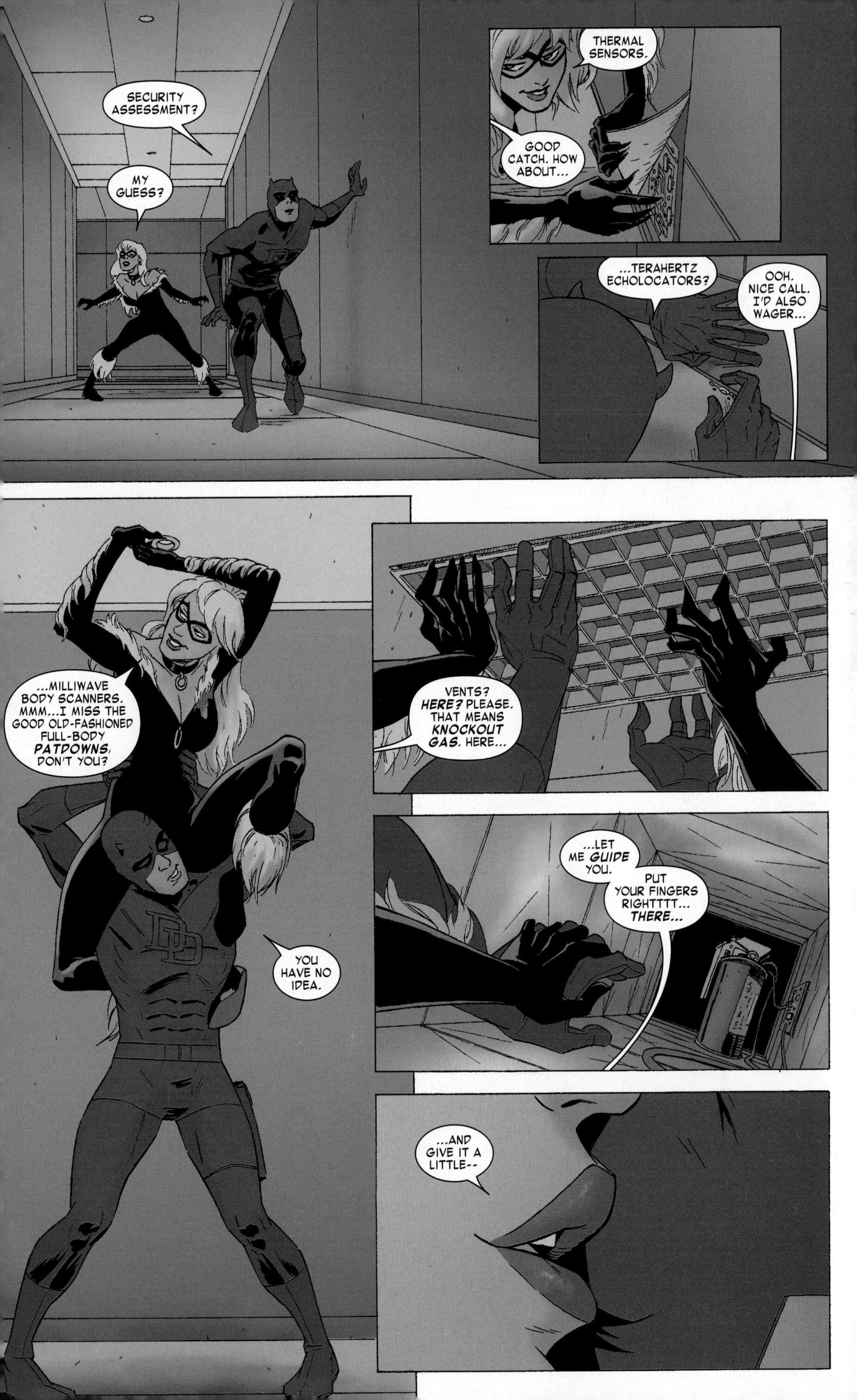

SECURITY ASSESSMENT?
MY GUESS?
THERMAL SENSORS.
GOOD CATCH. HOW ABOUT...
...TERAHERTZ ECHOLOCATORS?
OOH. NICE CALL. I'D ALSO WAGER...
...MILLIWAVE BODY SCANNERS. MMM...I MISS THE GOOD OLD-FASHIONED FULL-BODY PATDOWNS, DON'T YOU?
YOU HAVE NO IDEA.
VENTS? HERE? PLEASE. THAT MEANS KNOCKOUT GAS. HERE...
...LET ME GUIDE YOU.
PUT YOUR FINGERS RIGHTTTT... THERE...
...AND GIVE IT A LITTLE--

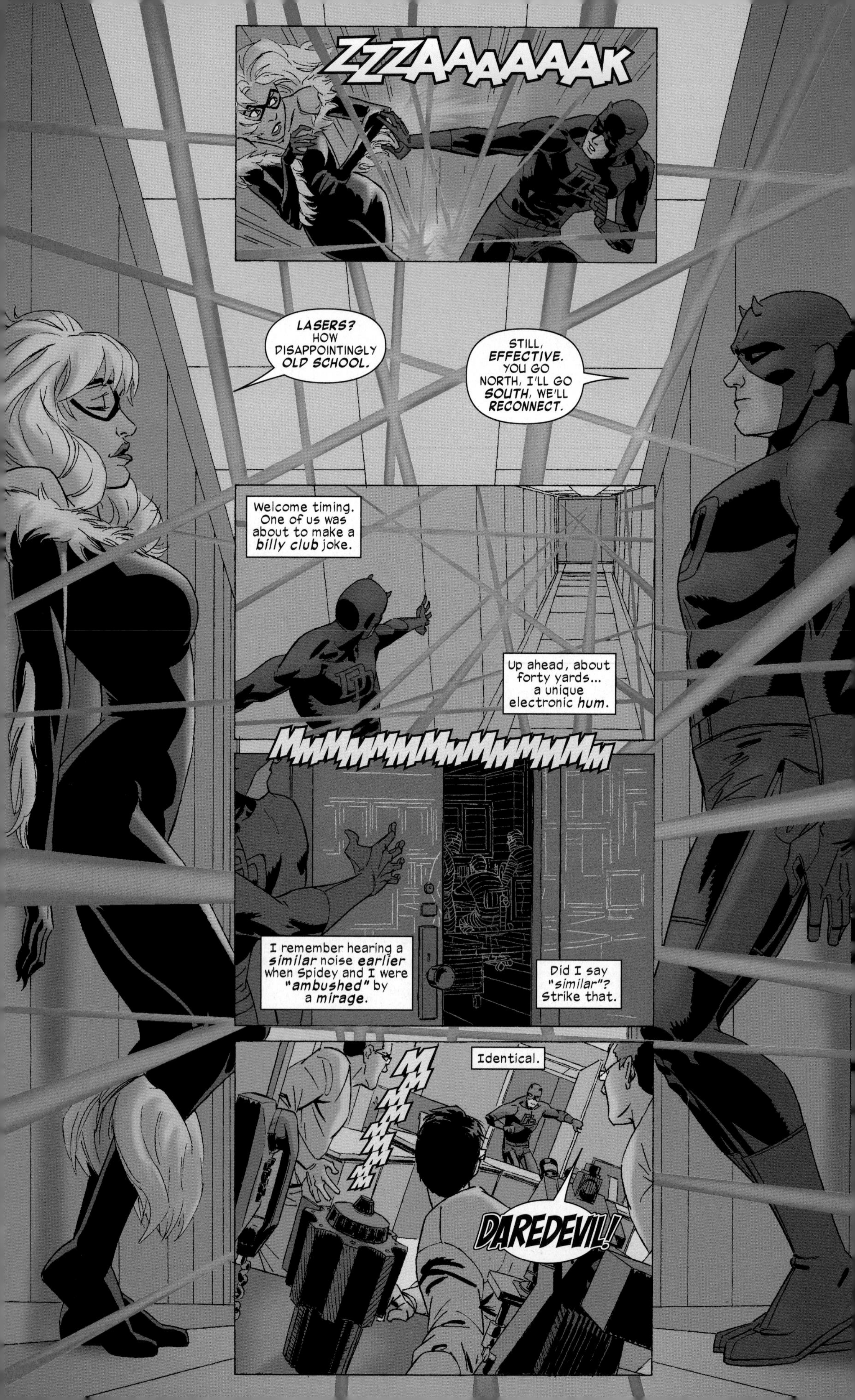
ZZZAAAAAAK
LASERS? HOW DISAPPOINTINGLY OLD SCHOOL.
STILL, EFFECTIVE. YOU GO NORTH, I'LL GO SOUTH, WE'LL RECONNECT.
Welcome timing. One of us was about to make a billy club joke.
Up ahead, about forty yards... a unique electronic hum.
MMMMMMMMMMMMMMMMMM
I remember hearing a similar noise earlier when Spidey and I were "ambushed" by a mirage.
Did I say "similar"? Strike that.
Identical.
MMMMMMMMM
DAREDEVIL!

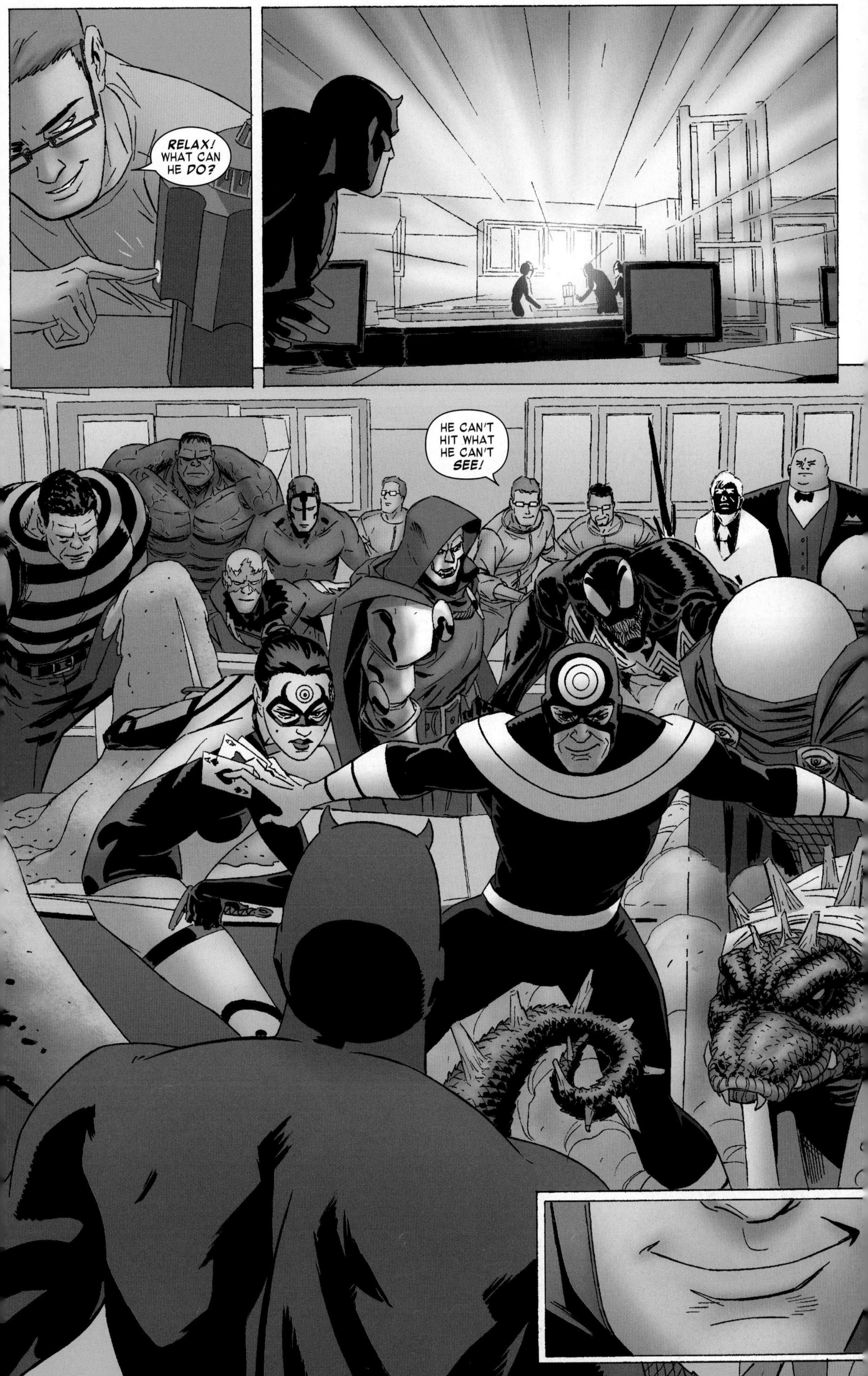
RELAX! WHAT CAN HE DO?
HE CAN'T HIT WHAT HE CAN'T SEE!

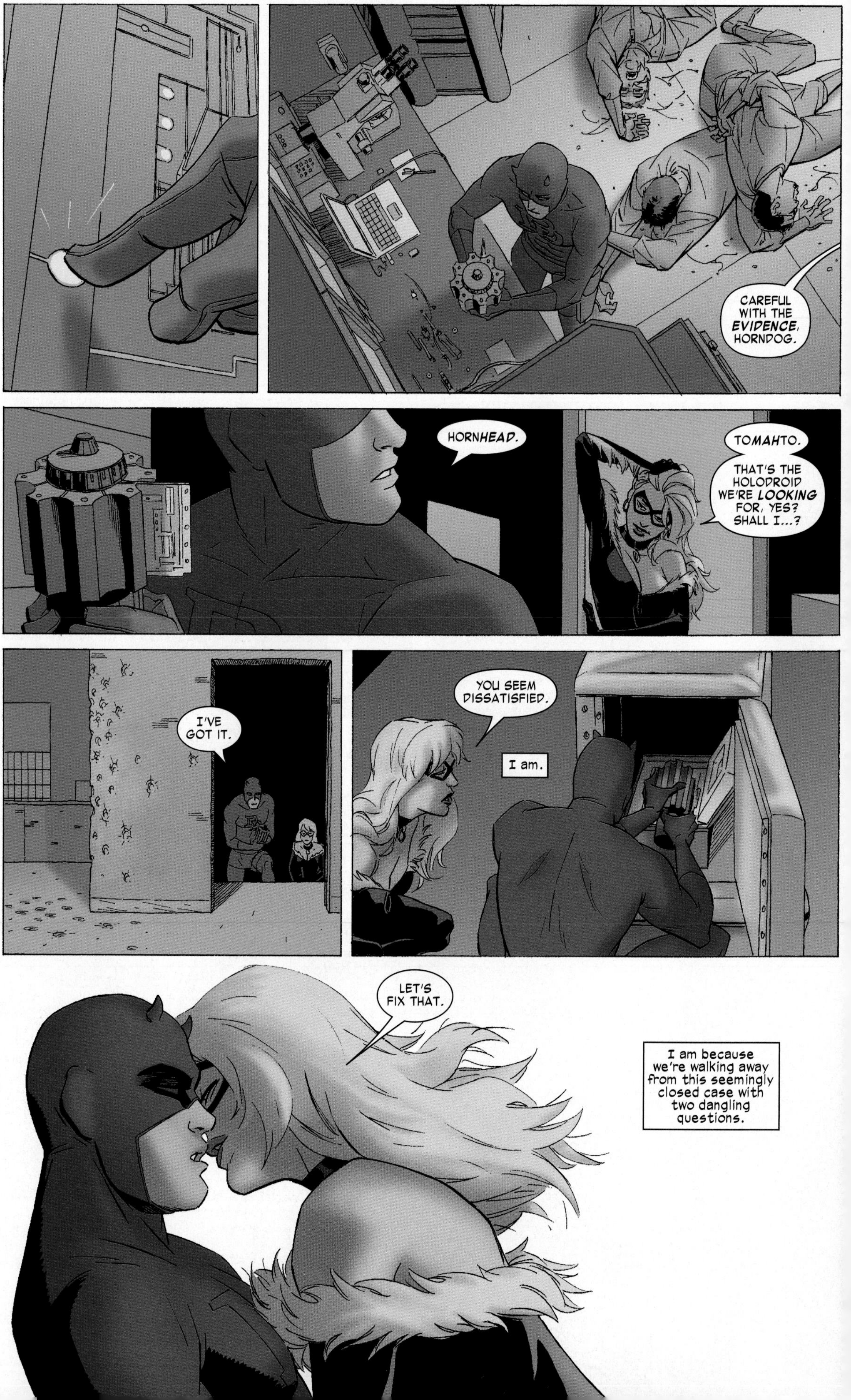
CAREFUL WITH THE EVIDENCE, HORNDOG.
HORNHEAD.
TOMAHTO.
THAT'S THE HOLODROID WE'RE LOOKING FOR, YES? SHALL I...?
I'VE GOT IT.
YOU SEEM DISSATISFIED.
I am.
LET'S FIX THAT.
I am because we're walking away from this seemingly closed case with two dangling questions.

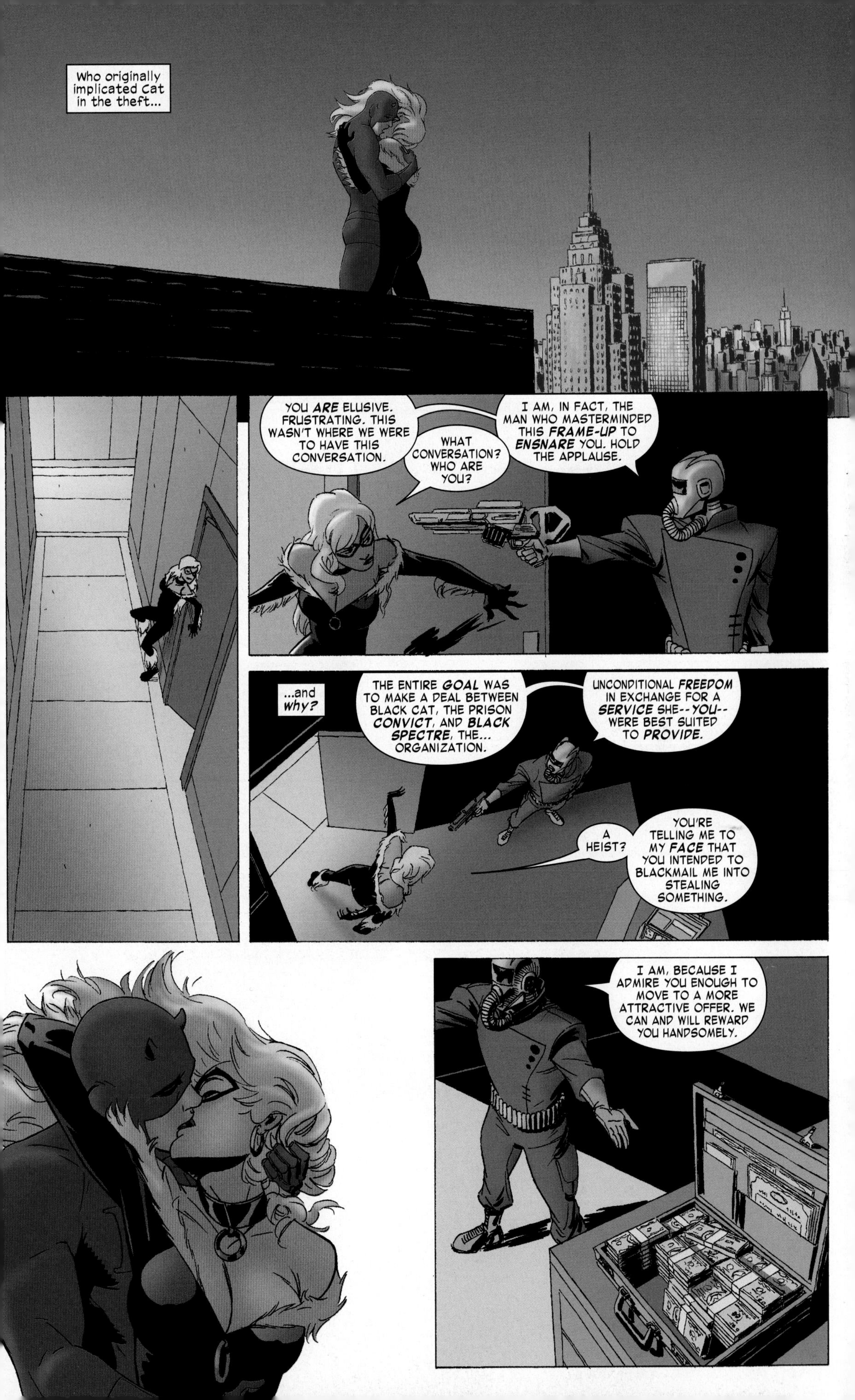
Who originally implicated Cat in the theft...
YOU ARE ELUSIVE. FRUSTRATING. THIS WASN'T WHERE WE WERE TO HAVE THIS CONVERSATION.
WHAT CONVERSATION? WHO ARE YOU?
I AM, IN FACT, THE MAN WHO MASTERMINDED THIS FRAME-UP TO ENSNARE YOU. HOLD THE APPLAUSE.
...and why?
THE ENTIRE GOAL WAS TO MAKE A DEAL BETWEEN BLACK CAT, THE PRISON CONVICT, AND BLACK SPECTRE, THE... ORGANIZATION.
UNCONDITIONAL FREEDOM IN EXCHANGE FOR A SERVICE SHE--YOU--WERE BEST SUITED TO PROVIDE.
A HEIST?
YOU'RE TELLING ME TO MY FACE THAT YOU INTENDED TO BLACKMAIL ME INTO STEALING SOMETHING.
I AM, BECAUSE I ADMIRE YOU ENOUGH TO MOVE TO A MORE ATTRACTIVE OFFER. WE CAN AND WILL REWARD YOU HANDSOMELY.

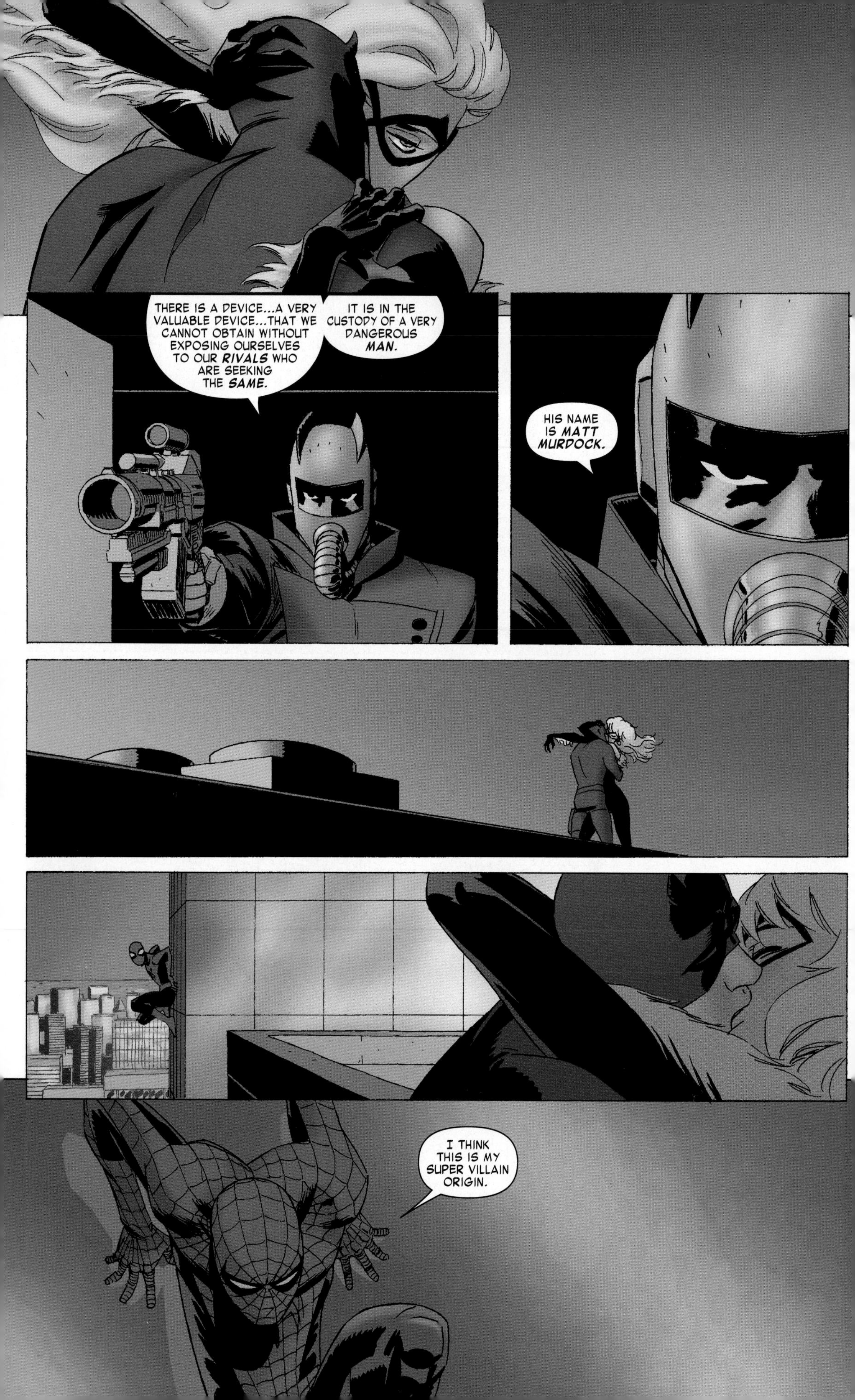
THERE IS A DEVICE...A VERY VALUABLE DEVICE...THAT WE CANNOT OBTAIN WITHOUT EXPOSING OURSELVES TO OUR RIVALS WHO ARE SEEKING THE SAME.
IT IS IN THE CUSTODY OF A VERY DANGEROUS MAN.
HIS NAME IS MATT MURDOCK.
I THINK THIS IS MY SUPER VILLAIN ORIGIN.

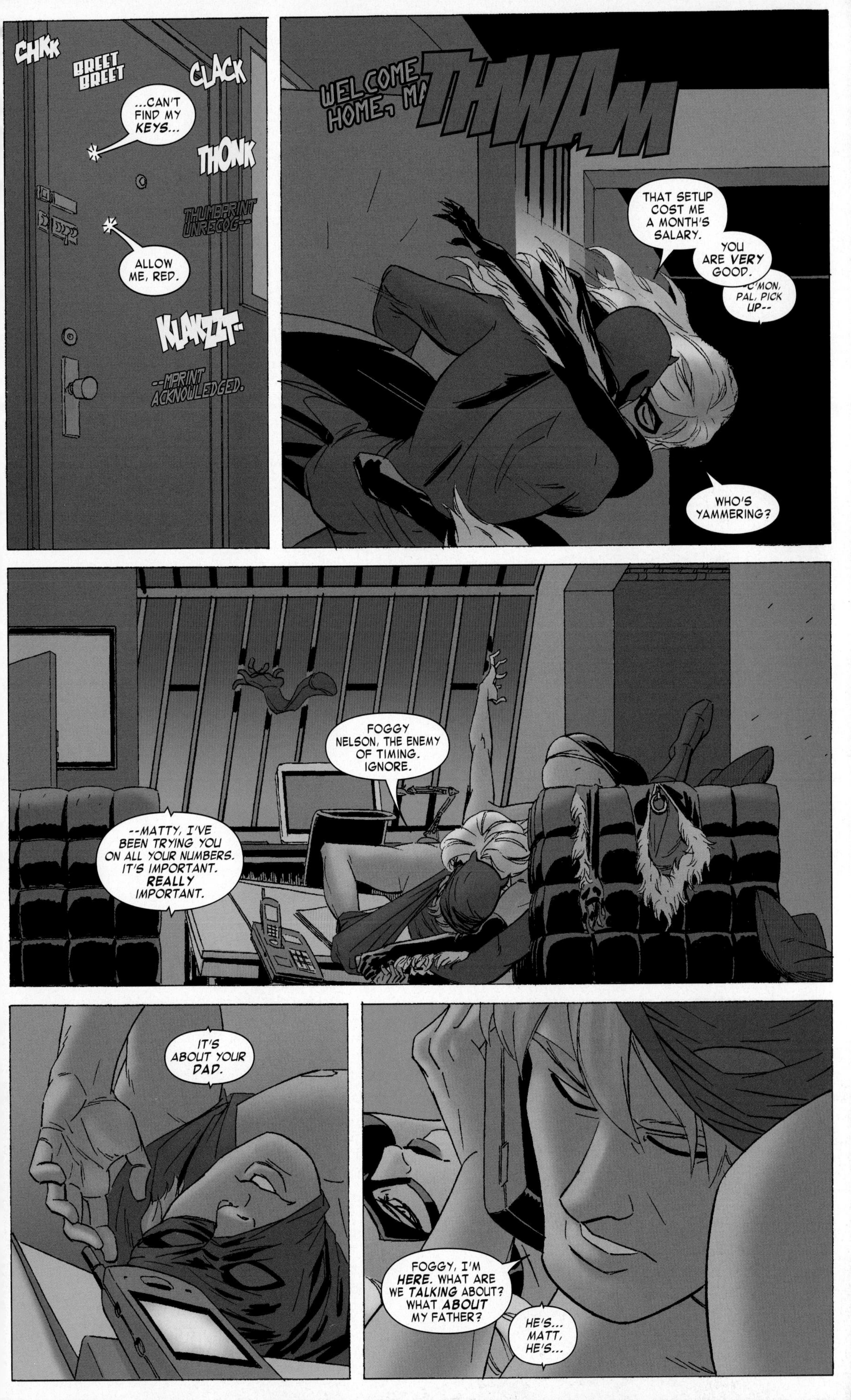
CHKK
BREET BREET
CLACK
...CAN'T FIND MY KEYS...
THONK
THUMBPRINT UNRECOG--
ALLOW ME, RED.
KLAKZZT--
--MPRINT ACKNOWLEDGED.
WELCOME HOME, MA
THWAM
THAT SETUP COST ME A MONTH'S SALARY.
YOU ARE VERY GOOD.
C'MON, PAL, PICK UP--
WHO'S YAMMERING?
FOGGY NELSON, THE ENEMY OF TIMING. IGNORE.
--MATTY, I'VE BEEN TRYING YOU ON ALL YOUR NUMBERS. IT'S IMPORTANT. REALLY IMPORTANT.
IT'S ABOUT YOUR DAD.
FOGGY, I'M HERE. WHAT ARE WE TALKING ABOUT? WHAT ABOUT MY FATHER?
HE'S... MATT, HE'S...

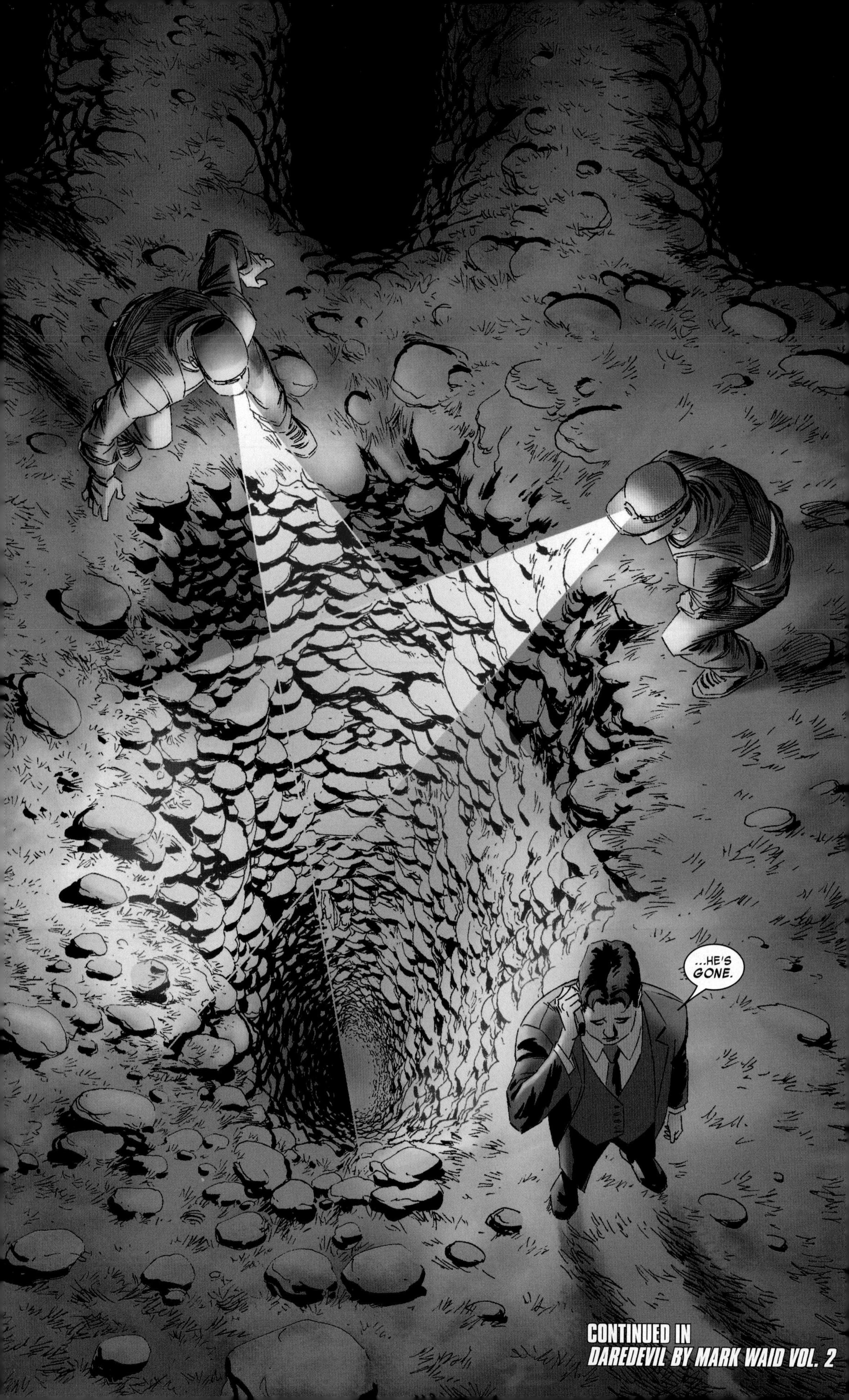
...HE'S GONE.

CONTINUED IN
DAREDEVIL BY MARK WAID VOL. 2

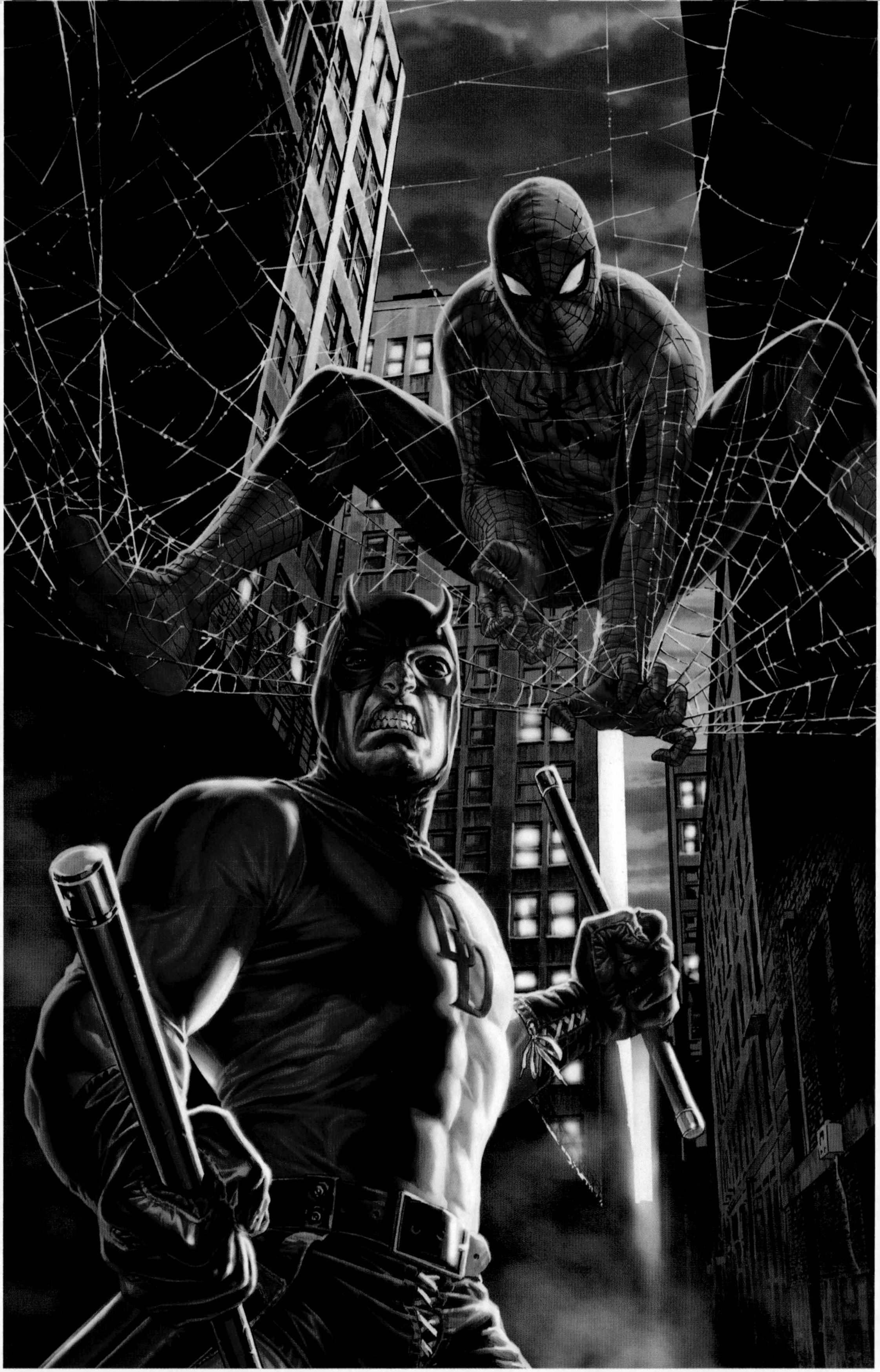

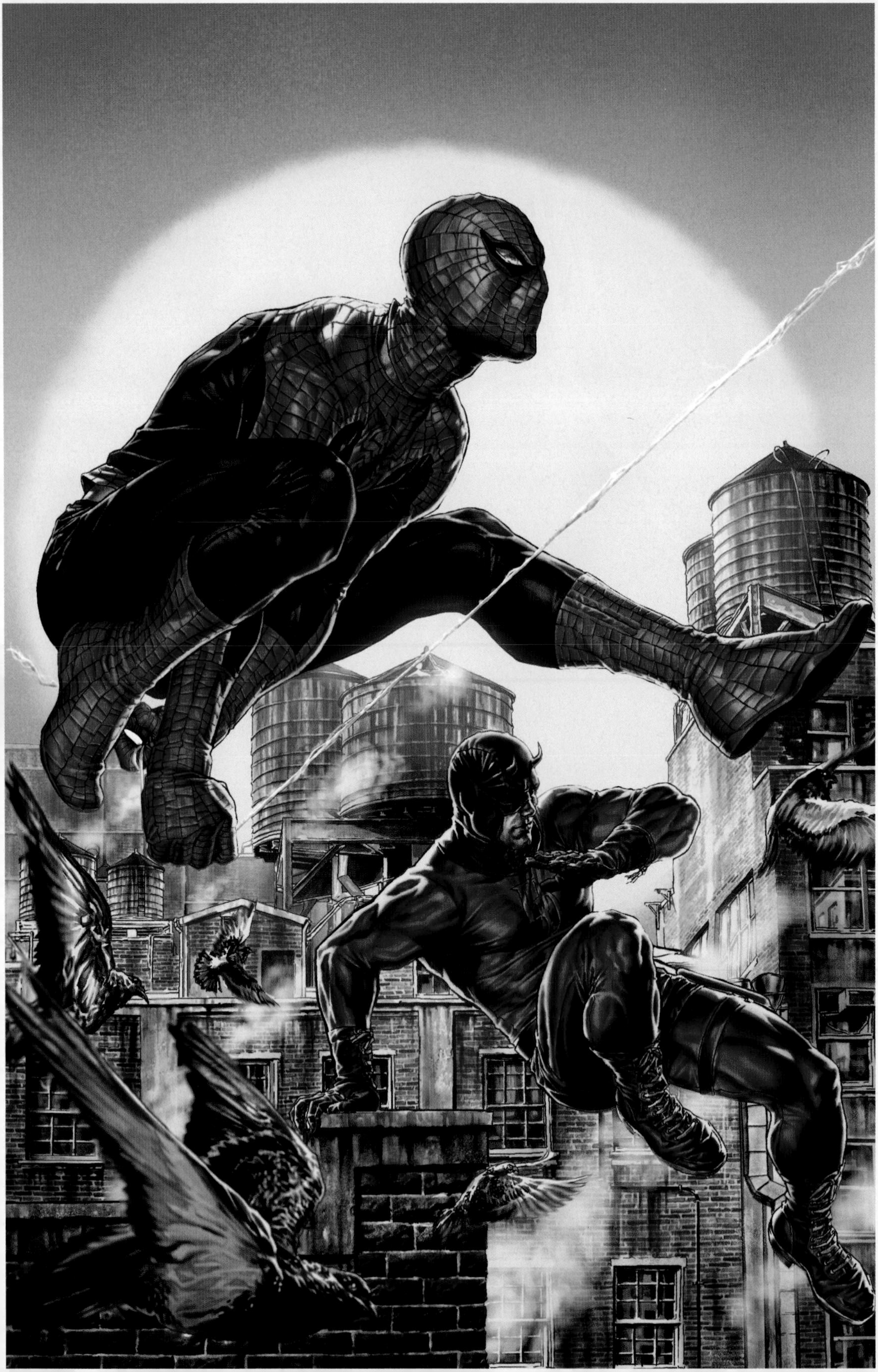

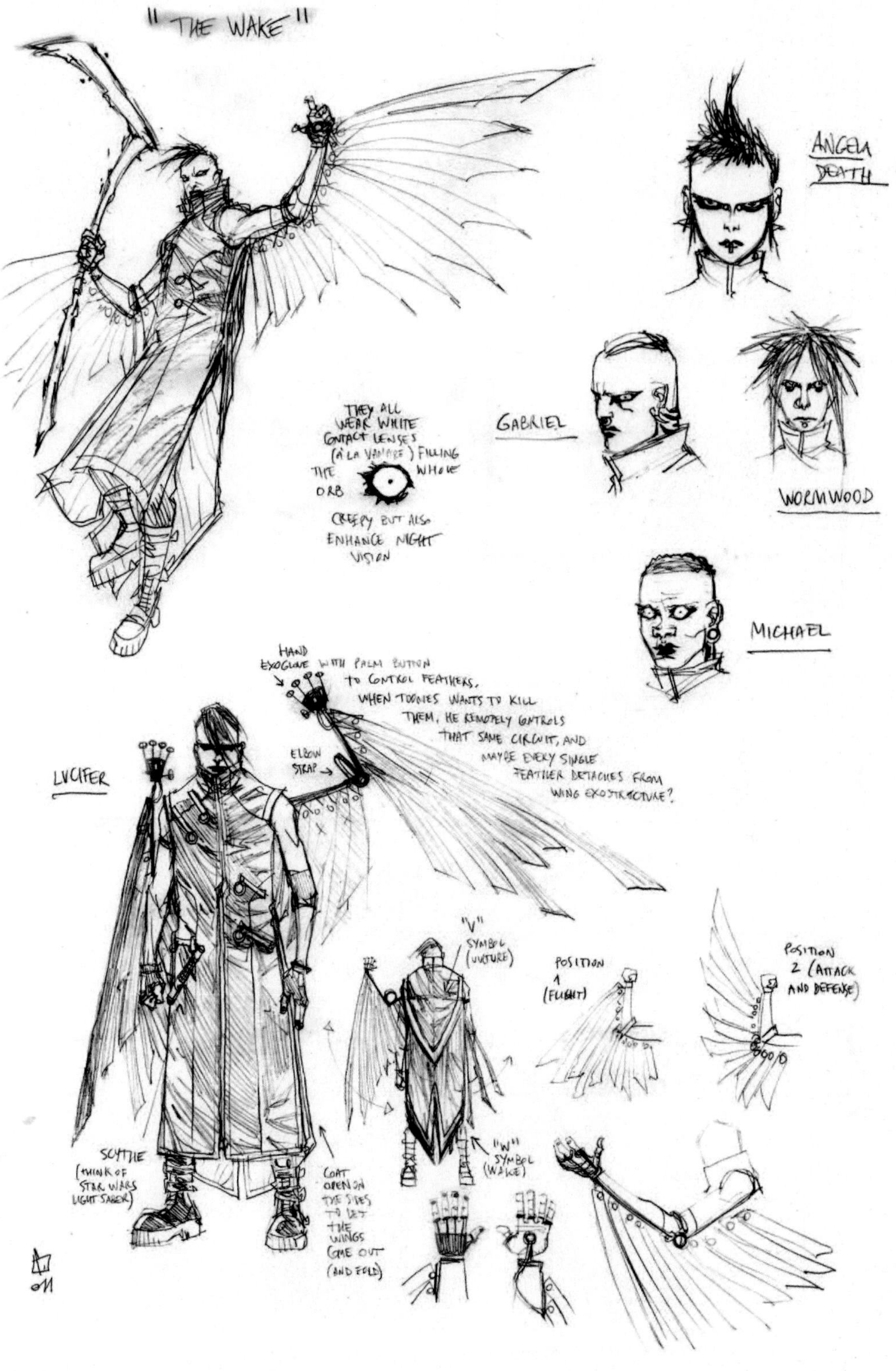
"THE WAKE"
ANGEL OF DEATH
THEY ALL WEAR WHITE CONTACT LENSES (À LA VAMPIRE) FILLING THE WHOLE ORB
CREEPY BUT ALSO ENHANCE NIGHT VISION
GABRIEL
WORMWOOD
MICHAEL
HAND EXOGLOVE WITH PALM BUTTON TO CONTROL FEATHERS. WHEN TODNIES WANTS TO KILL THEM, HE REMOTELY CONTROLS THAT SAME CIRCUIT, AND MAYBE EVERY SINGLE FEATHER DETACHES FROM WING EXOSTRUCTURE?
ELBOW STRAP
LUCIFER
"V" SYMBOL (VULTURE)
POSITION 1 (FLIGHT)
POSITION 2 (ATTACK AND DEFENSE)
SCYTHE (THINK OF STAR WARS LIGHT SABER)
COAT OPEN ON THE SIDES TO LET THE WINGS COME OUT (AND FOLD)
"W" SYMBOL (WAKE)

1

the
LIVE TON

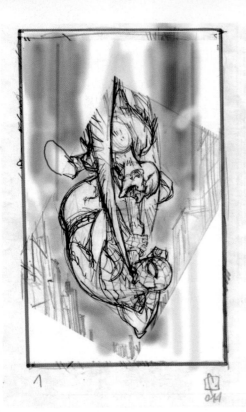

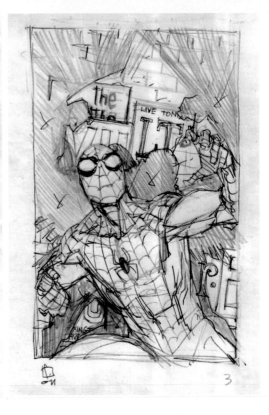

3

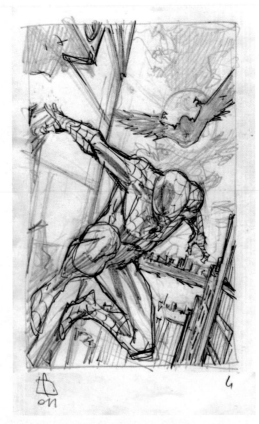

4

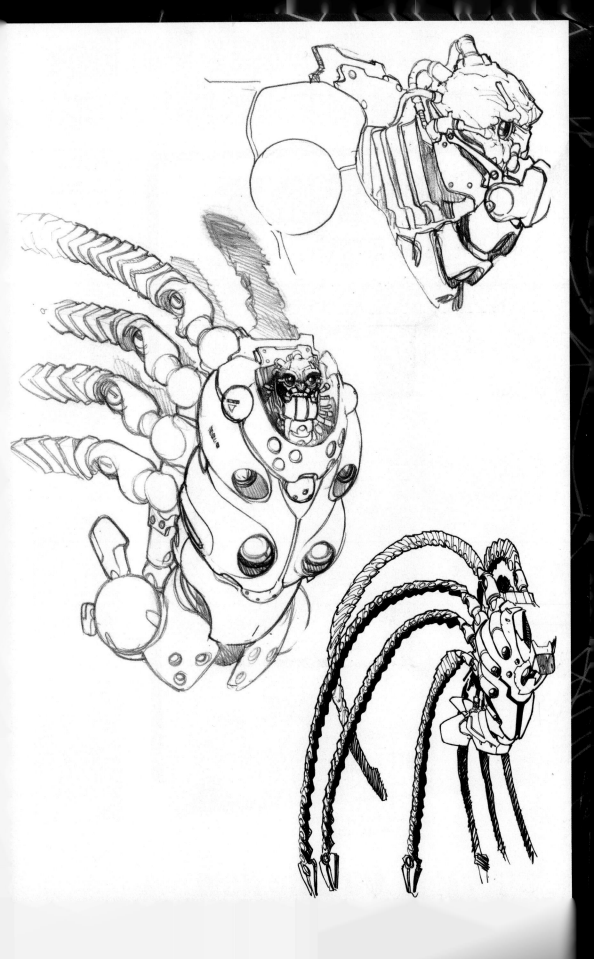

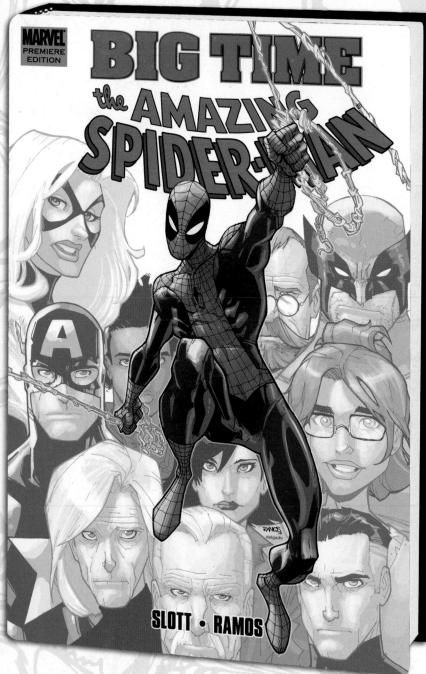